The Myth of Mental Illness

Books by Thomas S. Szasz

Pain and Pleasure

The Myth of Mental Illness

Law, Liberty, and Psychiatry

The Ethics of Psychoanalysis

Psychiatric Justice

Ideology and Insanity

The Manufacture of Madness

The Second Sin

The Age of Madness (*Editor*)

THE MYTH OF
MENTAL ILLNESS

Foundations of a Theory of Personal Conduct

by Thomas S. Szasz, M.D.

REVISED EDITION

HARPER & ROW, PUBLISHERS

NEW YORK, EVANSTON
SAN FRANCISCO
LONDON

1817

Designed by Sidney Feinberg

Library of Congress Cataloging in Publication Data

Szasz, Thomas Stephen, 1920–
    The myth of mental illness: foundations of a theory of personal conduct.
    Bibliography: p.
    1. Psychiatry—Philosophy. 2. Mental illness.
3. Hysteria. I. Title.
RC437.5.S9 1974   616.8′9′07   73–14296
ISBN 0–06–014196–4

Contents

v

Part Two

Foundations of a Theory of Personal Conduct

III. SEMIOTICAL ANALYSIS OF BEHAVIOR

IV. RULE-FOLLOWING ANALYSIS OF BEHAVIOR

V. GAME-MODEL ANALYSIS OF BEHAVIOR

Preface to the Second Edition

Every book is, inevitably, part autobiography. I started to work on this book in 1954, when, having been called to active duty in the Navy, I was relieved of the burdens of a full-time psychoanalytic practice and could turn my energies to putting on paper something of what had long been on my mind. The first publisher to whom I submitted the manuscript, in 1957 or 1958 I think, deliberated about it at length and then rejected it. I next sent it to Mr. Paul Hoeber, then the director of the medical division of Harper & Brothers (now Harper & Row, Publishers), to whom I am grateful for publishing a work which, especially then, must have seemed to fly in the face of nearly everything that was known about psychiatry and psychoanalysis.

Within a year of its publication, the Commissioner of the New York State Department of Mental Hygiene demanded, in a letter citing specifically *The Myth of Mental Illness,* that I be dismissed from my university position because I did not "believe" in mental illness. Neither the details of that affair nor the other consequences of my publishing this book belong in this Preface. Suffice it to say that much has happened to me since. And much, in part perhaps because of this book, has happened to psychiatry also.

Obviously, then, were I to write this book today, I would write it differently. But I am, on the whole, still quite satisfied with the original work. However, the original version of *The Myth of Mental Illness* now appears to me too detailed in the development of its thesis, overdocumented in its citations, and often couched in unnecessarily technical language. I have decided, therefore, that for this second edition I would eliminate everything that does not bear directly on its main themes, reduce the documentation, and rewrite the text, where necessary, in more straightforward English prose. At the same time, I have rejected the temptation to bring the arguments up to date or to add any significant new material—except for this Preface and a brief Summary—partly because, once begun, such rewriting would have been difficult to control, and partly because, in several of my books published since 1961, I have elaborated on the ideas first presented here.[1]

The problems to which I address myself in this book are easy to state but, because of the powerful cultural and economic pressures that define the "correct" answers to them, are difficult to clarify. They have to do with such questions as: What is disease? What are the ostensible and actual tasks of the physician? What is mental illness? Who defines what constitutes illness, diagnosis, treatment? Who controls the vocabulary of medicine and psychiatry, and the powers of the physician-psychiatrist and citizen-patient? Has a person the right to call himself sick? Has a physician the right to call a person mentally sick? What is the difference between a person complaining of pain and calling himself sick? Or between a physician complaining of a person's misbehavior and calling him a mentally sick patient? Without attempting to answer these questions or trying to anticipate the contents of this book, let me show briefly the sort of reasoning I bring to it.

It is impossible to undertake an analysis of the concept of mental illness without first coming to grips with the concept of ordinary or bodily illness. What do we mean when we say that

a person is ill? We usually mean two quite different things: first, that he believes, or that his physician believes, or that they both believe, that he suffers from an abnormality or malfunctioning of his body; and second, that he wants, or is at least willing to accept, medical help for his suffering. The term "illness" thus refers, first, to an abnormal biological condition whose existence may be claimed, truly or falsely, by patient, physician, or others; and second, to the social role of patient, which may be assumed or assigned.

If a person does not suffer from an abnormal biological condition, we do not usually consider him to be ill. (We certainly do not consider him to be physically ill.) And if he does not voluntarily assume the sick role, we do not usually consider him to be a medical patient. This is because the practice of modern Western medicine rests on two tacit premises—namely, that the physician's task is to diagnose and treat disorders of the human body, and that he can carry out these services only with the consent of his patient. In other words, physicians are trained to treat bodily ills—not economic, moral, racial, religious, or political "ills." And they themselves (except psychiatrists) expect, and in turn are expected by their patients, to treat bodily diseases, not envy and rage, fear and folly, poverty and stupidity, and all the other miseries that beset man. Strictly speaking, then, disease or illness can affect only the body. Hence, there can be no such thing as mental illness. The term "mental illness" is a metaphor.

To understand current psychiatric practices, it is necessary to understand how and why the idea of mental illness arose and the way it now functions. In part, the concept of mental illness arose from the fact that it is possible for a person to act and to appear as if he were sick without actually having a bodily disease. How should we react to such a person? Should we treat him as if he were not ill, or as if he were ill?

Until the second half of the nineteenth century, persons who imitated illness—that is, who claimed to be sick without

being able to convince their physicians that they suffered from bona fide illnesses—were regarded as faking illness and were called malingerers; and those who imitated medical practitioners—that is, who claimed to heal the sick without being able to convince medical authorities that they were bona fide physicians—were regarded as impostors, and were called quacks.

As a result of the influence of Charcot, Janet, and especially Freud, this perspective, both medical and lay, on imitations of illness and healing was radically transformed. Henceforth, persons who imitated illness—for example, who had "spells"—were regarded as genuinely ill, and were called hysterics; and those who imitated physicians—for example, who "hypnotized"—were regarded as genuine healers, and were called psychotherapists. This profound conceptual transformation was both supported and reflected by an equally profound semantic transformation—one in which "spells," for example, became "seizures," and quacks became "psychoanalysts."

The upshot of this psychiatric-psychoanalytic "revolution" is that, today, it is considered shamefully uncivilized and naïvely unscientific to treat a person who acts or appears sick as if he were not sick. We now "know" and "realize" that such a person is sick; that he is obviously sick; that he is mentally sick.

But this view rests on a serious, albeit simple, error: it rests on mistaking or confusing what is real with what is imitation; literal meaning with metaphorical meaning; medicine with morals. In other words, I maintain that mental illness is a metaphorical disease: that bodily illness stands in the same relation to mental illness as a defective television set stands to a bad television program. Of course, the word "sick" is often used metaphorically. We call jokes "sick," economies "sick," sometimes even the whole world "sick"; but only when we call minds "sick" do we systematically mistake and strategically

misinterpret metaphor for fact—and send for the doctor to "cure" the "illness." It is as if a television viewer were to send for a television repairman because he dislikes the program he sees on the screen.[2]

Furthermore, just as it is possible for a person to define himself as sick without having a bodily illness, so it is also possible for a physician to define as "sick" a person who feels perfectly well and wants no medical help, and then act as if he were a therapist trying to cure his "patient's" disease. How should we react to such a physician? Should we treat him as if he were a malevolent meddler or a benevolent healer? Today, it is considered quite unscientific and uncivilized to adopt the former posture, everyone—except the victim, and sometimes even he, himself—regarding such a physician as obviously a therapist, that is, a psychiatric therapist. I believe this is a serious error. I hold that psychiatric interventions are directed at moral, not medical, problems; in other words, that psychiatric help sought by the client stands in the same relation to psychiatric intervention imposed on him as religious beliefs voluntarily professed stand to such beliefs imposed by force.

It is widely believed that mental illness is a type of disease, and that psychiatry is a branch of medicine; and yet, whereas people readily think of and call themselves "sick," they rarely think of and call themselves "mentally sick." The reason for this, as I shall try to show, is really quite simple: a person might feel sad or elated, insignificant or grandiose, suicidal or homicidal, and so forth; he is, however, not likely to categorize himself as mentally ill or insane; that he is, is more likely to be suggested by someone else. This, then, is why bodily diseases are characteristically treated with the consent of the patient, while mental diseases are characteristically treated without his consent. (Individuals who nowadays seek private psychoanalytic or psychotherapeutic help do not, as a rule, consider themselves either "sick" or "mentally sick," but rather view their difficulties as problems in living and the help they receive as a type of counseling.[3]) In short, while medical diagnoses are the names of genuine diseases, psychiatric diagnoses are stigmatizing labels.

Such considerations lead to two diametrically opposed points of view about mental illness and psychiatry. According to the traditional and at present generally accepted view, mental illness is like any other illness; psychiatric treatment is like any other treatment; and psychiatry is like any other medical specialty. According to the view I have endeavored to develop and clarify, however, there is, and can be, no such thing as mental illness or psychiatric treatment; the interventions now designated as "psychiatric treatment" must be clearly identified as voluntary or involuntary: voluntary interventions are things a person does for himself in an effort to change, whereas involuntary interventions are things done to him in an effort to change him against his will; and psychiatry is not a medical, but a moral and political, enterprise. This book is an attempt to demonstrate the fallacy of the former view and the validity of the latter.

I wish to thank my brother, Dr. George Szasz, for his help with the revisions; and my publisher, Harper & Row, and especially Mr. Hugh Van Dusen and Mrs. Ann Harris, for their decision to bring out a new edition of *The Myth of Mental Illness,* and for their help in preparing it.

THOMAS S. SZASZ, M.D.

Syracuse, New York
July 1, 1973

Preface to the First Edition

I became interested in writing this book approximately ten years ago when, having become established as a psychiatrist, I became increasingly impressed by the vague, capricious, and generally unsatisfactory character of the widely used concept of mental illness and its corollaries, diagnosis, prognosis, and treatment. It seemed to me that although the notion of mental illness made good *historical* sense—stemming as it does from the historical identity of medicine and psychiatry—it made no *rational* sense. Although mental illness might have been a useful concept in the nineteenth century, today it is scientifically worthless and socially harmful.

Although dissatisfaction with the medical basis and conceptual framework of psychiatry is not of recent origin, little has been done to make the problem explicit, and even less to remedy it. In psychiatric circles it is almost indelicate to ask: What is mental illness? In nonpsychiatric circles mental illness all too often is considered to be whatever psychiatrists say it is. The answer to the question, Who is mentally ill? thus becomes: Those who are confined in mental hospitals or who consult psychiatrists in their private offices.

Perhaps these answers sound silly. If they do, it is because they are silly. However, it is not easy to give better answers without going to a good deal of trouble, first, by asking other questions, such as, Is mental illness an illness? and second, by resetting one's goals from understanding mental diseases to understanding human beings.

The need to re-examine the problem of mental illness is both timely and pressing. There is confusion, dissatisfaction, and tension in our society concerning psychiatric, psychological, and social issues. Mental illness is said to be the nation's number one health problem. The statistics marshaled to prove this contention are impressive: more than a half-million hospital beds for mental patients, and 17 million persons allegedly suffering from some degree of mental illness.

The concept of mental illness is freely used in all the major news media—the newspapers, radio, and television. Sometimes famous persons are said to be mentally ill—for example, Adolf Hitler, Ezra Pound, Earl Long. At other times the label is attached to the most lowly and unfortunate members of society, especially if they are accused of a crime.

The popularity of psychotherapy, and people's alleged need for it, is rapidly increasing. At the same time it is impossible to answer the question, What is psychotherapy? The term "psychotherapy" encompasses nearly everything that people do in the company of one another. Psychoanalysis, group psychotherapy, religious counseling, rehabilitation of prisoners, and many other activities, are all called "psychotherapy."

This book was written in an effort to dispel the perplexities mentioned, and thereby to clear the psychiatric air. Parts I and II are devoted to laying bare the socio-historical and epistemological roots of the modern concept of mental illness. The question, What *is* mental illness? is shown to be inextricably tied to the question, What do psychiatrists *do?* My first task, accordingly, is to present an essentially "destructive" analysis of the concept of mental illness and of psychiatry as a pseudomedical enterprise. I believe that such "destruction," like tearing down old buildings, is necessary if we are to construct a new, more habitable edifice for the science of man.

Since it is difficult to scrap one conceptual model without having another with which to replace it, I had to search for a new point of view. My second aim, then, is to offer a "constructive" synthesis of the knowledge which I have found useful for filling the gap left by the myth of mental illness. Parts III, IV, and V are devoted to presenting a systematic theory of personal conduct, based partly on materials culled from psychiatry, psychoanalysis, and other disciplines, and partly on my own observations and ideas. The omission from psychiatric theories of moral issues and normative standards, as explicitly stated goals and rules of conduct, has divorced psychiatry from precisely that reality which it has tried to describe and explain. I have endeavored to correct this defect by means of a game theory of human living, which enables us to combine ethical, political, religious, and social considerations with the more traditional concerns of medicine and psychiatry.

Although my thesis is that mental illness is a myth, this book is not an attempt to "debunk psychiatry." There are altogether too many books today that attempt either to sell psychiatry and psychotherapy or to unsell them. The former usually set out to show why and how this or that form of behavior *is* "mental illness," and how psychiatrists *can* help a person so afflicted. The latter often employ a two-pronged attack suggesting that psychiatrists themselves are "mentally ill," and that psychotherapy is a poor method for "treating" a sickness that manifests itself in symptoms as serious as those of mental illness.

I should like to make clear, therefore, that although I consider the concept of mental illness to be unserviceable, I believe that psychiatry could be a science. I also believe that psychotherapy is an effective method of helping people—not to recover from an "illness," but rather to learn about themselves, others, and life.

In sum, then, this is not a book on psychiatry, nor is it a book on the nature of man. It is a book *about* psychiatry—inquiring, as it does, into what people, but particularly psychiatrists and patients, have done with and to one another. It is also a book about human conduct—since in it observations and hypotheses are offered concerning how people live.

THOMAS S. SZASZ, M.D.

Syracuse, New York
June 30, 1960

The Myth of Mental Illness

Science must begin with myths and with the criticism of myths.

—Karl R. Popper

Introduction

Psychiatry is conventionally defined as a medical specialty concerned with the diagnosis and treatment of mental diseases. I submit that this definition, which is still widely accepted, places psychiatry in the company of alchemy and astrology and commits it to the category of pseudoscience. The reason for this is that there is no such thing as "mental illness." Psychiatrists must now choose between continuing to define their discipline in terms of nonexistent entities or substantives, or redefining it in terms of the actual interventions or processes in which they engage.

In the history of science, thinking in terms of entities has always tended to precede thinking in terms of processes. Alchemists and astrologers thus spoke of mysterious substances and concealed their methods from public scrutiny. Psychiatrists have similarly persisted in speaking of mysterious mental maladies and have continued to refrain from disclosing fully and frankly what they do. Indeed, whether as theorists or therapists, they may do virtually anything and still claim to be, and be accepted as, psychiatrists. The actual behavior of a particular psychiatrist may thus be that of a physician, psychologist, psychoanalyst, policeman, clergyman, historian, literary critic, friend, counselor, or teacher—or sundry

1

combinations of these roles. A physician is usually accepted as a psychiatrist so long as he insists that what concerns him is the problem of mental health and mental illness.

But let us suppose that there is no such thing as mental health or mental illness, that these terms refer to nothing more substantial or real than did the astrological notions of the influence of planetary positions on personal conduct. What then?

Methods of Observation and Action in Psychiatry

Psychiatry stands at the crossroads. Until now, thinking in terms of entities or substantives—such as illness, neurosis, psychosis, treatment—has been the rule. The question now is: Shall we continue along the same road or branch off in the direction of thinking in terms of interventions or processes? Viewed in this light, my efforts in this study are directed, first, at demolishing the major false substantives of contemporary psychiatric thought, and second, at laying the foundations for a process theory of personal conduct.

Discrepancies between what people say they do and what they actually do are encountered in all walks of life—science, medicine, and psychiatry among them. It was precisely against such discrepancies that Einstein warned his fellow physicists when he declared:

If you want to find out anything from the theoretical physicists about the methods they use, I advise you to stick closely to one principle: Don't listen to their words, fix your attention on their deeds.[1]

Actions do speak louder than words. Clearly, there is no reason to assume that this proverb, or the principle proposed by Einstein, are not equally valid for understanding the methods, and hence the very nature, of psychiatry.

The foregoing principle now also forms the basis of a

systematic philosophy of science known as operationalism.[2] Simply stated, an operational definition of a concept is one that refers to actual interventions or operations. This sort of definition may be contrasted with an idealistic one, which refers to the basic or "essential" qualities of the object or idea. Modern physical concepts are defined in terms of physical operations, such as measurements of time, temperature, distance, and so forth. Earlier physical definitions made use of such ideal notions as phlogiston or ether. In the same way, psychiatric, psychological, or social concepts, defined operationally, would have to relate to actual interventions and observations. Actually, many contemporary psychosocial concepts are defined in terms of the expert's self-proclaimed intentions, interests, and values. Virtually all current psychiatric concepts are of this sort.

Hence, if we try to answer the question, What do psychiatrists do? our reply will necessarily depend on the kind of psychiatrist we have in mind. Actually, psychiatrists engage in all of the following activities (and the list is by no means complete): they physically examine patients, prescribe and administer drugs and electric convulsions, sign commitment papers, examine criminals at the request of judicial authorities, testify in legal proceedings, listen and talk to persons, offer speculations about ancient and modern historical events and personages, engage in research in biochemistry and neurophysiology, study monkeys and other animals, and so forth almost *ad infinitum*.

In this book I shall be concerned mainly with psychiatry as a discipline whose special method is, derisively but quite correctly, often said to be "only talking." If we disregard the "only" as gratuitous condemnation before the facts, and if under the term "talking" we encompass communications of all sorts, we arrive at a formulation of a basic method of psychiatry to which, although it is accurate, surprisingly few psychiatrists really subscribe. There is, as I noted before, a serious discrepancy between what psychotherapists and psychoanalysts *do* and what they *say they do*. What they do, quite simply, is to communicate with other persons (often called "patients") by means of language, nonverbal signs, and rules; they analyze—that is, discuss, explain, and speculate about— the communicative interactions which they observe and in which they themselves engage; and they often recommend engaging in some types of conduct and avoiding others. I believe that these phrases correctly describe the actual operations of psychoanalysts and psychosocially oriented psychiatrists. But what do these experts tell themselves and others concerning their work? They talk as if they were physicians, physiologists, biologists, or even physicists. We hear about "sick patients" and "treatments," "diagnoses" and "hospitals," "instincts" and "endocrine functions," and, of course, "libido" and "psychic energies," both "free" and "bound." All this is fakery and pretense whose purpose is to "medicalize" certain aspects of the study and control of human behavior.

A psychiatry based on and using the methods of communication analysis has actually much in common with the disciplines concerned with the study of languages and communicative behavior, such as symbolic logic, semiotic,* semantics, and philosophy. Nevertheless, so-called psychiatric problems continue to be cast in the traditional framework of medicine. The conceptual scaffolding of medicine, however, rests on the principles of physics and chemistry, as indeed it should, for it has been, and continues to be, the task of medicine to study, and if necessary to alter, the physicochemical structure and function of the human body. Yet the fact remains that human sign-using behavior does not lend itself to exploration and understanding in these terms. We thus remain shackled to the wrong conceptual framework and terminology. No science, however, can be better than its linguistic apparatus allows it to be. And the language of psychiatry (and psychoanalysis) is

* The term "semiotic" designates the science of signs.[3]

fundamentally unfaithful to its own subject: in it, imitating medicine comes before telling the truth. We shall not, however, be able to hold on to the morally judgmental and socially manipulative character of our traditional psychiatric and psychoanalytic vocabulary without paying a price for it. Indeed, we are well along the road of having purchased superiority and power over patients at the cost of scientific self-sterilization and imminent professional self-destruction.

Causality and Historicism in Modern Psychiatry

Psychoanalytic theory was fashioned after the pattern of the causal-deterministic model of classical physics. The erroneousness of this transfer has been amply documented in recent years.[4] I wish to call attention here to that particular application of the principle of physical determinism to human affairs which Karl Popper called "historicism."[5] Briefly stated, historicism is a doctrine according to which historical events are as fully determined by their antecedents as are physical events by theirs. Hence, historical prediction is not essentially different from physical prediction. In principle, at least, the prediction of future events is possible, and is indeed the task of the human sciences. Popper's models of important historicist thinkers are Plato, Marx, and the modern totalitarian dictators and their apologists.

While Popper himself alludes to Freud as a historicist thinker, he does not fully develop a critique of psychoanalysis as a historicist doctrine. It is obvious, however, that not only psychoanalysis but also much of traditional and modern psychiatric theory assumes that personal conduct is determined by prior personal-historical events. All these theories downgrade and even negate explanations of human behavior in terms such as freedom, choice, and responsibility. "Every version of historicism," writes Popper, "expresses the feeling of being swept into the future by irresistible forces."[6] No more

perfect description of the Freudian imagery of human conduct—"swept into the future" by the Unconscious—could be
wished for. Moreover, in psychoanalysis, not only are "unconscious forces" regarded as the causes of behavior, but these
forces themselves are considered to be the results of instinctual drives and early life experiences. Here, then, lie the
crucial similarities between Marxism and Freudianism: each is
a historicist doctrine attributing all-pervasive causal influences
on conduct to a single type of "cause" or human circumstance. Marx singled out the economic arrangements prevailing in society as the overwhelming causes and explanations of
countless subsequent human events; Freud assigned the same
powers to family-historical, or so-called genetic-psychological
circumstances. Both of these unsupported—and, as Popper
shows, unsupportable and palpably false—doctrines have
nevertheless become widely accepted in our day. The sanction
of legal recognition has, of course, long supported the psychiatric view that certain kinds of "abnormal" behaviors were
"caused" by antecedently acting "mental diseases." This view
was simply extended to behaviors of all kinds by Freud and his
supporters, and has been embraced even by many of his
opponents, especially the behaviorists.

My opposition to deterministic explanations of human behavior does not imply any wish to minimize the effects, which
are indeed significant, of past personal experiences. I wish
only to maximize the scope of voluntaristic explanations—in
other words, to reintroduce freedom, choice, and responsibility into the conceptual framework and vocabulary of psychiatry.

In human affairs, and hence in the social sciences that try to
explain these affairs, we are faced with a full and complicated
interplay between observer and observed. This alone should
suffice to demonstrate what Popper has aptly called the "poverty of historicism." In particular, the prediction of a social
event itself may cause it to occur or may serve to prevent it

from occurring. The self-fulfilling prophecy stands as a stark symbol of the hazards of prediction in social affairs.

In view of the glaring inadequacies of historicist theories, the question arises as to why people subscribe to them. The answer seems to be that historicist doctrines function as religions masquerading as science. Popper puts it this way:

It really looks as if historicists were trying to compensate themselves for the loss of an unchanging world by clinging to the belief that change can be foreseen because it is ruled by an unchanging law.[7]

Curiously, Freud—himself a devout determinist and historicist—proposed a similar explanation for why men cling to religion: he attributed religious belief to man's inability to tolerate the loss of the familiar world of childhood, symbolized by the protective father.[8] Man thus creates a heavenly father and an imaginary replica of the protective childhood situation to replace the real or longed-for father and family. The differences between traditional religious doctrine, modern political historicism, and psychoanalytic orthodoxy thus lie mainly in the character of the "protectors": they are, respectively, God and the priests, the totalitarian leader and his apologists, and Freud and the psychoanalysts.

While Freud criticized revealed religion for the patent infantilism that it is, he ignored the social characteristics of closed societies and the psychological characteristics of their loyal supporters.[9] He thus failed to see the religious character of the movement he himself was creating. It is in this way that the paradox that is psychoanalysis—a system composed of a historicist theory and an antihistoricist therapy—came into being. Perhaps we should assume that historicism fulfilled the same needs for Freud, and for those who joined him in the precarious early development of psychoanalysis, as it had for others: it provided him with a hidden source of comfort and security against the threat of unforeseen and unpredictable change. This view is consistent with the contemporary use of psychoanalysis and dynamic psychiatry as means for obscuring and disguising moral and political conflicts as mere personal problems.

What, then, can we say about the relationship between psychosocial laws and physical laws? We can assert that the two are dissimilar. Psychosocial antecedents do not cause human sign-using behavior in the same way as physical antecedents cause their effects. Indeed, the use of terms such as "cause" and "law" in connection with human affairs ought to be recognized as metaphorical rather than literal. Finally, just as physical laws are relativistic with respect to mass, so psychological laws are relativistic with respect to social conditions. In short, the laws of psychology cannot be formulated independently of the laws of sociology.

Psychiatry and Ethics

In this book I shall view psychiatry, as a theoretical science, as consisting of the study of personal conduct. Its concerns are therefore to describe, clarify, and explain the kinds of games people play with each other and with themselves; how they learned these games; why they like to play them; what circumstances favor their continuing to play old games or learning new ones; and so forth.* Actual behavior is of course the datum from which the nature and rules of the game are inferred. Among the numerous types of behavior that persons engage in, the verbal form—that is, communications by means of conventional language—constitutes one of the central areas of interest for psychiatry. Hence, it is in the playing of language games that the interests of linguistics, philosophy, semiotic, and psychiatry meet. Each of these disciplines ad-

* A systematic analysis of personal conduct in terms of game-playing behavior will be presented in Part V. The model of games, however, is used throughout the book. Although it is difficult to give a concise definition of the concept of game, game situations are characterized by a system of set roles and rules binding for all of the players.

dresses itself to a different aspect of the language game: linguistics to its formal structure, philosophy and semiotic to its cognitive structure, and psychiatry to its personal significance and social usage.

I hope that this approach will effect a much-needed and long-overdue rapprochement between psychiatry on the one hand, and ethics and philosophy on the other. Questions such as, How does man live? and, How ought man to live? traditionally have been assigned to the domains of ethics, religion, and philosophy. Until the latter part of the nineteenth century, psychology and psychiatry were much more closely allied with ethics and philosophy than they are now. For example, much of what was formerly called "moral philosophy" is now called "social psychology" or simply "psychology." For the past century or so, psychologists have considered themselves, and have been accepted by others, as empirical scientists whose methods and theories are ostensibly the same as those of the biologist or physicist. Yet the fact remains that insofar as psychologists address themselves to the questions posed above, their work differs significantly from that of the natural scientist. Psychologists and psychiatrists deal with moral problems which, I believe, they cannot solve by medical methods.

In sum, then, inasmuch as psychiatric theories seek to explain, and systems of psychotherapy seek to change, human behavior, statements concerning goals and values must remain indispensable for all theories of personal conduct and psychotherapy.

Hysteria as a Paradigm of Mental Illness

If dated from Charcot's work on hysteria and hypnosis, modern psychiatry is approximately one hundred years old. How did the study of so-called mental illnesses begin and develop? What economic, moral, political, and social forces helped to mold it into its present form? And, perhaps most important, what effect has medicine, and especially the concept of bodily illness, had on the development of the concept of mental illness?

My strategy in this inquiry will be to answer these questions using conversion hysteria as the historical paradigm of the sorts of phenomena to which the term "mental illness" refers. I chose hysteria for the following reasons:

Historically, it is the problem that captured the attention of the pioneer neuropsychiatrists Charcot, Janet, and Freud, and paved the way to the differentiation between neurology and psychiatry.

Logically, hysteria brings into focus the need to distinguish bodily illness from the imitations of such illness. It confronts the physician—and others as well—with the task of distinguishing "real" or genuine illness from "imaginary" or faked illness. This distinction—between fact and facsimile, object and sign, physics and psychology, medicine and morals—remains the core problem of contemporary psychiatric epistemology.

Psychologically and socially, hysteria offers a good example of how a so-called mental illness may now be most adequately conceptualized in terms of sign-using, rule-following, and game-playing. In other words, hysteria is (1) a form of nonverbal communication, making use of a special set of signs; (2) a system of rule-following behavior, making use of the rules of illness, helplessness, and coercion; and (3) an interpersonal game characterized by, among other things, strategies of deceit to achieve the goal of domination and control.

Furthermore, I believe that the interpretation of hysteria which I shall present pertains fully—with appropriate modifications—to all so-called mental illnesses, and indeed to personal conduct generally. The manifest diversity among mental illnesses—for example, the differences between hysteria, depression, paranoia, schizophrenia, and so forth—may be regarded as analogous to the manifest diversity among languages. In each case, behind the apparent phenomenological differences there are certain basic similarities. Within a particular family of languages, for example the Indo-European, there are important similarities of both structure and function. Thus, English, French, German, and Dutch have much in common with one another, whereas each differs from Hungarian. In the same way, hysteria and dreaming—that is to say, the picture languages of hysterical conversions and dreams—closely resemble each other: both are composed of iconic signs. And both differ from, say, the language of paranoia—which makes use of ordinary language, and which owes its characteristic form and impact not to the peculiarity of its symbols, but to the peculiar uses which ordinary linguistic signs serve in it.

But if hysteria is not a mental illness—if, indeed, there are no mental illnesses at all—why do we call the things we now call "mental illnesses" by that name?

The Invention of Mental Illness

Until the middle of the nineteenth century, and beyond, illness meant a bodily disorder whose typical manifestation was an alteration of bodily structure: that is, a visible deformity, disease, or lesion, such as a misshapen extremity, ulcerated skin, or a fracture or wound. Since in this original meaning of it, illness was identified by altered bodily structure, physicians distinguished diseases from nondiseases according to whether or not they could detect an abnormal change in the structure of a person's body. This is why, after dissection of the body was permitted, anatomy became the basis of medical science: by this means, physicians were able to identify numerous alterations in the structure of the body which were not otherwise apparent. As more specialized methods of examining bodily tissues and fluids were developed, the pathologist's skills in detecting hitherto unknown bodily diseases grew explosively. Anatomical and pathological methods and criteria continue to play a constantly increasing role in enabling physicians to identify alterations in the physicochemical integrity of the body and to distinguish between persons who display such identifiable signs of illness and those who do not.

It is important to understand clearly that modern psychiatry—and the identification of new psychiatric diseases—began not by identifying such diseases by means of the established methods of pathology, but by creating a new criterion of what constitutes disease: to the established criterion of detectable alteration of *bodily structure* was now added the fresh criterion of alteration of *bodily function;* and, as the former was detected by observing the patient's body, so the latter was detected by observing his behavior. This is how and why conversion hysteria became the prototype of this new class of diseases—appropriately named "mental" to distinguish them from those that are "organic," and appropriately called also "functional" in contrast to those that are "structural." Thus, whereas in modern medicine new diseases were *discovered,* in modern psychiatry they were *invented.* Paresis was *proved* to be a disease; hysteria was *declared* to be one.

It would be difficult to overemphasize the importance of this shift in the criteria of what constitutes illness. Under its impact, persons who complained of pains and paralyses but were apparently physically intact in their bodies—that is, were healthy, by the old standards—were now declared to be suffering from a "functional illness." Thus was hysteria invented. And thus were all the other mental illnesses invented—each identified by the various complaints or functional-behavioral alterations of the persons affected by them. And thus was a compelling parallel constructed between bodily and mental illness: for example, as paresis was considered to be a structural disease of the brain, so hysteria and other mental illnesses were considered to be functional diseases of the same organ. So-called functional illnesses were thus placed in the same category as structural illnesses and were distinguished from imitated or faked illnesses by means of the criterion of voluntary falsification. Accordingly, hysteria, neurasthenia, depression, paranoia, and so forth were regarded as diseases that *happened* to people. Mentally sick persons did not "will" their pathological behavior and were therefore considered "not responsible" for it. These mental diseases were then contrasted with malingering, which was the voluntary imitation of illness. Finally, psychiatrists have asserted that malingering, too, is a form of mental illness. This presents us with the logical absurdity of a disease which, even when it is deliberately counterfeited, is still a disease.

But, clearly, this is the inescapable consequence of confusing discovering diseases with inventing them: the enterprise of trying to discover bodily diseases, constrained by fixed criteria and the requirements of empirical evidence, *cannot* eventuate in the conclusion that every phenomenon observed by the investigator is a disease; but the enterprise of inventing mental diseases, unconstrained by fixed criteria or the requirements of empirical evidence, *must* eventuate in the conclusion that any phenomenon studied by the observer may be defined as a disease.

Part One

■

The Myth
of Mental Illness

1 Charcot and the Problem of Hysteria

Since the modern concept of hysteria was cut from the cloth of malingering, and since the physician most responsible for establishing "hysteria" as a medically legitimate illness was Charcot, I shall start with an examination of his work; and I shall then trace the development of the concept of hysteria to the present time.

Charcot and Hysteria

Jean-Martin Charcot (1825–1893) was a neurologist and neuropathologist. In other words, he was a physician who specialized in diseases of the nervous system. Exactly what did this mean at that time? It is important that we understand what a physician like Charcot did, how he practiced, and how his work differed from that of his counterparts today.

One hundred years ago, physicians possessed practically no effective therapeutic methods with which to help their patients. This was especially true for the neurologist, who dealt almost entirely with what were then incurable diseases. Charcot, moreover, was not just a physician in private practice. He was also a professor of pathological anatomy at the Sorbonne, and, as such, his duties were educational and scientific; in addition he was a physician in charge of the care of patients at the Salpêtrière. In short, there was nothing therapeutic, in the contemporary medical sense of this word, about much of his work. Most of Charcot's hospitalized patients, whether those with or without organic neurological diseases—and, as we shall see, it was often extremely difficult to make this distinction at that time—were hospitalized not so much because they were sick as because they were poor, unwanted, or disturbing to others. From an economic, social, and political point of view, these patients were similar to those who today are committed to mental hospitals with psychiatric diagnoses of "major" mental disorders.[1] The families of these patients either could not care for their disabled relative because they were too poor to do so and it was cheaper to have the patient hospitalized, or, if they could, they did not want to do so because the patient was too offensive or troublesome. Overwhelmingly, then, Charcot's hospital patients came from the lower classes and thus stood socially far beneath their physician. What was Charcot's personal attitude toward his patients? We can infer the answer to this question from Freud's obituary of his great teacher:

Having at his disposal a considerable number of patients afflicted with chronic nervous disease he was enabled to take full advantage of his peculiar talent. He was not much given to cogitation, was not of the reflective type, but he had an artistically gifted temperament —as he said himself, he was a *visuel,* a seer. He himself told us the following about his method of working. He was accustomed to look again and again at things that were incomprehensible to him, to deepen his impression of them day by day until suddenly understanding of them dawned on him. Before his mind's eye, order then came into the chaos apparently presented by the constant repetition of the same symptoms; the new clinical pictures which were characterized by the constant combination of certain syndromes took shape; the complete and extreme cases, the "types," were then distinguishable with the aid of a specific kind of schematic arrangement, and with these as a starting point the eye could follow down

the long line of the less significant cases, the *formes frustes,* showing some one or other peculiar feature of the type and fading into
the indefinite. He called this kind of mental work, in which he had
no equal, "practising nosography" and he was proud of it.[2]

Charcot's own term for this work—"practising nosography"—is indeed an apt expression to describe his charting
of human misery and cataloguing it in the language of medicine. It is obvious that what Charcot here describes was of no
more help to his unknown patients than is a biologist's description of unknown bacteria to the microbes; indeed, depending
on the subsequent uses to which such information is put, the
objects catalogued may be as easily harmed as helped.

Freud then continues:

But to his pupils, who made the rounds with him through the wards
of the Salpêtrière—the museum of clinical facts for the greater part
named and defined by him—he seemed a very Cuvier, as we see him
in the statue in front of the Jardin des Plantes, surrounded by the
various types of animal life which he had understood and described;
or else he reminded them of the myth of Adam, who must have experienced in its most perfect form that intellectual delight so highly
praised by Charcot, when the Lord led before him the creatures of
Paradise to be named and grouped.[3]

To Charcot and Freud, these patients are mere objects or
things to be classified and manipulated. It is an utterly dehu-
manized view of the sick person. But then, we might recall
that even today physicians often speak of "cases" and "clinical
material" rather than of persons, thus betraying the same bias.

Charcot's sole clinical interest was thus to identify, describe, and classify neurological diseases—diseases of the nervous system. He therefore had to establish which phenomena
constituted such diseases, and which did not. As the geologist
must differentiate gold from copper, and both from other
metals which glitter, so the neurologist-nosographer must
differentiate multiple sclerosis, tabes, and hysteria. How does
he do this?

In Charcot's days the most important tool, besides the clinical examination, was the post-mortem study of the brain. Freud provided us with an interesting glimpse of how Charcot carried out his taxonomic work:

During his student days chance brought him into contact with a charwoman who suffered from a peculiar form of tremor and could not get work because of her awkwardness. Charcot recognized her condition to be "choreiform paralysis," already described by Duchenne, of the origin of which, however, nothing was known. In spite of her costing him a small fortune in broken plates and platters, Charcot kept her for years in his service and, when at last she died, could prove in the autopsy that "choreiform paralysis" was the clinical expression of multiple cerebro-spinal sclerosis.[4]

Guillain's biography of Charcot furnishes considerable additional information consistent with the picture sketched so far.[5] For example, we learn that Charcot moved in the highest social circles. He was a friend of Premier Gambetta and also of the Grand Duke Nicholas of Russia. He is said to have paved the way for the Franco-Russian Alliance. By all accounts, he aspired to the role of aristocratic autocrat. It requires no great feat of the imagination to infer what sort of personal relationship must have prevailed between him and his destitute and near-illiterate patients.

A firsthand account, although perhaps somewhat embellished, of the human side of Charcot's work may be obtained from Axel Munthe's beautiful autobiography, *The Story of San Michele*.[6] Of particular interest is Munthe's story of a young peasant girl who took refuge in hysterical symptoms to escape the drudgery of her home life. Munthe felt the "treatment" she was receiving at the Saltpêtrière was making her a lifelong invalid, and that Charcot was, in a way, keeping her imprisoned. He tried to "rescue" the girl, took her to his apartment, and hoped to convince her to return home. It appears from Munthe's story, however, that the young woman preferred the social role of hysterical patient at the Salpêtrière to that of peasant girl in her village. Evidently, life in the hospital was more exciting and rewarding than her "normal" existence—a contingency Munthe seriously underestimated. What emerges from this account, too, is that the Salpêtrière, under Charcot, was a special type of social institution. In addition to its similarities to present-day state mental hospitals, its function could also be compared to armies and religious organizations. In other words, the Salpêtrière provided its inmates with certain comforts and gratifications lacking in their ordinary social environment. Charcot and the other physicians who worked there functioned as rulers vis-à-vis their subjects. Instead of intimacy and trust, their relationship to each other was based on fear, awe, and deception.

As Charcot's knowledge of neuropathology increased and as his prestige grew, his interest shifted from neurological disorders to disorders which simulated such conditions. Such patients were then classified either hysterics or malingerers, depending on the observer's point of view. Those labeled "hysterics" were declared relatively more respectable and fit objects for serious study. They were regarded as suffering from an illness, rather than as trying to fool the physician or exhibiting willful misbehavior. This is the most fundamental connection, although by no means the only one, between the notions of hysteria and malingering. Freud's account of Charcot's work is again illuminating:

He explained that the theory of organic nervous diseases was for the present fairly complete, and he began to turn his attention almost exclusively to hysteria, thus suddenly focusing general attention to this subject. This most enigmatic of all nervous diseases— no workable point of view having yet been found from which physicians could regard it—had just at this time come very much into discredit, and this ill-repute related not only to the patients but was extended to the physicians who treated this neurosis. The general opinion was that anything may happen in hysteria; hysterics found no credit whatsoever. First of all Charcot's work restored dignity to the subject; gradually the sneering attitude, which the hysteric could reckon on meeting when she told her story, was given up; she was no longer a malingerer, since Charcot had thrown the whole weight of his authority on the side of the reality and objectivity of hysterical phenomena.[7]

This passage reveals how the study of hysteria was prejudged by the importance of its investigator, Charcot. Certain crucial issues were, therefore, obscured and must now be reexamined. Even the simple statement that Charcot turned his attention to "hysteria" rests on the tacit assumption that *this* was the patient's trouble. It was decided by fiat that, in contrast to organic neurological disease, these people had "functional nervous illnesses." And most of these "illnesses" were then named "hysteria." Freud's interesting comment should now be recalled: hysterics were no longer diagnosed as malingerers because of Charcot's authority. Freud offered no evidence or reason for preferring the category of hysteria to that of malingering. Instead, he appealed to ethical considerations, although without explicitly saying so:

Charcot had repeated on a small scale the act of liberation commemorated in the picture of Pinel which adorned the lecture hall of the Salpêtrière. Now that the blind fear of being fooled by the poor patient which had stood in the way of a serious study of the neurosis was overcome, the question arose which mode of procedure would most speedily lead to the solution of the problem.[8]

This situation is historically significant on two counts: first, because it marks the beginning of the modern study of so-called mental illnesses; second, because it contains what I regard as the major logical and procedural error in the evolution of modern psychiatry.

Is Every Form of Suffering Illness?

Freud compared Charcot's work to Pinel's. But, as I see it, Pinel's liberation of the mental patient from the dungeon was not a psychiatric achievement at all. It was a moral achievement. He claimed that the sufferers who had been placed in his charge were human beings, and as such entitled to the rights and dignities which, in principle at least, motivated the French Revolution. Pinel did not advocate that the patient should be better treated because he was sick. Indeed, the social role of the sick person was not an enviable one at that time. Hence, an appeal for better treatment on this ground would not have been effective.

Pinel's liberation of the mental patient should thus be viewed as social reform rather than as innovation in medical treatment. This is an important distinction. For instance, during the Second World War the removal of venereal infection from the classification of disciplinary offenses among military personnel was an act of social reform. The discovery of penicillin, while bearing on the same problem—namely, the control of venereal disease—was a scientific discovery.

What were the effects of Charcot's insistence that hysterics were ill and not malingering? Although this diagnosis did not alter the hysteric's disability, it did make it easier for him to be "ill." Like a little knowledge, this type of assistance can be dangerous. It makes it easier for both sufferer and helper to stabilize the situation and rest content with what is still a very unsatisfactory state of affairs. A comparison of Charcot with another famous French physician, Guillotin, may be illuminating in this connection.

Guillotin's highly questionable contribution to human welfare consisted of the reinvention and advocacy of the guillotine. This resulted in a relatively painless and, therefore, less cruel form of execution than those previously in vogue. In our day, the guillotine and the rope have been succeeded in America by the gas chamber and electric chair. Clearly, Guillotin's work is humane or inhuman, depending on which side of the issue we examine. From the point of view of making execution less painful for the executed, it was humane.

Since it also made things easier for the executioner and his employers, it was inhuman. What Charcot did was similar. To put it succinctly, Guillotin made it easier for the condemned to die, and Charcot made it easier for the sufferer, then commonly called a malingerer, to be sick. It may be argued that when dealing with the hopeless and the helpless, these are real accomplishments. Still, I would maintain that Guillotin's and Charcot's interventions were not acts of liberation, but were rather processes of narcotization or tranquilization.

In short, Charcot and Guillotin made it easier for people—particularly for the socially downtrodden—to be ill and to die. Neither made it easier for people to be well and to live. They used their medical knowledge and prestige to help society shape itself into an image it found pleasing. Efficient and painless execution fitted well into the self-image of Guillotin's society. Similarly, late-nineteenth-century European society was ready to view almost any disability—and particularly one, such as hysteria, that looked so much like a disorder of the body—as illness. Charcot, Kraepelin, Breuer, Freud, and many others lent their authority to the propagation of this socially self-enhancing image of what was then "hysteria," and what in our day has become the problem of "mental illness." The weight of authority of contemporary medical and psychiatric opinion continues, of course, to support and to expand this image.

The foregoing events have had far-reaching consequences in shaping contemporary consciousness and practices with respect to the so-called mentally ill. It might seem, at first glance, that to advocate, and indeed to insist, that an unhappy or troubled person is sick—and that he is sick in exactly the same sense and way in which a person suffering from cancer is sick—is humane and well-intentioned, as it aims to bestow upon such a person the dignity of suffering from a genuine illness over which he has no control. However, there is a hidden weight attached to this tactic which pulls the suffering person back into the same sort of disrepute from which this semantic and social reclassification was intended to rescue him. Indeed, labeling individuals displaying or disabled by problems in living as "mentally ill" has only impeded and retarded the recognition of the essentially moral and political nature of the phenomena to which psychiatrists address themselves.

Another error in decreeing that some malingerers be called hysterics was that it led to obscuring the similarities and differences between organic neurological disease and phenomena that only resembled them. In analyzing hysteria, we have a choice between emphasizing the similarities or the differences between it and neurological illness. Actually, both are readily apparent. The similarities between hysteria and bodily illness lie chiefly in the patient's complaints, his clinical appearance, and the fact that he is disabled. The differences between them lie in the empirical findings on physical, laboratory, and post-mortem examination. Moreover, these similarities and differences do not really stand in opposition to one another: there is no reason to believe that every person who complains of being ill or who looks ill or who is disabled —or who manifests all three of these features—must also have a physicochemical disorder of his body! This does not deny the possibility that there may be a connection between such complaints and bodily diseases. The nature of this connection, however, is empirical, not logical. Once this is clear, it becomes a matter of scientific and social choice whether we prefer to emphasize the similarities—and place hysteria in the category of illness; or whether we prefer to emphasize the differences— and place it in the category of nonillness.

The Double Standard in Psychiatry

The aim of my analysis of the problem of hysteria up to here has been to make explicit the values which influenced members of the psychiatric profession in the late nineteenth century. I dwelled on Charcot's attitude toward patients to show, first, that he never considered himself to be the patient's agent, and second, that his principal goal was to identify accurately specific diseases. As a result, Charcot tended to define all of the phenomena he studied as neurological disorders. If this accomplished nothing else, it at least justified the attention he paid to these phenomena and the pronouncements he made about them. In this respect, Charcot and his group stood in the same sort of relationship to hysteria as the contemporary physicist stands to nuclear war. The fact that atomic energy is used in warfare does not make international conflicts problems in physics; likewise, the fact that the brain is used in human behavior does not make moral and personal conflicts problems in medicine.

The point is that the prestige of the scientist—whether of a Charcot or of an Einstein—can be used to lend power to its possessor. He then may be able to achieve social goals that he could not otherwise attain. Once a scientist becomes so engaged, however, he has a powerful incentive to claim that his opinions and recommendations rest on the same grounds as his reputation! In Charcot's case, this meant that he had to base his case about hysteria on the premise that it was an organic neurological illness. Otherwise, if hysteria and hypnosis were problems in human relations and psychology, why should anyone have taken Charcot's opinions as authoritative? He had no special qualifications or competence in these areas. Hence, had he openly acknowledged that he was speaking about such nonmedical matters, he might have encountered serious opposition.

These historical developments lie at the root of a double standard in psychiatry that still persists. I refer to the dual orientation of physicians and psychiatrists to certain occurrences which they encounter in their practices. Charcot's informal, off-the-record comment about hysteria illustrates this phenomenon:

Some years later, at one of Charcot's evening receptions, I happened to be standing near the great teacher at a moment when he appeared to be telling Brouardel a very interesting story about something that had happened during his day's work. I hardly heard the beginning, but gradually my attention was seized by what he was talking of: a young married couple from a distant country in the East—the woman a severe sufferer, the man either impotent or exceedingly awkward. *"Tachez donc,"* I heard Charcot repeating, *"je vous assure, vous y arriverez."* Brouardel, who spoke less loudly, must have expressed his astonishment that symptoms like the wife's could have been produced by such circumstances. For Charcot suddenly broke out with great animation, *"Mais, dans des cas pareils c'est toujours la chose genitale, toujours . . . toujours";* and he crossed his arms over his stomach, hugging himself and jumping up and down on his toes several times in his own characteristically lively way. I know that for a moment I was almost paralyzed with amazement and said to myself: "Well, but if he knows that, why does he never say so?" But the impression was soon forgotten; brain anatomy and the experimental induction of hysterical paralyses absorbed all available interest.[9]

Why was Charcot so insistent? With whom was he arguing? With himself! Charcot must have known that he was deceiving himself when he believed that hysteria was a disease of the nervous system. Herein lies the double standard. The organic viewpoint is dictated by social expediency insofar as the rules of the game of medicine are defined so that adherence to this position will be rewarded. Adherence to the psychological viewpoint is required by the physician's loyalty to the truth and his identification or empathy with the patient. This dichotomy is reflected in the two basic contemporary psychiatric methods, namely, the physicochemical and the psychosocial. In the days of Charcot and Freud, however, only the former was recognized as belonging to science and medicine. Interest in the latter was synonymous with charlatanry and quackery.

Adherence to the organic or physicochemical viewpoint was, and continues to be, dictated also by the difficulty in many cases of differentiating hysteria from, say, multiple sclerosis or brain tumor (especially in their early stages). Conversely, patients with neurological illnesses may also exhibit so-called hysterical behavior or may show signs of other types of mental illness. This problem of the so-called differential diagnosis between "organic" and "psychological" illness has constituted one of the major stumbling blocks in the way of a systematic theory of personal conduct free of brain-mythological components.

Although the problem of malingering will be examined in detail in the next chapter, it is necessary here to say a few words concerning Charcot's view of the relationship between hysteria and malingering. In one of his lectures he said:

This brings me to say a few words about malingering. It is found in every phase of hysteria and one is surprised at times to admire the ruse, the sagacity, and the unyielding tenacity that especially the women, who are under the influence of a severe neurosis, display in order to deceive . . . especially when the victim of the deceit happens to be a physician.[10]

Already, during Charcot's lifetime and at the height of his fame, it was suggested, particularly by Bernheim, that the phenomena of hysteria were due to suggestion. It was also intimated that Charcot's demonstrations of hysteria were faked, a charge that has since been fully substantiated. Clearly, Charcot's cheating, or his willingness to be duped—whichever it was seems impossible to ascertain now—is a delicate subject. It was called "the slight failing of Charcot" by Pierre Marie. Guillain, more interested in the neurological than in the psychiatric contributions of his hero, minimized Charcot's involvement in and responsibility for faking experiments and demonstrations on hypnotism and hysteria. But he was forced to concede that "Charcot obviously made a mistake in not checking his experiments. . . . Charcot personally never hypnotized a single patient, never checked his experiments and, as a result, was not aware of their inadequacies or of the reasons of their eventual errors."[11]

To speak of "inadequacies" and "errors" here is to indulge in euphemisms. What Guillain described, and what others have previously intimated, was that Charcot's assistants had coached the patients on how to act the role of the hypnotized or hysterical person. Guillain himself tested this hypothesis with the following results:

In 1899, about six years after Charcot's death, I saw as a young intern at the Salpêtrière the old patients of Charcot who were still hospitalized. Many of the women, who were excellent comedians, when they were offered a slight pecuniary remuneration imitated perfectly the major hysteric crises of former times.[12]

Troubled by these facts, Guillain asked himself how this chicanery could come about and how it could have been perpetuated? All of the physicians, Guillain hastened to assure us, "possessed high moral integrity."[13] He then suggested the following explanation:

It seems to me impossible that some of them did not question the unlikelihood of certain contingencies. Why did they not put Charcot on his guard? The only explanation that I can think of, with all the reservation that it carries, is that they did not dare alert Charcot, fearing the violent reactions of the master, who was called the "Caesar of the Salpêtrière."[14]

We must conclude that Charcot's orientation to the problem of hysteria was neither organic nor psychological. He recognized and clearly stated that problems in human relationships may be expressed in hysterical symptoms. The point is that he maintained the medical view in public, for official purposes, as it were, and espoused the psychological view only in private, where such opinions were safe.

The Definition of Hysteria as Illness: A Strategy

My criticism of Charcot rests not so much on his adherence to a conventional medical model of illness for his interpretation of hysteria as on his covert use of scientific prestige to gain certain social ends. What were these ends? They were the acceptance of the phenomena of hypnotism and hysteria by the medical profession in general, and particularly by the French Academy of Sciences. But at what cost was this acceptance won? This question is rarely raised. As a rule, only the conquest over the resistance of the medical profession is celebrated. Zilboorg describes Charcot's victory over the French Academy as follows:

These were the ideas which Charcot presented to Académie des Sciences on February 13, 1882, in a paper on the diverse nervous states determined by the hypnotization of hysterics. One must not forget that the Académie had already condemned all research on animal magnetism three times and that it was a veritable *tour de force* to make the Académie accept a long description of absolutely analogous phenomena. They believed, and Charcot himself believed, that this study was far removed from animal magnetism and was a definite condemnation of it. That is why the Académie did not revolt and why they accepted with interest a study which brought to a conclusion the interminable controversy over magnetism, about which the members of the Académie could not fail to have some remorse. And remorse they well might have, for, from the standpoint of the actual facts observed, Charcot did nothing more than what Georget had asked the Académie to do fifty-six years previously. Whether one called the phenomenon animal magnetism, mesmerism, or hypnotism, it stood the test of time. The scientific integrity of the Académie did not. Like a government reluctant, indecisive, and uncertain of itself, it did nothing whenever it was safe to do nothing and yielded only when the pressure of events forced it to act and the change of formulatory cloak secured its face-saving complacency.[15]

I believe that this "change of formulatory cloak," which secured the admittance of hysteria into the French Academy, constitutes a historical paradigm. Like the influence of an early but significant parental attitude on the life of the individual, it continues to exert a malignant effect on the life of psychiatry.

Such "pathogenic" historical events may be counteracted in one of two ways. The first is by reaction-formation—that is, by an overcompensation against the original influence. Thus, to correct the early organic bias the significance of psychogenic factors in so-called mental illness is exaggerated. Enormous efforts have been expended in modern psychiatry, psychoanalysis, and psychosomatic medicine to create the impression that "mental illness is like any other illness."

The second way to remedy such a "trauma" is exemplified by the psychoanalytic method itself. By helping the person become explicitly aware of the events that have influenced his life in the past, the persistent effects of these events on his future can be mitigated and indeed radically modified. In my epistemological analysis of the problem of mental illness, I have relied in part on the same method and premise—namely, that by becoming explicitly aware of the historical origins and philosophical foundations of current psychiatric ideas and practices, we may be in a better position to modify them than we would be without such self-scrutiny.

2 Illness and Counterfeit Illness

The Logic of Classification

Persons said to be schizophrenic often exhibit a certain uncon-
ventional manner of using language. For example, such an
individual may say that a stag is an Indian, or that he is Jesus.
In traditional psychiatry, this sort of behavior is called
"schizophrenic thought disorder," and is attributed to the
patient's following "primitive" or non-Aristotelian logic.[1]
Since both stags and Indians move swiftly, he equates the two
and says that stags are Indians; since he wants to be admired
and loved like Jesus, he says he is Jesus. In short, such a
person uses any kind of likeness or similarity—in appearance
or intention—as the basis for classifying objects or ideas as
belonging in the same group or as establishing a common
identity between them.

In contrast, Aristotelian logic—which psychiatrists often
call "normal" or "mature" logic[2]—consists of deductive reasoning of the following sort. From the major premise that "All
men are mortals" and the minor premise that "Socrates is a
man," we conclude that "Socrates is mortal." This sort of
reasoning presupposes an understanding that a class called
"man" consists of specific individuals, bearing proper names.

I will show later[3] that the former type of logical operation
is intimately connected with a simple type of symbolization,

namely, that resting on a similarity between the object and the sign used to represent it. Such signs are called *iconic,* because they stand for the object represented much as a photograph stands for the person photographed. Languages composed of iconic signs lend themselves to, and are best suited for, codification on the basis of manifest or structural similarities. On the other hand, logically more complex languages, for example those using conventional signs, permit the classification of objects and phenomena on the basis of hidden or functional similarities.

On the Notions of Real and False

Identification and classification are fundamental to the need to order the world about us. The activity of ordering, while of special importance to science, is ubiquitous. For example, we classify some substances as solid, and others as liquid; we call certain objects "money," others "masterpieces of art," and still others "precious stones." Expressed logically, we declare that some things belong in class A, and others in class non-A. In some instances it may be difficult or impossible to establish in what class a particular item belongs. There are two general reasons for this: first, the classifier may lack the knowledge, skill, or tools necessary for distinguishing A from non-A; second, he may deliberately be deceived by other persons into believing that non-A is A. An unsophisticated person may thus misidentify copper as gold. Or a sophisticated art dealer may mistake a forgery for a masterpiece.

Ordinary language recognizes and reveals the importance of the human proclivity to imitate things, making one thing look like another. Many words denote a particular kind of relationship between two items, A and B, so that A signifies a designated object or event, and B signifies what may be called "counterfeit-A." The latter is characterized by looking, more or less, like A, this similarity in appearance being deliberately created by a human operator for some purpose. For example, money may be "real" or "counterfeit"; a painting or sculpture may be an "original" or a "forgery"; a person may be telling the "truth" or "lying"; an individual complaining of bodily symptoms may be a "sick patient" or a "healthy malingerer."

What is the relevance of this discussion of the logic of classification to hysteria and the problem of mental illness? The answer is that we cannot have a clear and meaningful concept of illness as a class of phenomena (say, class A) without recognizing, first, that there are occurrences which look like illnesses but are not (class B); and second, that there are occurrences which are counterfeit illnesses (class B'). All this is logically inherent in classifying certain phenomena that persons exhibit as illnesses (or as the symptoms of illnesses). If blindness or the paralysis of a leg are diseases—to take the simplest cases—then we must be prepared to deal, epistemologically, medically, and politically, with imitations of blindness and paralysis and with the persons who perform these imitations. Throughout this book I regard bodily diseases as "real" or literal, and consider mental diseases as "counterfeit" or metaphorical illnesses. In the final analysis, whether we classify behaviors that, in some way, however obscure or remote, resemble bodily diseases but are in fact not such diseases as "illnesses" or as "nonillnesses" has, of course, the most profound implications not only for the individuals directly affected, but for the whole social and political system which authenticates the classification.

Illness, Counterfeit Illness, and the Physician's Role

Confronted with a counterfeit, the observer may be deceived because the imitation is very good, because he is relatively unskilled in differentiating A from non-A, or because he wants to believe that non-A is A. Translating this into the language of bodily versus mental illness, we may assert that the physician may be deceived because certain hysterical or hypochondriacal bodily symptoms might be exceedingly difficult to distinguish from physicochemical disorders; or he may be unskilled in recognizing the manifestations of problems in living and might mistake bodily symptoms for physical illness; or, lastly, committed to the role of expert engineer of the body as a physicochemical machine, the physician may believe that all the human suffering he encounters is illness.

The differentiation of A from non-A rests on empirical *observations* and ends in the rendering of a *judgment*. The observer's role is similar to that of arbiter, umpire, or judge. For example, a painting may be brought to an art expert so that he can decide if it is a Renaissance masterpiece or a forgery. He may correctly identify the painting as falling into one or the other category. Or he may err either way. Or he may decide that he cannot determine whether the painting is an original or a forgery. In medical terms, this corresponds to the well-known "differential diagnosis" between organic and mental disease. In making a differential diagnosis, the physician functions as expert arbiter. If he limits himself to this role, he will simply classify the item brought to him as either A or non-A (including counterfeit-A); in other words, the physician will limit himself to telling the patient that the allegedly or apparently diseased body which he has brought for examination is sick or not sick.[4]

If the observer distinguishes two classes of items, so that he can identify some as members of class A and others as their imitations, he usually has certain reactions to his own judgment. His judgment may then be implemented by appropriate actions toward the items or persons concerned. For example, if money is identified as counterfeit, the police will attempt to arrest the counterfeiters. What will the physician do when confronted with counterfeit bodily illness? The physician's behavior in this situation has varied through the ages. Today, too, his reaction depends heavily on the personalities and social circumstances of both doctor and patient. I shall comment only on those reactions to this challenge which are pertinent to our present concerns.

1. The physician may react as a policeman confronted by a counterfeiter. This was the usual response before Charcot, when hysteria was regarded as the patient's attempt to deceive the doctor. It was as if the patient had been a counterfeiter who wanted to pass his worthless bills to the physician. Accordingly, the doctor's reaction was anger and a desire to retaliate. For real money—that is, real illness—physicians rewarded people. For fake money—that is, fake illness—they punished them. Many physicians still conduct themselves according to these unwritten rules of the Original Medical Game.

2. The physician may react as a pawnbroker who, trying to avoid loaning money on paste jewelry, behaves as if all his clients wanted to cheat him. The pawnbroker refuses to lend money on imitation jewelry. Similarly, the physician may refuse to treat the so-called hysterical patient. He sends him away, declaring, as it were: "I treat only genuine—bodily—illness; I do not treat fake—hysterical—illness."

3. The physician may react by redefining illness and treatment, that is, by changing the rules of the Original Medical Game. This is what Charcot began and Freud perfected. The change of game-rules thus introduced may be summarized as follows. Under the old rules, illness was defined as a physico-chemical disorder of the body which eventually manifested itself in the form of a disability. When disabled, the patient was to be protected and, if possible, treated for his illness; and he was usually excused from working and from other social obligations. On the other hand, when a person imitated being ill and disabled, he was considered and called a malingerer and was to be punished by physicians and social authorities alike. Under the new rules, the attitude toward this latter

group—or at least toward many members of it—was rede-fined. Henceforth, persons disabled by phenomena that resembled bodily diseases but were in fact not such diseases—in particular so-called hysterics—were also classified as ill—that is, "mentally ill"; and they were to be treated by the same rules that applied to persons who were bodily ill.

I maintain, therefore, that Freud did not *discover* that hysteria was a mental illness. He merely asserted and advocated that so-called hysterics be *declared* ill. The adjectives "mental," "emotional," and "neurotic" are semantic strategies to codify—and, at the same time, to conceal—the differences between two classes of disabilities or "problems" in meeting life: one consists of bodily diseases which, by impairing the functioning of the human body as a machine, create difficulties in social adaptation; the other consists of difficulties in social adaptation not attributable to a malfunctioning machinery but, on the contrary, inherent in the purposes the machine was made to serve by those who "built" it (parents, society) or by those who "use" it (individuals).

Changes in the Rules of Conduct and the Reclassification of Behavior

To illustrate the far-reaching implications of the foregoing process of reclassification, let us return to our analogy between the art expert and the doctor as diagnostician.

The expert may be commissioned to determine whether, for example, a beautiful French painting of uncertain origin was painted by Cézanne, as claimed by the art dealer, or whether it is a forgery, as feared by the prospective buyer. If the expert plays the game properly, he can reach only one of two answers: he concludes either that the painting is a genuine Cézanne or that it is a fake Cézanne.

But suppose that in the process of examining the painting, studying its origin, and so on, the art expert becomes increasingly impressed by the craftsmanship of the artist and by the beauty of his work. Might he then not conclude that, although the painting is not a genuine Cézanne, it is nevertheless a "real masterpiece"? In fact, if the painting is truly excellent, he might even declare that it is a greater masterpiece than a real Cézanne. The artist—let us call him Zeno, hitherto an unknown painter of Greek descent—may then be "discovered" as a "great impressionist painter." But did the expert "discover" Zeno and his masterpiece? Or did he "make" him a famous artist, and his painting a valuable canvas, by the weight of his expert opinion, seconded of course by the weight of many other art experts?

This analogy is intended to show that, strictly speaking, no one discovers or makes a masterpiece. And no one "falls ill with hysteria." Artists paint pictures, and people become, or act, disabled. But the *names,* and hence the *values,* we give to paintings—and to disabilities—depend on the rules of the system of classification that we use. Such rules, however, are not God-given, nor do they occur "naturally." Since all systems of classification are made by people, it is necessary to be aware of who has made the rules and for what purpose. If we fail to take this precaution, we run the risk of remaining unaware of the precise rules we follow, or worse, of mistaking the product of a strategic classification for a "naturally occurring" event. I believe this is exactly what has happened in psychiatry during the past sixty or seventy years, during which time a vast number of occurrences were reclassified as "illnesses." We have thus come to regard addiction, delinquency, divorce, homosexuality, homicide, suicide, and so on almost without limit, as psychiatric illnesses. This is a colossal and costly mistake.

But immediately someone might object that this is not a mistake, for does it not benefit addicts, homosexuals, or so-called criminals to be regarded as "sick"? To be sure, such labeling might benefit some people, sometimes. But this is so largely because people tolerate uncertainty poorly and insist that misbehavior be classified either as sin or as sickness. This dichotomy must be rejected. Socially deviant or obnoxious behavior may be classified in numerous ways, or may be left unclassified. Placing some physically healthy persons in the class of sick people may indeed be justified by appeals to ethics or politics; but it cannot be justified by appeals to logic or science.

For greater precision, we should ask: for whom, or from what point of view, is it a mistake to classify nonillnesses as illnesses? It is a mistake from the point of view of intellectual integrity and scientific progress. It is also a mistake if we believe that good ends—say, the social rehabilitation of criminals—do *not* justify the use of morally dubious means; in this case, deliberate or quasi-deliberate misrepresentation and mendacity.

This reclassification of nonillnesses as illnesses has, of course, been of special value to physicians and to psychiatry as a profession and social institution. The prestige and power of psychiatrists have been inflated by defining ever more phenomena as falling within the purview of their discipline. Mortimer Adler had noted long ago that psychoanalysts "are trying to swallow everything in psychoanalysis."[5] It is difficult to see why we should permit, much less encourage, such expansionism in a profession and so-called science. In international relations, we no longer treasure the Napoleonic ideal of national expansion at the expense of the integrity of neighboring peoples. Why, then, do we not consider psychiatric expansionism—even though it might be aided and abetted from many sides, that is, by patients, medical organizations, lawyers, and so forth—equally undesirable?

The role of the psychiatrist as expert arbiter charged with deciding who is or is not ill has not ceased with the renaming of malingering as hysteria and with calling the latter an illness. It has merely made his job more arbitrary and nonsensical.[6]

Let us now take a closer look at the logic of reclassifying some nonillnesses as illnesses. On the basis of certain criteria, we may decide to place all A's in one class and all non-A's in another. Subsequently, we may choose to adopt new criteria, revise our classification, and transfer some members of the latter class into the former. It is clear, however, that if we transferred all non-A's into the class of A's, class A would encompass all of the things we want to classify and would therefore be utterly useless. The usefulness of any class and of its name depends on the fact that it includes some things and excludes others. For example, there are many colors, but only a few are called "green." If we called more colors "green" than we now do, we could do so only at the expense of the names of other colors. Emphasizing that it is possible to see not only by green light but also by white, blue, yellow, and so forth, we might indeed insist on calling all colors "green."

It is just this sort of thing that has taken place in medicine and psychiatry during the past century. Beginning with such clear-cut bodily diseases as syphilis, tuberculosis, typhoid fever, cancer, heart failure, and fractures and other injuries, we have created the class called "disease" or "illness." This class had only a limited number of members, all of which shared the common characteristic of reference to a physico-chemical state of bodily disorder. This, then, is the *literal meaning* of disease or illness. As time went on, new items were added to this class. Some, like brucellosis or tularemia, were added because new medical methods made the identification of new bodily diseases possible. Others, like hysteria and depression, were added, not because it was dis-covered that they were bodily diseases, but because the criteria of what constitutes disease have been changed—from the physicochemical derangement of the body to the disability and suffering of the person. This is the *metaphorical meaning* of disease or illness. In this way, at first slowly and soon at an increasingly rapid rate, many new members were added to the class called disease. Hysteria, hypochondriasis, obsessions, compulsions, depression, schizophrenia, psychopathy, homosexuality—all these and many others thus became diseases. Soon, physicians and psychiatrists were joined by philosophers and journalists, lawyers and laymen, in labeling as "mental illness" any and every kind of human experience or behavior in which they could detect, or to which they could ascribe, "malfunctioning" or suffering. Divorce became an illness because it signaled the failure of marriage; bachelorhood, because it signaled the failure to marry; childlessness, because it signaled the failure to assume the parental role. All these things are now said to be mental illnesses or the symptoms of such illnesses.

Malingering as Mental Illness

The metamorphosis of malingering from the imitation of illness to mental illness illustrates my foregoing thesis.

As we saw, before Charcot entered on the stage of medical history, a person was considered to be ill only if there was something wrong with his body. Persons who imitated illness, or who were thought to imitate illness, were considered to be malingerers and hence the legitimate objects of the physician's scorn. It is, after all, a natural reaction to feel angry toward those who try to deceive us. Why shouldn't physicians feel angry toward those who try to deceive them? This view of malingering made it medically and morally acceptable for physicians to act antagonistically and punitively toward such persons. Although this perspective on malingering is old-fashioned, it is by no means passé: it is still held by respectable physicians and published in prestigious journals—as the following excerpt from the *Journal of the American Medical Association* illustrates:

Physicians in the United States may be unaware of the patient who spends his time going from place to place, resulting in wide travels, and presenting himself to hospitals, with a fanciful history and extraordinary complaints. It is not uncommon for these patients to have many surgical scars crisscrossing their abdomens, and willingly to allow further surgical procedures to be performed, regardless of the dangers. Publicizing case histories of such patients seems to be the only way of coping with the problem, which exploits medical services that could be put to better use.[7]

The article concludes with the following paragraph:

The case of a 39-year-old merchant seaman is a remarkable example of hospital vagrancy and spurious hemoptysis. Similar patients in Britain have been said to have Münchausen's syndrome because their wide travels and fanciful histories are reminiscent of the travels and adventures of fiction's Baron Münchausen. Such patients constitute an economic threat and an extreme nuisance to the hospital they choose to visit, for their deception invariably results in numerous diagnostic and therapeutic procedures. Publicizing their histories in journals, thereby alerting the medical profession, seems the only effective way of coping with them. Appropriate disposition would be confinement in a mental hospital. Such patients have enough social and mental quirks to merit permanent custodial care, otherwise their exploitation of medical facilities will go on indefinitely.[8]

These excerpts show that physicians often play the medical game without self-reflection, unaware of the rules by which the game is played. It is important to note, also, that the author advocates the "permanent custodial care" as the proper punishment—although he calls it "care"—of those persons who try to deceive physicians into believing they are sick. Since physicians often have the social power to make such punishment enforceable, this view is not without serious consequences.[9]

Freud and the psychoanalysts created a new system of psychiatric classification, especially with respect to hysteria and malingering. Bodily illness remained, of course, class A, so to speak. Hysteria was still regarded as a type of counterfeit illness, but as a very special form of it: the patient himself did not know he was simulating. And the concept of malingering, too, was retained, but it was redefined as the conscious imitation of illness. Classes B and B', hysteria and malingering, were thus distinguished by whether the patient's imitative behavior was "unconscious" or "conscious."

The role of the psychiatrist-as-arbiter changed accordingly: previously his task was to distinguish bodily illness from all that did not fit into this class; now it became, in addition, to distinguish the "unconscious" imitation of illness, or hysteria, from the "conscious" imitation of it, or malingering. These judgments are, of course, even more arbitrary than were the previous ones. This is why, in part, the concepts of hysteria, neurosis, and mental illness have come to be used in an increasingly capricious and strategic, rather than consistent and descriptive, way. Typical is Freud's assertion that "There are people who are complete masochists without being neurotic."[10] Of course, Freud never explained which masochists are neurotic and which are not.

The disposition to view virtually all forms of personal conduct—especially if it is unusual or is studied by the psychiatrist—as illness is reflected by the contemporary psychoanalytic view of malingering. According to it, malingering is an illness—in fact, an illness "more serious" than hysteria. This is a curious logical position, for it amounts to nothing less than a complete denial of the human ability to imitate—in this instance, to imitate certain forms of disability. When simulation of mental illness is regarded as itself a form of mental illness, the rules of the psychiatric game are so defined as to explicitly exclude the class of "counterfeit illness." Only two classes are recognized: A—illness, and non-A—nonillness. Counterfeit illness, or malingering, is now defined as itself an illness. The good imitation of a masterpiece is redefined as itself a masterpiece! Since a good imitation of a masterpiece is as pleasing to the eye as the original, this is not an entirely unreasonable point of view. But it entails a radical redefinition of the idea of forgery. In the case of so-called psychiatric illnesses, such redefinitions have apparently occurred without anyone quite realizing what had happened.

It was probably Bleuler who first suggested that the simulation of insanity be regarded as a manifestation of mental illness. In 1924 he writes: "Those who simulate insanity with some cleverness are nearly all psychopaths and some are actually insane. Demonstration of simulation, therefore, does not at all prove that the patient is mentally sound and responsible for his actions."[11]

The view that malingering is a form of mental illness became popular during the Second World War, especially among American psychiatrists, when it was believed that only a "crazy" or "sick" person would malinger. Eissler's interpretation of malingering is typical of this modern psycho-imperialistic attitude toward moral and political problems of all kinds:

It can be rightly claimed that malingering is always the sign of a disease often more severe than a neurotic disorder because it concerns an arrest of development at an early phase. It is a disease which to diagnose requires particularly keen diagnostic acumen. The diagnosis should never be made but by the psychiatrist. It is a great mistake to make a patient suffering from the disease liable to prosecution, at least if he falls within the type of personality I have described here.[12]

This proposition has obvious advantages for the physician. For one thing, it buttresses the potentially shaky morale of the erstwhile civilian psychiatrist conscripted into the military service. It supports—at the patient's expense, of course—the physician's uncritical endorsement of the aims and values of the war effort. Although the patient might have been treated more or less kindly when regarded as sick, he was, at the same time, deprived of this particular opportunity to rebel against the demands placed on him. This form of protest was disallowed, and those who resorted to it were labeled "mentally ill" and were given "N.P. discharges."[13]

Concluding Remarks on Objects and Their Representations

The unifying thread that runs through this chapter is the idea of similarity. An iconic sign—say, a photograph—resembles the object it represents; a map represents the terrain of which it is a two-dimensional model. Photographs and maps imply, moreover, that they merely represent "real" things. In everyday life, it makes a vast practical difference whether objects are clearly recognized as representations or are accepted and treated as objects in their own rights. The difference between stage money and counterfeit money illustrates this point. Although stage money might look like real money, it is usually clearly identified as make-believe. It is of course possible to imagine a situation in which stage money is mistaken for real money. My point here is that the context of a message forms an integral part of the total communicational package. Thus, whether bills are regarded as stage money or counterfeit may depend not so much on how the objects appear as on who passed them to whom, where, and how. The stage setting itself implies that the monies used are props. Similarly, the setting of an economic transaction implies that the monies are real, and if they are not real, that they are counterfeit.

Let us apply these considerations to the problem of hysteria. Now it is disabled behavior that is under scrutiny, but the communicational package must include the situation in which such behavior is presented. If it is presented in a physician's office, we must ask: should the disabled behavior be viewed as an object in its own right or as a representation? If the phenomena presented are regarded and treated as real objects, then they must be classified as illness or as malingering, depending solely on one's definition of what constitutes illness. If, however, the phenomena are regarded as representations—the metaphors, models, or signs of other things—then a totally different interpretation becomes necessary. We may then speak of illness-imitative behavior. This, however, can under no circumstances be called illness unless we are prepared to do the nonsensical thing of placing an item and its known imitation in the same class.

Even if there is agreement that both malingering and hysteria refer to illness-imitative behavior, there still remains the uncertainty concerning the cognitive quality and the intent of the imitation. Is it deliberate or unwitting, conscious or unconscious? Is the person doing the imitation seeking to advance his own interests, or is he doing it for some other reason? In the theater, for example, it is clear that both actors and spectators know that what looks like money is in fact an imitation, a prop. In ordinary life, on the other hand, only the counterfeiters know that the bills they pass to others are counterfeit; those to whom the bills are passed, and who may pass them on to others, do not know this. Believing that they possess a real object when in fact they only possess its imitation, they are deceived.

What, then, is the comparable situation with respect to the imitation of illness? Does the so-called hysterical patient believe that he is "really ill," or does he know that he only "feels ill" but is not? Some insist that the patient offers illness in good faith; others insist that he is faking. There is often evidence to support both of these views. As a rule, the question cannot be answered unequivocally. Indeed, the patient's failure to come to grips with whether he suffers from bodily disease or personal problems, whether his message is about objects or representations, is one of the most important characteristics of his behavior.[14]

So much for the patient, in his role as actor or message sender. What about the spectators, the recipients of the message? Their reaction to the drama of hysteria will depend on their personality and relationship to the patient. Stranger and relative, foe and friend, nonpsychiatric physician and psycho-analyst—each will react differently. I shall comment briefly on the characteristic reactions of the last two only. The non-psychiatric physician tends to view and treat all forms of disability as objects proper, not as representations: that is, as illness or potential illness. On the other hand, the psychoanalyst tends to view and treat the same phenomena as representa-tions: that is, as symbols or communications. But since he fails to clearly recognize and articulate this distinction, he persists in describing his observations and interventions as if he were talking about objects instead of representations. The latter are, of course, just as "real" as the former. A photograph of a person is just as real as the person in the flesh. But the two are clearly not the same, and do not belong in the same class.

If we take this distinction seriously, we shall be compelled to regard psychiatry as dealing not with mental illness but with communications. Psychiatry and neurology are therefore not sister sciences, both belonging to the superordinate class called *medicine*. Rather, psychiatry stands in a *meta relation* to neurology and to other branches of medicine. Neurology is concerned with certain parts of the human body and its func-tions *qua* objects in their own rights—not as signs of other objects. Psychiatry, as defined here, is expressly concerned with signs *qua* signs—not merely with signs as things pointing to objects more real and interesting than they themselves.

3   The Social Context of Medical Practice

Traditionally, psychiatrists have regarded mental illness as a phenomenon apart from and independent of the social context in which it occurred. The symptomatic manifestations of diseases of the body, for instance of diphtheria or syphilis, are indeed independent of the sociopolitical conditions of the country in which they occur. A diphtheritic membrane was the same and looked the same whether it occurred in a patient in Czarist Russia or Victorian England.

Since mental illness was considered to be basically like bodily illness, it was logical that no attention was paid to the social conditions in which the alleged disease occurred. This is not to say that the effects of social conditions on the causation of illness were not appreciated. On the contrary, this sort of relationship had been recognized since antiquity. It was known, for example, that poverty and malnutrition favored the development of tuberculosis, or sexual promiscuity the spread of syphilis; but it was held, and rightly so, that once these diseases made their appearance, their manifestations were the same whether the patient was rich or poor, nobleman or serf. The phenomenology of bodily illness is indeed independent of the socio-economic and political character of the society in which it occurs. But this is emphatically not true for the phenomenology of so-called mental illness, whose manifestations depend upon and vary with the educational, economic, religious, social, and political character of the individual and the society in which it occurs.

When persons belonging to different religions or social classes become ill—for example with pneumonia or bronchogenic carcinoma—their bodies display the same sorts of physiological derangements. Hence, for a given bodily disease all patients might, in principle, receive the same treatment. This, indeed, is considered to be the scientifically correct position regarding the treatment of bodily diseases. If mental illnesses are truly like ordinary diseases, it becomes logical, and in fact necessary, to apply the same medical standard of treatment to them. This use of the medical model—namely, the idea that psychiatric treatment must be based on psychiatric diagnosis —has, in my opinion, led to a disastrous abuse of patients.

To demonstrate the importance of social and cultural influences on all therapeutic relationships, and in particular to show the differential effects of such influences on psychiatric interventions, I shall briefly review the therapeutic situations typical of three different socio-cultural settings; namely, the situations characteristic of late-nineteenth-century Europe, of the contemporary Western democracies, and of the Soviet Union.

I shall use the term "therapeutic situation" to refer to both medical and psychotherapeutic practice. And, because the connections between social contexts, moral values, and therapeutic arrangements are numerous and complex, I shall focus on two particular aspects of this problem. They may be best stated in the form of questions: (1) Whose agent is the therapist? (2) How many persons or institutions are directly involved in the therapeutic situation?

Nineteenth-Century Liberalism, Capitalism, and Individualism

Since antiquity, medical care was regarded much as were other economic goods or services. It was a commodity that could be purchased by the rich only. To the poor, when given, it had to be given free, as charity. This social arrangement was firmly established by the time modern scientific advances in medicine began, during the latter half of the nineteenth century. It should be recalled, too, that this period was characterized by the flowering of liberal thoughts and deeds in Europe, as manifested, for example, by the abolition of serfdom in Austria-Hungary and Russia.

As industrialization and urbanization flourished, the proletariat replaced the socially unorganized peasant class. Thus, a self-conscious and class-conscious capitalism developed, and with it recognition of a new form of mass suffering and disability, namely, poverty. The phenomenon of poverty, as such, was of course nothing new. However, the existence of huge numbers of impoverished people, crowded together within the confines of a city, was something new. At the same time, and undoubtedly out of the need to alleviate mass poverty, there arose "therapists" for this new "disease" of the masses. Among them, Karl Marx is, of course, the best known. He was no solitary phenomenon, however, but rather exemplified a new social role and function—the revolutionary as "social therapist." Along with these developments, the ethics of individualism also gained momentum. The basic value of the individual—as opposed to the interests of the masses or the nation—was emphasized, especially by the upper social classes. The professions, medicine foremost among them, supported the ethics of individualism. This ethic gradually became pitted against its opposite, collectivism.

Although the ethics of individualism and collectivism are polar opposites, their present forms were achieved through a simultaneous development, and they often exist side by side. This was already the case, to some extent, in the days of Charcot, Breuer, and Freud. This contention may be illustrated by some observations concerning the therapeutic situations characteristic of that period.

The physician in Charcot's Paris, or in his counterpart's Berlin, Moscow, or Vienna, was usually engaged in two diametrically opposite types of therapeutic practices or situations. In one, he was confronted by an affluent private patient. Here the physician served, by and large, as the patient's agent, having been hired by him to make a diagnosis and, if possible, achieve a cure. The physician, for his part, demanded payment for services rendered. He thus had an economic incentive, in addition to other incentives, to help his patient. Furthermore, since some bodily illnesses were considered shameful—among these being not only venereal diseases but tuberculosis and certain dermatological ailments as well—a wealthy person could also avail himself of the social protection of privacy. In fact, just as a wealthy person could buy a house large enough to provide several rooms for his sole occupancy, so he could also buy the services of a physician for his sole use. In its extreme form, this amounted to having a personal physician, much as one had a valet, maid, or cook. This custom is by no means extinct. In some parts of the world, wealthy or socially prominent people still have personal physicians whose duty is to care only for them or perhaps their families. A modification of this arrangement is the private, two-person medical situation, which affords the patient the time, effort, and privacy necessary for his care but leaves the physician free to care for other patients within the limits of his available time and energy. The development and safeguarding of therapeutic privacy are, of course, closely tied to the individualistic-capitalist socio-economic system. Such privacy cannot be maintained, and is even officially devalued, in collectivistic-communist societies, where the physician's primary loyalty is to the state rather than to the patient.

It is implicit in this discussion that having access to a private therapeutic relationship is something desirable. Why is this so? The answer lies in the connections between illness or disability and shame, and between shame and privacy. The feeling of shame is closely related to what other people think of one. Exposure and humiliation are feared both as punishments for shameful acts and as stimuli for increasingly intense feelings of shame. Secrecy and privacy protect the person from public exposure and hence from shame. Regardless of whether the shame is occasioned by physical disability, psychological conflict, or moral weakness, it is more easily acknowledged if it is shared with only a single person—as it is in the confessional or in private psychotherapy—than if it is communicated to many people. Privacy in medical or psychotherapeutic relationships is thus useful because it protects the patient from undue embarrassment and humiliation, and thus facilitates psychological mastery of his problem.

In addition, privacy and secrecy in the therapeutic situation are desirable and necessary also to protect the patient from "real"—that is, social rather than emotional—harm. Social isolation and ostracism, loss of employment, and injury to family and social status are some of the hazards that threaten a person should his condition or diagnosis become public knowledge. In this connection, such possibilities as syphilis in a schoolteacher, psoriasis in a cook, or schizophrenia in a judge should be kept in mind. These, however, are merely illustrative examples. The possibilities both of reward and penalty for publicly established diagnoses are virtually limitless. The precise character of the rewards and penalties will vary, once again, with the moral, political, and scientific character of the society.

The second type of therapeutic situation I want to consider is charity practice. The differences between it and private practice are often overlooked as a result of concentrating on the patient's disease and the physician's alleged desire to cure it. In traditional charity practice, the physician was not the patient's agent. Hence, a truly confidential relationship between patient and physician could not develop. The physician was professionally and legally responsible to his superiors and employers. He was, therefore, bound to orient himself for his rewards, at least to some extent, to his employer, rather than to his patient. It is often maintained nowadays that removing the financial involvement with the patient enables the physician better to concentrate on the technical task at hand—provided that he is adequately remunerated. While this might be true in thoracic surgery, it is assuredly not true in psychotherapy. In any case, it is clear that the financial inducement which the private patient offers the physician is absent in charity practice. The main features of these two types of therapeutic situations are summarized in Table 1.

The contrast between private and public medical care is often represented as if it were like the difference between a palace and a hovel. One is fine and expensive; anyone who could afford it would be foolish if he did not secure it, especially if he needed it. The other is inferior and second-rate; at

Table 1. Private Versus Charity Practice

Characteristics of the Situation	Private Practice	Charity Practice
Number of participants	Two (or few) Two-person situation "Private"	Many Multiperson situation "Public"
Whose agent is the therapist?	Patient's Patient's guardian's (e.g., pediatrics) Patient's family's	Employer's (e.g. institution, state, etc.)
Sources and nature of the therapist's rewards	Patient: money, referrals, etc.	Employer: money, promotion, prestige through status
	Patient's relatives and friends: satisfaction from having helped	Patient's relatives and friends: satisfaction from having helped
	Self: satisfaction from mastery	Self: satisfaction from mastery
	Colleagues: satisfaction from proven competence	Colleagues: satisfaction from proven competence

best, it makes life livable. Hence, although physicians and politicians have tried to assure the poor that their medical care was equally as good as that of the rich, this pious message usually fell on deaf ears. Instead, people have tried to raise their standard of living. In this effort, so far the people of the United States, Japan, and some European countries have been the most successful. This has resulted in certain fundamental changes in the patterns of medical care—and hence in the sociology of the therapeutic situation—in these countries. I shall comment on these changes now, and shall then consider the socio-medical situation in the Soviet Union.

Contemporary Society and Its Pattern of Health Care

Progressive technological and socio-cultural sophistication has led to the development of several means of protection against future poverty, want, and helplessness. One of these is insurance. We shall here be especially concerned with the effects of health insurance on medical and psychotherapeutic relationships.

Insured Practice

From our present point of view it matters little whether protection from illness is guaranteed for the individual by a private insurance company or is furnished by the state.

Health insurance introduces a completely new phenomenon into the practice of medicine. The most significant feature of insured practice—a name which I suggest to distinguish it from both private and charity practice—is that it is neither private nor public. The physician-patient relationship is so structured that the doctor is neither the patient's sole agent nor that of a charitable institution. This arrangement cannot be reduced to the old patterns of medical care and cannot be understood in their terms. It is commonly believed that the insured situation does not differ significantly from the private practice situation, the only difference being that the physician is paid by the insurance company instead of by the patient. Rarely is insured medicine regarded as similar to charity practice. I submit, however, that there are more important similarities between insured and charity practice than between insured and private practice. For the insurance arrangement, like the charitable one, makes a two-person, confidential relationship between doctor and patient virtually impossible.

Without penetrating further into the sociological intricacies of insured medicine, I should like to offer some generalizations which may be useful for our understanding of the problem of mental illness. It appears to be a general rule that the more clear-cut, objective, or socially acceptable a patient's disease is, the more closely insured practice resembles private practice. For example, if a woman slips on a banana peel in her kitchen and fractures her ankle, her treatment may not be significantly influenced by who pays for it—she, or an insurance company, or the state.

On the other hand, the more an illness deviates from something that happens to a person, and the more it is something that the person does or makes happen, the greater are the differences between the insured situation and the private, two-person situation. For example, if a woman falls in a factory rather than in her kitchen, she will not only receive compensation for her injury, but will also be granted a medical excuse to stay away from work. Furthermore, if she has a young child at home whom she would like to care for herself, she will have a powerful incentive to be disabled for a longer period than she might be otherwise. Obviously, this sort of situation requires an arbiter or judge to decide whether a person is or is not sick and disabled. The physician is the logical candidate for this role. It may be argued that physicians in private practice also perform this task. But this is not so. The physician in private practice is primarily the patient's agent. Should there be a conflict between his opinion and the presumed "real facts"—as may occur when the patient is involved with draft boards, insurance companies, or industrial concerns—the latter groups rely on the judgments of their own physicians. In the case of the draft board, for example, the examining physician has absolute power to overrule a private physician's opinion. And if he does not have such power, as in the case of an industrial concern, the conflict of opinion is arbitrated in a court of law.

In the case of insured practice, the answer to the question, Whose agent is the physician? is not—and indeed cannot be—clearly defined. As a result, the physician may sometimes be for the patient and sometimes against him—it being understood that "for" and "against" are here used in accordance with the patient's judgments of his own needs and wants.

In short, so-called mental illnesses share only a single significant characteristic with bodily diseases: the sufferer or "sick person" is, or claims to be, more or less disabled from performing certain activities. The two differ from one another in that mental illnesses can be understood only if they are viewed as occurrences that do not merely happen to a person but rather are brought about by him (perhaps unconsciously or unwittingly), and hence are of some value to him. This assumption is unnecessary—indeed, it is unsupportable—in the typical cases of bodily illness.

The premise that the behavior of persons said to be mentally ill is meaningful and goal-directed—provided one is able to understand the patient's behavior from his particular point of view—underlies virtually all forms of psychotherapy. Furthermore, if the psychotherapist is to perform his task properly, he must not be influenced by socially distracting considerations concerning his patient. This condition can be met best if the relationship is rigidly restricted to the two people involved in it.

The Private Practice Situation

It is necessary now to refine our conception of private practice. So far I have used this term in its conventional sense, to denote the medical activities of any physician not employed by an agency, institution, or the state. According to this definition, such a physician is engaged in private practice regardless of how he is paid or by whom. This definition will no longer suffice. Instead, we shall now have to adopt a much stricter definition of private practice. I suggest that we define the Private Practice Situation as a contract between a patient and a physician: the patient hires the doctor to assist him with his own health care and pays him for it. If the physician is hired by someone other than the patient, or is paid by another party, the medical relationship will no longer fall in the category of Private Practice Situation. This definition highlights, first, the two-person nature of the relationship; and second, the autonomy and self-determination of the patient. I shall continue to use the expression "private practice" in its conventional sense, to refer to all types of noncharity, non-institutional practice; and shall reserve the term Private Practice Situation (with initials capitalized) to designate the two-person therapeutic situation (see Table 2).

It is important to note, in this connection, that affluence fosters not only health insurance but also private practice. In the United States, a considerable proportion of the latter is psychiatric or psychotherapeutic practice. This proportion becomes even more significant if it is considered not in relation to the general category of private practice, but rather in relation to the narrowly defined Private Practice Situation. Psychotherapeutic practice is, indeed, the most important contemporary representative of a truly two-person therapeutic

Table 2. Private Practice Situation Versus Insured Practice

Characteristics of the Situation	Private Practice Situation	Insured Practice
Number of participants	Two Two-person situation	Three or more Multiperson situation

Whose agent is the therapist?	Patient's	Therapist's role is poorly defined and ambiguous:
		  Patient's agent, when in agreement with his aspirations
		  Society's agent, when in disagreement with patient's aspirations
		  His own agent, trying to maximize his own gains (e.g., compensation cases)

Sources and nature of therapist's rewards	Patient: money, referrals, etc. Self: satisfaction from mastery Colleagues	Patient: cure, gratitude, etc. Self: satisfaction from mastery Colleagues System or state: money, promotion, etc.

relationship. Deterioration in the privacy of the traditional medical situation may in fact be one of the reasons for the increased demand for psychotherapeutic services. Since the general physician ceased to be the true representative of the patient, the suffering person has turned to the psychiatrist and to the nonmedical psychotherapist as new representatives of his best interests.

To be sure, increasing economic affluence also serves to stimulate the demand for psychotherapeutic services. As soon as people have more money than they need for whatever they consider the necessities of life, they expect to be happy. And since most people still will not be happy, some will use some of their money to seek happiness through psychotherapy. From this point of view, the social function of psychotherapy is similar not only to that of religion, but also to that of alcohol, tobacco, cosmetics, and various recreational activities.

These considerations touch on the relationship between social class, mental illness, and the type of treatment received for it. It has always been known that educated, rich, and important persons receive very different kinds of psychiatric treatments than do uneducated, poor, and unimportant persons. The validity of this impression was solidly established by the careful studies of Hollingshead and Redlich,[1] who demonstrated that, in the United States, affluent psychiatric patients are generally treated by psychotherapy, while poor patients are treated by physical interventions.

The over-all social impact of economic affluence on medicine generally, and on psychiatry in particular, is complex and contradictory; it seems both to promote and to inhibit the free play of a confidential two-person therapeutic situation. Better education and economic security favor the conditions necessary for a two-person therapeutic contract; whereas the spread of insured health protection and government-sponsored medical care impair the conditions necessary for it. It is also worth noting that while the Private Practice Situation is being displaced by patterns of insured care in the democracies, in the Soviet Union it was liquidated when physicians became state employees. I shall now turn to a survey of medical practice in Soviet Russia. This will help us to sharpen the contrast between the role of the physician as agent of the patient and as agent of the state.

Soviet Medicine

Most of the Russian people depend on medical services furnished by the state. Private practice exists but is available only to persons occupying the uppermost layers of the Soviet social pyramid. One of the characteristic features of the Russian medical scheme is the consequence of the government's strong emphasis on agricultural and industrial production. The necessity of hard work is impressed on the people in every possible way. It follows that those who wish to avoid working find in falling sick and remaining disabled one of the few means of escape from what they experience as a sort of enslavement. Since the presence of genuine illness is not always obvious to the layman, it falls upon the physician to act as expert arbiter: he must decide which persons claiming to be ill are "really ill," and which only "malinger." Here is how Field describes this situation:

It stands to reason that certification of illness cannot be left, under most circumstances, to the person who claims to be sick. This would make abuses too easy. It is the physician, then, as the only person technically qualified to do so, who must "legitimize" or "certify" sickness in the eyes of society. This means, in turn, that abuses of the patient's role will consist in conveying to the physician the impression that one's sickness is independent of one's conscious motivation—whereas it actually is not. This possibility beclouds the classical assumption that the person who comes to the physician must necessarily be sick (independently of motivation): on the contrary, in certain cases, just the opposite assumption may be held. . . . [A] society (or social group) which, for any number of reasons, cannot offer its members sufficient incentives of motivation for the faithful and spontaneous performances of their social obligations must rely on coercion to obtain such performances. Because of the presence of coercion such a society will also generate a high incidence of deviant behavior to escape coercion. Simulation of illness (technically known as malingering) will be one form of such behavior. Malingering can be considered as a medical, a social, and a legal problem. It is a medical problem only insofar as it is the physician's task to certify who is a *bona fide* patient and who is a faker. It is a social problem insofar as the assumption that the person who comes to the physician must necessarily be sick (independently of motivation) is no longer tenable. The opposite assumption may sometimes be just as valid. It is often a legal problem because a fraud has been perpetrated.

Malingering may have far-reaching consequences because the "business" of society (or the group) is not done and because ordinary social sanctions are inadequate to close this escape valve. This means, in turn, that some provision must be made, some mechanism devised, to control the granting of medical dispensations. The logical point at which to apply this control is the physician.[2]

Field further notes that, because of a widespread anxiety among physicians that every patient is a potential spy or *agent provocateur,* doctors are afraid to be lenient with individuals who do not suffer from objectively demonstrable diseases.

Most Russian physicians are women, and their social status is relatively low—comparable to that of American schoolteachers or social workers. Indeed, the members of these three groups share an important feature: each of them functions as an *agent of society.* In other words, persons fulfilling these roles are employed by the government or the state to minister to the "needs" of certain socially defined and designated groups—for example, schoolchildren, persons on relief, the sick, and so forth. These agents—who are quite literally "social workers"—are generally not sought out, and are never paid, by their customers, clients, or patients, and hence do not owe their primary loyalties to them. In fact, they may not feel that they owe any loyalty to their clients at all, whom they may regard more as wicked persons to be controlled than as sick persons to be treated.

A revealing similarity between the role of the modern Soviet physician on the one hand, and that of the nineteenth-century European physician doing charity work on the other hand, now emerges. Both were given to diagnosing many of their patients as malingerers. The reasons for this are now evident: in each case the physician is an agent of society (or of some social agency) and not of the patient; and in each case the physician tacitly espouses and supports society's dominant values, especially as these relate to the patient's "proper role" in the group. The Soviet physician is identified with, and serves the interests of, the communist state: he believes, for example, that hard work where "one is needed" is necessary for the welfare of both the individual and society. Similarly, the nineteenth-century European physician was identified with, and often served the interests of, the capitalist state: he believed, for example, that the woman's duty was to be wife and mother. Escape from either role—that is, from that of downtrodden worker or downtrodden wife—was and is left open along only a few routes, illness and disability being perhaps the most important among them.

In his study of Soviet medicine, Field remarks on how intensely the Russian physician is committed to the role of agent of society, if necessary in opposition to the personal needs of any particular patient:

It is perhaps significant to note that the Hippocratic oath, which was taken by tsarist doctors (as it is in the West), was abolished after the revolution because it "symbolized" bourgeois medicine and was considered incompatible with the spirit of Soviet medicine. "If," continues a Soviet commentator in the *Medical Worker,* "the prerevolutionary physician was proud of the fact that for him 'medicine' and nothing else existed, the Soviet doctor on the other hand is proud of the fact that he actively participated in the building of socialism. He is a worker of the state, a servant of the people . . . the patient is not only a person, but a member of socialist society."[3]

The Hippocratic oath was abolished, I submit, not because it symbolized "bourgeois medicine"—for charity practice is as much a part of bourgeois medicine as private practice—but rather because the oath tends to define the physician as an agent of the patient. For the Hippocratic oath is, among other things, a Bill of Rights for the patient. In short, the conflict

Table 3. Western Versus Soviet Practice

Characteristics of the Situation	Western Practice	Soviet Practice
Number of participants	Two or few Private, insured, state-supported	Many State-supported
Whose agent is the therapist?	Patient's Employer's His own	Society's Patient's (insofar as patient is positively identified with the values of the state)
	Physician's role is ambiguous	Physician's role is clearly defined as agent of society
Ethical basis of therapeutic actions	Individualistic	Collectivistic
Relative social status of physician	High	Low

with which the Russian physician struggles is an ancient one—the conflict between individualism and collectivism. (A brief summary of the contrasting characteristics of Western and Soviet medical systems is presented in Table 3.)

The Significance of Privacy in the Physician-Patient Relationship

Two features of Soviet medicine—first, the Russian physician's fear lest by being sympathetic with an agent-provocateur-malingerer he bring ruin on himself, and second, the abolition of the Hippocratic oath—make it necessary to examine further the role of privacy in the therapeutic situation. The first shows that the privacy of the physician-patient relationship is not solely for the benefit of the patient. The belief that it is stems, in part, from the Hippocratic oath, which explicitly commands that the physician not abuse his patient's trusted communications. The contemporary legal definition of confidential communications to physicians lends support to this view, since it gives the patient the power to waive confidentiality. The patient "owns" his confidential communications: he can, to a large extent, control when and how they will be used.

However, in the psychoanalytic situation—at least as I understand it[4]—the contract is that the therapist will not communicate with others, regardless of whether or not the patient gives permission for the release of information. Indeed, even the patient's explicit request for such action on the part of the analyst must be denied if the two-person, confidential character of the relationship is to be preserved.

The common-sense view that confidentiality serves solely the patient's interests makes it easy to overlook that the privacy of the physician-patient relationship provides indispensable protection for the therapist as well. By making the patient a responsible participant in his own treatment, the therapist is to a very large extent protected against the patient's accusations of wrongdoing. If the patient is kept at all times fully informed as to the nature of the treatment, it becomes largely his responsibility to assess his therapist's performance, to make his demands known, and to leave his therapist if he is dissatisfied with him.

In short, the private, two-person therapeutic situation maximizes mutuality and cooperation in the relationship between the participants; whereas the public, multiperson therapeutic situation maximizes deception and coercion in the relationship among them. In Western institutional psychiatry as well as in Soviet medicine, physicians and patients can thus force one another to do things they do not want to do: for example, physicians can coerce patients by "certifying" them as insane, or by certifying or refusing to certify that they are genuinely ill; and patients, in retaliation as it were, can sue physicians for illegally imprisoning them, or can denounce them to the authorities on a wide variety of charges.[5]

These considerations also help to account for the nonexistence of psychoanalysis, or of any other type of confidential psychotherapy, in the Soviet Union. The communists attribute their antagonism to these practices to the various theoretical claims of psychotherapists. It seems to me, however, that the reason for the conflict between psychoanalysis (and other forms of confidential psychotherapy) and communism lies simply in the fact that, in a collectivist society, therapeutic privacy poses an intolerable affront against the core-value of the political system.

The Physician and the Poor

The roots of the physician's role as "social worker" may be traced to antiquity. The fusion of priestly and medical functions made for a strong bond which was split asunder only in recent times—then to be reunited, explicitly in Christian Science, implicitly in some aspects of charity practice, psychotherapy, and Soviet medicine. Rudolf Virchow (1821–1902), the great German pathologist, supposedly asserted that "The physicians are the natural attorneys of the poor."[6] This concept of the physician's role must now be scrutinized and challenged. There is, of course, nothing "natural" about it; nor is it clear why it should be desirable for doctors to act as if they were attorneys.

I have suggested earlier[7] that the change from diagnosing some persons as malingerers to diagnosing them as hysterics was not a medical act, but rather an act of social promotion. Charcot had indeed acted as an "attorney for the poor." Since then, however, social developments in Western countries have resulted in the creation of social organizations whose explicit duty is to be "attorneys for the poor." Socialism and communism were among the earliest of these. There were many others as well—the labor unions, social work agencies, private philanthropies, and so forth. The modern, scientifically trained and equipped physician may have many duties, but being the protector of the poor and oppressed is hardly one of them. In the United States, the poor and downtrodden have their own representatives, and the American Medical Association is not one of them. They have, instead, the Salvation Army, the National Association for the Advancement of Colored People, and a host of other organizations. If we value explicitness and honesty in such matters, then this is all to the good. If an individual or group wishes to act in behalf of the interests of the poor—or the Negro, the Jew, the immigrant, etc.—it is desirable that this be made clear. By what right and reason, then, do physicians arrogate to themselves—as physicians— the role of protectors of this or that group? Ironically, among contemporary physicians, it is the psychiatrist who, more than any other specialist, has assumed the mantle of protector of the downtrodden.

Concurrently with the development of appropriate social roles and institutions for the protection of the poor, the medical profession has witnessed the development of countless new diagnostic and therapeutic techniques. For two good reasons, then, it is now quite unnecessary and inappropriate for the physician to function as an "attorney for the poor." First, the poor have genuine attorneys of their own and hence need no longer to cheat their way to humane treatment by means of faking illness. Second, as the technical tasks which the physician is expected to perform have become more complex and difficult—that is, as modern pharmacotherapy, radiology, hematology, surgery, and so forth have evolved—the physician's role became more sharply defined by the particular technical operations in which he actually engages.[8] Hence, most contemporary physicians have neither the time nor the inclination to act as "attorneys for the poor."

Medical Care as a Form of Social Control

It is evident that anything that affects large numbers of people and over which the government or the state has control may be used as a form of social control. In the United States, for example, taxation may be used to encourage or inhibit the consumption of certain goods. In the Soviet Union, medicine may be used to control personal conduct and mold society in a desired direction. Moreover, just as taxation is also used as a method of social control in Russia, so medicine is also used in this way in the United States.

I have remarked already on the similarities between Soviet medicine and American social work. Both are, fundamentally, systems of social care and control. Both meet certain personal and social needs, while, at the same time, both may be used— and, indeed, are used—to exert a subtle but immensely power-ful control over those cared for. Both systems are thus ad-mirably suited for "gently" keeping "in line" the discontented and dissenting members or groups of society.

Employing medical care in such an ambivalent manner— that is, to care for some of the patient's needs and at the same time to oppress him—is not a new phenomenon invented in the Soviet Union. It was flourishing in Czarist Russia as well as in nineteenth-century Europe. The severity of life in Czarist prisons—and perhaps in jails everywhere—was mitigated by the intercessions of a relatively benevolent medical personnel, the latter themselves constituting an integral part of the prison system.[9] This sort of arrangement was and is extremely com-mon; we are, therefore, justified in placing a far-reaching interpretation on it. It is, I believe, a characteristic example of the way tensions generated in an oppressive social system are managed—and tranquilized, as it were. This sort of homeo-stasis is displayed perhaps most obviously for us today in the classic autocratic-patriarchal family—where the father is a brutal tyrant, cruel and punitive toward his children, domi-neering and deprecatory toward his wife; and the mother is gentle, kind, and all-suffering, who, through her protective intercessions, makes life bearable for the children. The Soviet state, ever-menacing and demanding of work and sacrifice, is like such a father; the Soviet physician and medical system, like such a mother; and the Soviet citizen, like a child in such a family.

In such a system, the protector—whether doctor or mother—not only shields the victim from the victimizer, but, by virtue of his or her very intervention, also shields the victimizer from the potentially more fully developed wrath of the victim. Such an intermediary thus serves to maintain a familial or political homeostasis, whose disruption may in turn depend heavily on the breakdown or cessation of the role of the intermediary.

The Soviet medical arrangement also represents a dramatic re-enactment of the basic human problem of dealing with so-called good and bad objects. The autocratic patriarchal family structure just mentioned offers a simple but quite effective solution for this problem. Instead of fostering the synthesis of love and hate for the same persons, with subsequent recognition of the complexities of human relationships, the arrangement permits and even encourages the child—and later the adult—to live in a world of devils and saints: the father is a monster, the mother a madonna.[10] This, in turn, leads the grown child to feeling torn between boundless righteousness and bottomless guilt. In Russia, communism is the idealized, nurturing-protective mother, the perfect "good object"; and, if need be, the physician is the perfect "bad object." Medical care in Russia is supposed to be both free and faultless; if it fails to fulfill these promises, the blame lies with the physician. Once again, the citizen-patient is caught in the struggle between good and evil, the glorified state and the vilified doctor. This view is supported by the fact that the Russian press gives much space to public accusations against physicians.[11] Although these complaints may be loud, the complainants have no real power. The Russian patient, unlike his American counterpart, cannot sue his doctor for malpractice, as doing so would be tantamount to suing the Soviet state itself. The relationship in Russia between doctors and patients continues to exemplify the wisdom of the old proverb that "He who pays the piper may call the tune": this arrangement—which gives enough power to both patients and doctors to harass each other, but not enough to alter their own situation—thus serves best the government that supports it.

The famous "doctors' plot" of early 1953 lends further support to the foregoing interpretation.[12] It was alleged then that a group of highly placed physicians—for good measure, many of them Jewish—had murdered several high-ranking Soviet officials and were also responsible for Stalin's rapidly declining health. After Stalin's death, the plot was branded a fabrication. The point I want to emphasize here is that, whatever might have been the specific political conflicts that triggered these charges, physicians—the erstwhile co-architects of the Soviet state[13]—were now accused of destroying the very edifice they had been commissioned to build.

In sum, I have tried to show that therapeutic interventions have two faces: one is to heal the sick, the other is to control the wicked. Since sickness is often considered to be a form of wickedness, and wickedness a form of sickness, contemporary medical practices—in all countries regardless of their political makeup—often consist of complicated combinations of treatment and social control. The temptation to embrace all medical interventions as forms of therapy, or to reject them all as forms of social control, must be firmly resisted. It behooves us, instead, to discriminate intelligently and to describe honestly the things doctors do to cure the sick and the things they do to control the deviant.

4   Breuer and Freud's *Studies on Hysteria*

The Historical Background

Freud's studies under Charcot centered on the problem of hysteria. When he returned to Vienna in 1886 and settled down to establish a practice in so-called nervous diseases, a large proportion of his clientele consisted of cases of hysteria.[1] Then, even as today, the hysterical patient presented a serious challenge to the physician whom he or she consulted. The comfortable and safe course lay in adhering to accepted medical attitudes and following established procedures. This meant that the patient as a person could be the object of sympathy, but could not be the object of medical or scientific interest. Medical science was interested only in afflictions of the body. Personal problems—problems of human living or existence—were either ignored or treated as if they were the manifestations of physical illnesses. Living and working in this setting, Breuer and Freud's singular achievement lay in adopting an attitude toward neurotic suffering that was at once humane and inquiring, compassionate and critical. Their actual observations still merit the closest possible attention; at the same time, we must bear in mind that most contemporary physicians and psychiatrists practice under entirely different circumstances.

It is often said that psychoanalysts no longer encounter the type of "hysterical illness" described by Breuer and Freud. This alleged change in, or even the disappearance of, hysteria is usually attributed to cultural changes, especially to a lessening of sexual repressions and to the social emancipation of women. Be that as it may, the social role of the physician has also changed. Thus, although it is true that psychoanalysts in their private offices rarely if ever encounter so-called classical cases of hysteria, general practitioners and various specialists in large medical centers do.[2] Indeed, there is little doubt that hysteria, much as Breuer and Freud described it, is still prevalent in America as well as in Europe. However, those who "suffer" from it do not, as a rule, consult psychiatrists or psychoanalysts. Instead, they consult their family physicians or internists and are then referred to neurologists, neurosurgeons, orthopedic and general surgeons, and other nonpsychiatric specialists. These physicians rarely define such a patient's difficulty as psychiatric. To do that would require redefining the patient's "illness" as personal rather than medical, a task they are, understandably, not eager to undertake.

Physicians also fear missing an "organic diagnosis." They tend to distrust psychiatry and psychiatrists and find it difficult to understand what psychotherapists do. These are the main reasons why hysterical patients have become relatively rare in private psychiatric practice. Finally, for reasons to be discussed later, conversion hysteria tends nowadays to be an affliction of relatively uneducated, lower-class persons. Hence, they are encountered least often in the private offices of psychoanalysts and most often in free or low-cost clinics or in state hospitals. The few hysterics who do finally consult a psychotherapist will have had so many medical and surgical experiences that they will no longer communicate in the pure language of "classical hysteria."

A Re-examination of the Observations

In their classic study, Breuer and Freud cite many examples of persons complaining of various bodily feelings, usually of an unpleasant nature. They mystify and prejudge the problem before them, however, by accepting all such persons as "patients," by regarding their complaints as "symptoms," and by viewing these symptoms as the manifestations of some obscure disorder in the physiochemical machinery of the complainant's body. In other words, Freud assumed and wrote as if everyone who consulted him as a patient were a patient. He thus failed to ask, Is the person sick? and asked instead, In what way is he or she sick? His observations were thus systematically misdescribed, as the following excerpt illustrates:

A highly intelligent man was present while his brother had an ankylosed hip-joint extended under an anaesthetic. At the instant at which the joint gave way with a crack, he felt a violent pain in his own hip-joint, which persisted for nearly a year. Further instances could be quoted. In other cases, the connection is not so simple. It consists only in what might be called a "symbolic" relation between the precipitating cause and the pathological phenomenon—a relation such as healthy people form in dreams. For instance, a neuralgia may follow upon mental pain or vomiting upon a feeling of moral disgust. We have studied patients who used to make the most copious use of this sort of symbolization.[3]

Freud speaks here in a language that is a complicated mixture of object and metalanguages[4]—of things one can observe and of things one cannot. For example, it is possible to observe a person who vomits or who is in pain or is disgusted; but it is impossible to observe a person who has "mental pain" or feels "moral disgust."[5]

Further, Freud speaks of "neuralgia" when he really means

"like neuralgia"; the former implies that the person has some sort of neurological disease, a disorder of his bodily machinery; the latter implies only that the pain resembles neuralgia and may or may not signify the presence of a bodily disease.

Although Freud regarded hysteria as a disease, he clearly understood it far better than his language allowed him to express it. He was in a sort of semantic and epistemological straitjacket from which he freed himself only rarely and for brief periods. The following passage is an example of description in plain language, unencumbered by the need to impress the reader that the "patient" is truly ill and a genuine patient:

Here, then, was the unhappy story of this proud girl with her longing for love. Unreconciled to her fate, embittered by the failure of all her little schemes for reestablishing the family's former glories, with those she loved dead or gone away or estranged, unready to take refuge in the love of some unknown man—she had lived for eighteen months in almost complete seclusion, with nothing to occupy her but the care of her mother and her own pains.[6]

But where is the "illness" in this passage—or "patient"? Freud lets the cat out of the bag here and provides his critics with ammunition to justify their charge that he is not a "real doctor" dealing with genuinely sick patients; in other words, that he, Freud, does not identify and treat diseases of organisms or bodies, as they do—but discourses on the troubles and unhappiness of human beings or persons, as moralists and writers do.

In Freud's day, the medicalization of personal problems was rooted in part also in the perennial dilemma which doctors faced in connection with so-called hysterical patients —namely, having to decide whether the patient had an organic illness or "only" hysteria. The business of having to make a "differential diagnosis" was never far from the mind of the young Freud or his neuropsychiatric colleagues. He mentions—with unconcealed and indeed justifiable pride—a "case" referred to him as one of hysteria in which he made the correct diagnosis of a neurological disease.[7] The presumption that every person who consults a doctor is sick was also consistent with and supported the presumption that the physician's first task is to make a differential diagnosis. Whereas formerly this often involved distinguishing between real and faked illness, in Freud's day it meant mainly distinguishing between organic and functional illness or between bodily and mental illness—and, in particular, between neurological illness and conversion hysteria. The following excerpt is illustrative:

In the autumn of 1892, I was asked by a doctor I knew to examine a young lady who had been suffering for more than two years from pains in her legs and who had difficulties in walking. All that was apparent was that she complained of great pain in walking and of being quickly overcome by fatigue both in walking and in standing, and that after a short time she had to rest, which lessened the pains but did not do away with them altogether . . . I did not find it easy to arrive at a diagnosis, but I decided for two reasons to assent to the one proposed by my colleague, viz., that it was a case of hysteria.[8]

Why this was a case of hysteria rather than a case of malingering or a case of no disease at all, Freud never says. In the passages cited, Freud describes an unhappy young woman and the bodily feelings and complaints by means of which she communicates her unhappiness—to herself and others. And elsewhere he remarks on how his work resembles the biographer's more than the regular physician's.[9] In short, if we stick to Breuer and Freud's observations as closely as possible, we would have to say that their patients were unhappy or troubled persons who expressed their distress through various bodily complaints. In none of these cases was there any evidence that that patient suffered from an anatomical or physiological disorder of his or her body. This did not deter Breuer and Freud, however, from entertaining an "organic" hypothesis regarding the "cause" of this "disease."

A Re-examination of the Theory

In his discussion of the case of Fräulein Elizabeth von R., Freud explains his original conception of hysterical conversion in this way:

According to the view suggested by the conversion theory of hysteria, what happened may be described as follows: She repressed her erotic idea from consciousness and transformed the amount of its affect into physical sensations of pain.

This theory calls for closer examination. We may ask: What is it that turns into physical pain here? A cautious reply would be: Something that might have become, and should have become, mental pain. If we venture a little further and try to represent the ideational mechanism in a kind of algebraical picture, we may attribute a certain quota of affect to the ideational complex of these erotic feelings which remained unconscious, and say that this quantity (the quota of affect) is what was converted.[10]

Here, then, is the problem of conversion hysteria in *statu nascendi*. Freud asks: What is being converted (to physical pain)? Why does the patient have physical pain? Implied are the additional questions: What causes conversion? How does a conflict, or affect, become converted to physical pain?

Freud answers these questions by taking recourse to what Colby has aptly called a "hydraulic metaphor."[11] It seems evident, however, that no such complicated explanation is required. All that is necessary is to frame our questions differently. We might then ask: Why does a patient complain of pain? Why does the patient complain about his or her body when it is physically intact? Why does the patient not complain about personal troubles? If we ask the second set of questions, then the answers must be phrased in terms of the complainant's personality and situation. Actually, Breuer and Freud's accounts of their patients go far in answering these questions.

How profoundly the idea of hysterical complaints as symptoms of bodily diseases has confused rather than clarified our problems is illustrated by the following passage:

The mechanism was that of conversion: i.e., in place of mental pains which she avoided, physical pains made their appearance. In this way a transformation was effected which had the advantage that the patient escaped from an intolerable mental condition: though, it is true, this was at the cost of psychical abnormality—the splitting of consciousness that came about, and of a physical illness—her pains, in which an astasia-abasia was built up.[12]

In this statement—which is typical of many others like it—the words "mental" and "physical" appear as if they described observations, when in fact they are theoretical concepts used to order and explain the observations. I submit, therefore, that the so-called problem of conversion hysteria is epistemological rather than psychiatric: there is no problem of conversion, unless we insist on so framing our questions that we inquire about physical disorders where, in fact, there are none.

Thus, despite the apparent novelty of some of Breuer and Freud's claims, their philosophical orientation was anything but novel or unorthodox. Both men were imbued with and committed to the contemporary scientific Weltanschauung, according to which science was synonymous with physics and chemistry. There was a tendency, therefore, to squeeze psychology into behaviorism or, that failing, to reduce it to its so-called physical and chemical bases. This goal of reducing psychological observations to physical explanations—or at least to "instincts"—was espoused by Freud from the very beginning of his psychological studies, and he never relinquished it.

Breuer and Freud approached hysteria as if it were a disease, essentially similar to physicochemical disorders of the body, for example, syphilis. The main difference between the two was thought to be that the physicochemical basis of hysteria was more elusive, and hence more difficult to detect with the methods then available. Hence, investigators had to content themselves with pursuing psychological methods of diagnosis and treatment until discovery of a physicochemical test of hysteria and its appropriate organic treatment became available. We might recall in this connection that when *Studies on Hysteria* was published—in 1895—the Wassermann test had not yet been devised, and proof of the syphilitic etiology of general paresis had not yet been histologically documented. The prevalent attitude toward psychopathology was—as it often still is—that the detection of physicochemical disorders in the human bodily machinery is the proper task facing the investigating physician. All else is an inferior substitute and must be relegated to a second-class position. Thus, psychology and psychoanalysis were given only second-class citizenship in the land of science, their emancipation remaining contingent on the discovery of the physicochemical basis of "mind" and behavior.

In my opinion, this sort of search for the biological and physical causes of so-called psychopathological phenomena is motivated more by the investigator's craving for prestige and power than by his desire for understanding and clarity. I have suggested earlier that patterning his beliefs and behavior on the medical model enables the psychiatrist to share in the prestige and power of the physician. The same applies to the psychiatric and psychological investigator or research worker. Because theoretical physicists enjoy greater prestige than theoreticians of psychology or human relations, psychiatrists and psychoanalysts stand to gain from claiming, as they do, that, at bottom as it were, they too are in quest of the physical or physiological causes of bodily illnesses. This impersonation makes them, of course, pseudo-physicists and pseudo-physicians, and has many regrettable consequences. Yet, this imitation of the natural scientist has been largely successful, at least in a social or opportunistic way: I refer to the widespread social acceptance of psychiatry and psychoanalysis as allegedly biological—and hence ultimately physicochemical—sciences, and to the prestige of their practitioners based, in part, on this connection between what they claim they do and what other scientists do.

A Summing Up

In effect, then, Freud's theory of hysterical conversion was an answer to the question, How and why does a psychological problem manifest itself in a physical form? This question rearticulated the classic Cartesian dualism of mind and body and generated the new psychoanalytic riddle of the so-called "jump from the psychic into the organic"[13]—which psychoanalysis, and especially the theory of conversion, then allegedly sought to clarify.

I consider this whole medical-psychoanalytic perspective false and misleading. In particular, I view the connection between the psychological and the physical not as a relationship between two different types of occurrences or processes, but as a relationship between two different types of languages or modes of representation.[14]

Despite its evident shortcomings, which have often been remarked on, the psychoanalytic theory of hysteria lingers on. The principal reason why it does is, I think, institutional and social. The notion of hysteria as a mental disease, the psychoanalytic theory of hysteria, and especially the idea of conversion have all become the symbols of psychoanalysis as a medical technique and profession. The psychoanalytic theory of hysteria, and of neurosis patterned after it, made it easy for physicians and others in the mental health professions to retain a seemingly homogeneous scheme of diseases.[15] According to this medical model, diseases are either somatic or psychical; and so are treatments. Any psychological phenomenon may thus be regarded as a mental disease or psycho-pathology, and any psychological intervention a form of mental treatment or psychotherapy. The only viable alternative to this familiar but false perspective is to abandon the entire medical approach to mental illness and to substitute new approaches for it appropriate to the ethical, political, psychological, and social problems from which psychiatric patients suffer and which psychiatrists ostensibly seek to remedy.

5   Hysteria and Psychosomatic Medicine

Conversion and Psychogenesis

The concept of hysterical conversion was modern psychiatry's answer to the question, How does the mind influence the body? As I have noted earlier, this is asking the wrong question: it is using "mind" as if it were brain.

Nevertheless, because the concept of conversion hysteria has had a profound impact not only on psychiatry but, through what has become known as psychosomatic medicine, also on medicine itself, it will be worth our while to critically review the connections between the theory of hysterical conversion and psychosomatic theories purporting to explain the "psychogenesis of organic symptoms."

To properly examine this problem, we must first identify what is meant by "organic symptoms." Like the meaning of any such term, its meaning must be inferred from the way psychiatrists use it. They use it in three distinct ways: first, to describe complaints about the body, for example, pain, palpitation, or itching; second, to denote bodily signs, for example, cough, tremor, or unsteady gait; and third, to identify certain special observations made on patients, for example, heart murmur, cardiac enlargement, or elevation of blood pressure. Calling all these things simply "organic symptoms" is like calling coal, graphite, and diamond simply "carbon." Let us try to disentangle this jumble and then turn to the so-called problem of psychogenesis.

The first category, bodily complaints, comprises what are often called "symptoms," and the second, bodily signs, what are often called "signs." From the point of view of the physician, both of these relate to observations made with the unaided eye and ear, whereas the third class of "symptoms" requires the use of certain extensions of our sense organs. Bodily complaints are observed by means of hearing: the patient communicates his complaint to the physician. Bodily signs are observed by means of vision: the patient displays his disability to the physician. These two classes of phenomena thus stand in exactly the same sort of relation to each other as do spoken and written words. This connection is not only remarkably unappreciated in medicine and psychiatry, but is actually often misapprehended—physicians believing that bodily signs are more reliable guides to diagnosis than bodily complaints. This is not necessarily true. To be sure, most people find it easier to utter deliberate falsehoods than to display faked bodily signs; in other words, people more often lie than malinger. But obviously, in any particular case, the observer cannot be certain of the veracity of either bodily complaints or signs; both can be, and often are, falsified.

The third class of "organic symptoms" also consists of records of observation,[1] but of a particular kind: these observations are obtained by special methods, often called "tests," which not only supplement the physician's unaided eye and ear, but also circumvent the patient's mind or self. This is why tests are considered to be more "objective" and reliable guides to ascertaining what ails the patient than bodily complaints: the patient can falsify complaints, but he cannot, as a rule, falsify tests. Tests, then, do not lie or deliberately misinform, although those who perform them may. Accordingly, while tests can eliminate errors of diagnosis due to the patient's deceptions, they can introduce fresh errors due to the accidental errors or deliberate fabrications of those who do the tests. For example, a shadow on a chest X-ray may be interpreted as a sign of tuberculosis, when it might actually be the sign of coccidioidomycosis or an artifact.

It is sometimes assumed that all three of the foregoing types of observations point, as it were, to bodily diseases; in other words, that bodily diseases "cause" certain symptoms, the symptoms being the "effects" of the diseases. While on rare occasions this rather simplistic view is correct enough, it is, as a general principle, quite false. Statements or records concerning bodily functions are observations; statements or hypotheses concerning diseases are inferences. The relationship between observations and inferences is the same in medicine as it is in any empirical science. As singular events, diagnostic inferences may be verified or falsified—for example, when a surgeon operates for a peptic ulcer: he either finds the ulcer or he does not. As generalizations, however, assertions of the type "All persons who complain of X symptoms . . . or who display Y signs . . . have Z diseases" can neither be verified nor falsified. Actually, some such patients will have Z diseases, and others will not.

To be sure, some inferences, whether diagnostic or other, are more accurate than others. What distinguishes accurate from inaccurate inferences? The essential connection between observations and correct inferences is that of regularity. Indeed, the modern conception of causality is nothing but the assumption that certain regularities will persist in the future: if you drop a glass, it will shatter; if you exsanguinate an animal, it will die; and so forth. Herein, too, lies the crucial distinction between physical causation and human volition: one is an account of recurrent regularities; the other is an account of an agent making something happen. For example, peptic ulcers do not "compel" patients to have pains in the same sense as lenders compel borrowers to repay loans.

Although there is never a point-to-point correlation between observations of bodily functions and inferences concerning bodily diseases, some observations are obviously more reliable than others. Since the context in which the observation is made is part of the observation, no simple generalizations about the connection between medical observation and medical inference can be offered. In ordinary or obvious cases, the simplest observations may suffice: for example, when we see a man who has just been hit by an automobile lying in the road bleeding, we need no further evidence to infer that he has been injured. On the other hand, we might come upon a similar scene staged for making a film, and mistake ketchup for blood and an actor for a patient. Finally, in obscure cases of suspected serious illness, simple observations of bodily complaints such as fatigue can of course never suffice as evidences for drawing a medical inference; for example, it would be absurd to base a diagnosis of leukemia on fatigue. In such cases, only repeated observations based on appropriate laboratory examinations can serve as the grounds for the inference of illness.

This empirical-scientific perspective on medical diagnosis has several implications which I now want to articulate.

One is that anyone, whether he complains of his body or not, may be healthy or sick, in the sense that he may or may not have a demonstrable physicochemical abnormality of his body. It is illogical, incorrect, and unwise to assume, as physicians and patients often do, that anyone with bodily complaints is sick until proven otherwise. This is simply a presumption of illness, analogous to a presumption of guilt in some codes of criminal law. In English and American law, of course, a person accused of a crime is considered innocent until proven guilty. As humane and rational physicians and patients, we should assume a similar posture vis-à-vis illness: we should assume that a person who complains that he is ill, or about whom others complain that he is ill, is healthy until it is proven—if not beyond a shadow of a doubt, at least to a degree of reasonable likelihood—that he is ill.[2] This, of course, would be a presumption of health. My point here is that in such situations we must be careful not to deceive ourselves: we either presume health or illness, or keep an open mind presuming neither.

A second important implication of this perspective is that we must realize, and act as if we realized, that anyone who complains of being ill might indeed be ill, but that—if, as proof of illness, we accept only demonstrable physicochemical alterations of the body—we may not now have the means to detect such alterations. A hundred years ago, physicians did not know how to detect paresis; fifty years ago, they did not know how to detect pellagra; no doubt there are diseases that they do not know how to detect today. But it is one thing to admit this, and quite another to maintain that, because of these historical facts, the persons psychiatrists now call schizophrenic suffer from an as yet undetectable form of organic disease, and that it is only a matter of time and research until medical science discovers the lesions "responsible" for this disease.

In all this, we must not lose sight of our criteria for diagnosing illness: they are either certain kinds of demonstrable physicochemical alterations of the body, or certain kinds of psychosocial communications about it. This brings us back to our core problem—namely, whether the mimicry of neurological illness, such as the hysteric exhibits, is to be regarded as a "physicochemical alteration" or as a "psychosocial communication," a happening or an action, an occurrence or a strategy.

Whereas the idea of mental illness is firmly rooted in the notion of complaint, whether by the patient or about him, the idea of bodily illness (in the sense defined above) is independent of it. It is easy to imagine cases—and such cases are of course quite real—where a person has an illness, even a very serious illness, but where neither he nor anyone else has any complaints referable to it. For example, a person may have a significant elevation of his blood pressure, but have no symptoms of it; we would nevertheless consider such a person to be suffering from the disease called "essential hypertension." Indeed, in their early stages, many serious diseases, such as arteriosclerosis, diabetes, or cancer, may be said to be present in a person without his or anyone else's knowledge of it or complaint about it. My point is that to speak of elevated blood pressure and hypertension, of sugar in the urine and diabetes, all as "organic symptoms," and to place them in the same category as hysterical pains and paralyses is a misuse of language; it is nonsensical; and it creates a linguistic and epistemological muddle which no amount of "psychosomatic research" can clarify. Long ago the philosopher Moritz Schlick warned that "The so-called 'psycho-physical problem' arises from the mixed employment of both modes of representation in one and the same sentence. Words are put side by side which, when correctly used, really belong to different languages."[3]

Here is a typical example of this muddle. The passage is from a paper by Leon Saul, characteristically titled "A Note on the Psychogenesis of Organic Symptoms":

Some psychogenic organic symptoms, such as tremor or blushing, are the *direct* expressions of emotions or conflicts, while others are only their *indirect* results. Examples of the latter are (a) the effects of acting out, such as catching cold from throwing off the bedclothes during sleep, (b) the incidental soreness of an arm due to an hysterical tremor.[4]

A sore arm, a hysterical tremor, and the common cold are here lumped together, each a member of the class called "psychogenic organic symptoms." A sore arm is a complaint; "it" might be a lie. A hysterical tremor is a psychiatric inference; "it" might be an organic tremor. And the common cold is a microbiological inference; "it" might be a bacterial infection or an allergic reaction.

Although it is a part of the unquestioned and unquestionable dogma of psychosomatic research to call all these phenomena organic symptoms, I maintain that these are not organic symptoms—indeed, that there are no such things as organic symptoms. A sore arm, as I have remarked, is a complaint; a tremor is a sign; and the common cold is a disease. If a sore arm is "organic" merely because it involves the body, then everything that people do with their bodies—from playing bridge to making love—is also "organic." And if all these things are "psychogenic" because they are preceded by some sort of conduct to which they might be related, then every illness is psychogenic, as every illness could be shown to be related to some antecedent act. In short, "psychogenic organic symptoms," like "mental illnesses," are phrases which are the products of linguistic misuse, palmed off on the public as the products of "psychosomatic research."[5]

Conversion and Organ Neurosis

Until the 1930s, all sorts of bodily complaints, signs, and diseases were, if they were thought to be "mental," called "hysteria." Accordingly, pains, paralyses, false pregnancies, asthma, diarrhea, and many other bodily symptoms were conceptualized as conversion hysteria and were so labeled. The early psychosomaticists wanted to distinguish among these phenomena and suggested that two separate classes be distinguished: conversion hysteria and organ neurosis. Ostensibly, this proposal was a matter of nosology, resting on accurate clinical description and adequate logical distinction. Actually, it rested on neither of these criteria, but was based simply on the well-known anatomical and physiological distinction between the cerebrospinal and autonomic, or the voluntary and involuntary, nervous systems. The person most responsible for these ideas was Franz Alexander, to whose pertinent views we shall now turn.

Recognizing the philosophical underpinnings of this problem, Alexander asserts that, in his view, "there is no logical distinction between 'mind' and 'body,' mental and physical";[6] and adds that while the division of medical disciplines into physiology, medicine, neurology, psychiatry, and so on "may be convenient for academic administration, . . . biologically and philosophically these divisions have no validity."[7] Alexander ignores the linguistic and legal, epistemological and social, and all the other distinctions between psychological and physiological events and pursuits, and simply asserts that "psychic and somatic phenomena take place in the same biological system and are probably two aspects of the same process."[8]

All this flies in the face of the most obvious objections which I do not want to belabor further.[9] Suffice it to say that if psychology and medicine are the same, why are religion and medicine not also the same? or law and medicine? or politics and medicine? For my part, I prefer the view of those contemporary philosophers who suggest that we regard the relationship between body and mind as similar to that between a football team and its team spirit.[10]

In any case, we cannot have it both ways: we must choose between the psychophysical symmetry of modern psychosomatic medicine, fashionable in medicine and psychiatry today, and the psychophysical hierarchy of modern philosophy, opposing contemporary efforts to medicalize moral problems.

It is interesting, and indeed revealing of the state of the art of psychiatry and psychoanalysis, that despite wide differences among various schools of thought, the distinction between hysterical conversion and organ neurosis has been embraced by workers of the most divergent orientations. Such consensus is, of course, no proof of correctness. In this case, it rests on and reflects, in my opinion, the widespread passion to describe the most diverse human experiences and phenomena in medical or pseudomedical terms.

As the distinction between these two types of neuroses was most clearly drawn by Alexander, let us consider his original statement on it:

It seems advisable to differentiate between hysterical conversion and vegetative neurosis. Their similarities are rather superficial: both conditions are psychogenic, that is to say, they are caused ultimately by a chronic repressed or at least unrelieved tension. The mechanisms involved, however, are fundamentally different both psychodynamically and physiologically. The hysterical conversion symptom is an attempt to relieve an emotional tension in a symbolic way, it is a symbolic expression of a definite emotional content. This mechanism is restricted to the voluntary neuromuscular or sensory perceptive systems whose function is to express and relieve emotions. A vegetative neurosis consists of a psychogenic dysfunction of a vegetative organ which is not under control of the voluntary neuromuscular system. The vegetative symptom is not a substitute expression of the emotion, but its normal physiological concomitant.[11]

All this sounds rather attractive, especially to those whose ears are attuned to the music of medical metaphors. I shall limit my following critical remarks to those aspects of Alexander's views on which I have not touched before.

In writing about certain bodily phenomena Alexander calls them "vegetative symptoms." It is not mere quibbling, however, to insist that body parts cannot have symptoms; only persons can. Alexander's usage, which is traditional in psychiatry, leads to a hopeless confusion of affects with body parts, and of complaints with bodily diseases. One result of this confusion, which I discussed in detail elsewhere, is the characteristic psychiatric perspective on phantom pain: since in such cases persons lack certain body parts and yet assign painful feelings to them, physicians tend to deny the "reality" of such experiences and regard them as similar to "delusions."[12]

In describing why conversion symptoms are "pathological,"

Alexander uses the neurologistic language of old-fashioned psychoanalysis: it is because "substitute innervations never bring full relief."[13] Here is the familiar hydraulic metaphor again: one can "substitute" one choice for another, but how does one substitute one "innervation" for another? In the best—or worst—tradition of psychoanalytic theorizing, Alexander here mixes metaphor with observation and offers the old psychoanalytic theory of "personal neurosis" as the new psychosomatic theory of "vegetative neurosis": "A vegetative neurosis is not an attempt to express an emotion but is the physiological response of the vegetative organs to constant or to periodically returning emotional states."[14] Alexander's theory of the "psychogenesis" of hysteria and of organ neurosis may thus be paraphrased as follows: if dammed-up libido is discharged via the cerebrospinal system, it causes hysteria; and if via the autonomic system, it causes vegetative neurosis. It is a seemingly elegant expansion of the theory of hysteria. But what, exactly, does it tell us? What good is it?

To advance our analysis of this problem, let us consider an actual example of a case of vegetative neurosis. Alexander's paradigm of this illness is chronic gastric hypersecretion which, in time, may lead to a gastric or duodenal ulcer: ". . . emotional conflicts of long duration may lead as a first step to a stomach neurosis which in time may result in an ulcer."[15] The terminology is, again, crucially important: Alexander regards the ulcerated stomach as a regular "organic disease" and calls only the antecedent physiological dysfunction, the hypersecretion, a "vegetative neurosis." This is an utterly senseless distinction, not because hypersecretion without ulceration is not different from hypersecretion with it, but because objectively demonstrable gastric hypersecretion is an organic illness just as, say, objectively demonstrable pancreatic hyposecretion is an organic illness.

It is clear, then, that Alexander actually offers no clue of how we are to ascertain whether or not a person has a

vegetative neurosis. Is having gastric hypersecretion a sufficient criterion? Or must the patient also have complaints
referable to the stomach? Or must he also have an ulcer? As I
noted before, in the case of hysteria it would be absurd to say
that someone suffers from it who has no complaints and
displays no disability. But in Alexander's usage, one could say
that someone suffers from an organ neurosis, even though he
has no complaints and displays no disability. In this respect,
the concept is identical to that of ordinary bodily illness, say
diabetes. But then why call it a "neurosis"? Perhaps because
by the time Alexander invented vegetative neurosis it was no
longer clear what any neurosis was! Actually, the term "neurosis" has long been used to denote three quite distinct things:
observable behavior, such as a paralyzed arm; reported behavior, such as a facial pain; and a medico-psychiatric theory
regarding the pathogenetic process allegedly responsible for
certain kinds of disabilities—such as conversion hysteria as
the pathogenetic theory of certain kinds of seizures. In traditional psychoanalytic usage, the third meaning of the term is
the one most favored.[16]

It is this traditional psychoanalytic model of conversion
hysteria that is responsible for the idea of vegetative neurosis.
According to this model, which identifies hysteria with certain
kinds of accumulations and discharges of libido, not only can
persons be neurotic but so can parts of the body. For example,
in a phobia, the dammed-up impulses are imagined to be in
the person; in stuttering, in the speech organs; and in peptic
ulcer, in the stomach. This is what happens when explanatory
metaphors are mistaken for the things they are supposed to
explain.

Energy Conversion and Language Translation

Traditional psychoanalytic theory, as well as modern psychosomatic theory of the sort reviewed above, is based on the

physical model of energy discharge, of which a hydraulic system is an instance.[17] In such a system, a body of water behind a dam, representing potential energy, "seeks" release, and may be discharged through several pathways. First, through its proper channel into the riverbed into which the water is intended to flow; that is, through "normal" behavior. Second, through some other route, such as through a leak at one side of the dam; that is, through hysterical conversion. And third, through another route, such as through a leak at another side of the dam; that is, through organ neurosis.

I suggest that we entirely abandon this metaphor and model of energy conversion in psychiatry and psychoanalysis and replace it with the metaphor and model of language translation.[18] Let me indicate briefly some of the practical consequences of such a change in perspective.

By translation we mean rendering a message from one idiom into another, say a Hungarian sentence into an English sentence. When the translation is successfully consummated, we have two statements about which we say that they "mean the same thing." In such a process, neither energy nor information is transferred—from one place or person to another. What, then, is the point of translation? The answer to this question lies in the social situation that motivates the translation and gives sense to it. Typically, translation is necessary because two or more people who do not speak the same language want to communicate with one another; to do so, someone must translate for them or they must do so for themselves. In short, translation is that act which makes certain sorts of communications possible, which, as it were, unblocks blocked communication.[19] This, in my opinion, is the model that best fits the situation of the so-called mental patient facing himself and others. A hypothetical example will illustrate this.

A patient who speaks only Hungarian visits a physician who speaks only English. The patient wants help and the physician wants to help him. How are they to proceed? How can they communicate with each other? There are four discreet possibilities in this situation: 1. The patient learns to speak English. 2. The physician learns to speak Hungarian. 3. An interpreter is brought in who translates from Hungarian into English and vice versa. 4. The patient not only learns to speak English, but realizing and reflecting upon the problem of communication which he faces, also undertakes an explicit study of his own problems.

To understand hysteria, we must substitute complaints about the body for Hungarian/patient, and demonstrable bodily disorders for English/physician. (For other mental diseases, we must substitute the patient's particular complaints or symptoms for Hungarian, and the psychiatrist's particular orientation or perspective for English.) Every patient knows how to tell others how he feels; this, as it were, is the mother tongue of all sick persons. Similarly, every physician knows how genuine diseases express themselves; this, as it were, is the way physicochemical disorders betray themselves to medical experts. In short, the patient speaks (listens) in the language of complaints; and the physician listens (and speaks) in the language of illness. The task that faces them is therefore similar to the task I sketched above; in this case, it is to translate from the language of complaints to the language of illness and vice versa. The same four choices are now open to the participants.

1. The patient learns to address the physician in the language of illness. He seeks and finds physicians who will take medical action in the face of slight or nonexistent evidences of bodily malfunctioning. He may thus receive vitamins, tranquilizers, or hormones, or may have his teeth or her uterus removed.

2. The physician learns to speak hysterical body language and understands the patient's message on the patient's terms rather than his own.

3. An interpreter is brought in who translates from body language to the language of bodily illness: this usually means that the patient is referred to a psychiatrist who talks to both patient and referring physician and mediates between them.

4. The patient not only learns to speak the language of real illness, but, realizing and reflecting upon the problem of communication he faces with physicians, also undertakes an explicit study of his own problem. He learns both about his own communications and about those of physicians; in particular, he learns about the history, aims, and uses and abuses of each of these languages. The patient may accomplish this either by undergoing psychoanalysis or some similar form of psychotherapy, by association with wise friends, or by reading and contemplation.

6 Contemporary Views of Hysteria and Mental Illness

In studying human behavior, we face the disconcerting fact that psychiatric theories are nearly as numerous and varied as psychiatric symptoms. This is true not only in historical and international perspectives but also within single nations. Thus, it would be difficult to identify and compare, say, American and English, or American and Swiss psychiatry, for none of these countries presents a psychiatrically united front. The reasons for this state of affairs, and its important implications for our efforts to build an internationally respectable science of psychiatry, cannot be considered here. I should like to emphasize only that I believe that much of the difficulty in the way of building a coherent theory of personal conduct lies in our inability—or sometimes unwillingness—to separate description from prescription. Questions such as, How *do* persons conduct themselves? and, What *are* the relations between society and the individual? can and must be separated from questions such as, How *should* persons conduct themselves? and, What *should* be the relations between society and the individual?

Actually, contemporary psychiatry is characterized by a multitude of diverse, competing, and often mutually exclusive beliefs and practices. In this respect—and indeed not only in this respect—psychiatry resembles religion rather than science, politics rather than medicine. In religion and politics we expect to find conflicting systems or ideologies. Broad consensus concerning the practical management of human affairs, and the ethical systems utilized in governing and justifying particular types of group formations, are regarded merely as a measure of the political success of the dominant ideology. In contrast, scientific theories do not, as a rule, concern vast populations. Hence, broad consensus concerning such matters is not an issue. At the same time, it is unusual for scientists widely and persistently to disagree among themselves concerning the ideas and actions appropriate to their special areas of competence. There is, for instance, relatively little disagreement among scientists concerning basic physiological, biochemical, or physical theories—even though individual scientists may believe in different religions, or in no religion, and may be members of different national groups. This is emphatically not true for psychiatry. In this chapter I want to remark briefly on a few of the principal contemporary views on hysteria and mental illness.

Psychoanalytic Theories

Fenichel, the author of a highly respected psychoanalytic text, distinguishes anxiety hysteria from conversion hysteria. He identifies anxiety hysteria, which is also a synonym for phobia, as the "simplest compromise between drive and defense."[1] The anxiety motivating the defense becomes manifest, he says, while the reason for the anxiety remains repressed. In other words, the person experiences anxiety without knowing why. Fenichel illustrates this process by citing the example of "Small children [who] are afraid of being left alone, which for them means not being loved any more."[2] The psychology of anxiety hysteria is laid bare here as simply a connection, on the part of the child, between being left alone and being unloved. Since it is considered normal for children to feel anxious when they are unloved, their being anxious for this reason is not considered to be "abnormal." However, being left alone, as such, is not considered to be a sufficient reason for feeling anxious. Hence, if such a reaction occurs, it must be due to something else. The *meaning* of being left alone is then advanced as the *cause* of the "abnormal reaction" called a "phobia."

Furthermore, the child's experience of anxiety on being left alone is open to two antithetical interpretations. First, it may be considered pathological—that is, "bad"— if it is assumed that the reaction signifies excessive susceptibility to feeling unloved. Second, it may be considered normal—that is, "good"—if it is assumed that the reaction signifies the child's ability to make connections between more or less dissimilar situations. According to the latter view, a phobia—and, indeed, nearly all "psychopathological symptoms"—are similar to scientific hypotheses. Both the making of mental symptoms and the making of hypotheses rests on the fundamental human propensity to construct symbolic representations and to use these as guides to action.

In his discussion of conversion hysteria, Fenichel consistently uses the mixed physical and psychological language which I have criticized earlier. For example, he writes about "physical functions" providing unconscious expression for repressed "instinctual impulses."[3] As in Breuer and Freud's writings, complaints about the body or communications by means of bodily signs are here erroneously described as alterations in physical functions. The following is an example of these sorts of unrecognized epistemological errors typical of psychoanalytic writings on hysteria:

A patient suffered from pain in the lower abdomen. The pain repeated sensations she had felt as a child during an attack of appendicitis. At that time she had been treated with unusual tenderness by her father. The abdominal pain expressed simultaneously a longing for the father's tenderness and a fear that an even more painful operation might follow a fulfilment of this longing.[4]

Here is a contrasting account of the same sort of phenomenon, written by a theoretical biologist. The account concerns a girl who developed abdominal pain and consulted a surgeon.

He [i.e., the surgeon] recommended an operation for the removal of the appendix and this was accordingly performed. But after recovery and convalescence the girl again complained of abdominal pain. This time she was advised to consult a surgeon with a view to treatment for adhesions resulting from the first operation. But the second surgeon referred the girl to a psychiatrist from whose inquiries it transpired that the girl's education had been such that she believed it to be possible to become pregnant by being kissed. The first abdominal pain had appeared after the experience of being kissed by an undergraduate during his vacation. After the recovery from the operation this girl was again kissed by the same undergraduate with a similar result.[5]

In an earlier passage, Fenichel speaks of a patient's "original physical pain," and contrasts this with his present "hysterical pain." In the passage cited, he translates "abdominal pain" into a "longing for tenderness." All such statements ignore the crucial issue of validating the nature of the complainant's pain. After all, Fenichel's patient's pain could conceivably have been "caused" by, say, a tubal pregnancy, and could also have "meant" that she longed for her father's love.

The problem of whether the "meaning" of pain could also be its "cause," and if so in what way, is far more complicated than the psychoanalytic theory of hysteria would have it. According to the latter, some pains are "organic," others "hysterical." Thus a longing, a wish, a need—broadly speaking, psychological "meanings" of all sorts—are regarded as "causal agents" similar, in all significant respects, to tumors, fractures, and other bodily lesions. Clearly, nothing could be more misleading, since fractures and tumors belong in one logical class, while desires, aspirations, and conflicts belong in another.[6] I am not saying that psychological motives can never be regarded as the "causes" of human conduct, for evidently this is often a useful way of describing social behavior. It should be kept in mind, however, that my desire to see a play is the "cause" of my going to the theater in a sense very different from that in which we speak of "causal laws" in physics.

Glover adheres to the usual psychiatric classification of hysteria. He asserts that "two major types of hysteria exist, namely, conversion hysteria and anxiety hysteria."[7] He thus implies that "hysteria" is an entity found in nature rather than an abstraction made by man. And he too uses a mixed physical and psychological language—for example, in speaking of "physical symptoms" and "psychic contents."

However, Glover makes a distinction which is both valid and important—namely, that conversion symptoms possess "specific psychic content," whereas so-called psychosomatic symptoms do not.[8] In other words, conversion symptoms are intentional signs: they are bits of behavior that are intended to convey a message. This is why they must be regarded as communications. In contrast, so-called psychosomatic symptoms are unintentional signs: they are occurrences, not actions, and are not intended to convey a message. This is why they must not be regarded as communications. They may, nevertheless, be interpreted as signs by certain observers— who may be astute and knowledgeable, or stupid and mistaken, as the case may be.

All this, though not clearly articulated, is implicit in the early papers of Freud and Ferenczi. The communicational possibilities of diseases of all types, and not only of a few specially labeled as "psychosomatic," for both diagnosis and treatment, inspired Groddeck[9] to propose far-reaching, and at times fantastic, interpretations of these phenomena. But Groddeck's ideas, though unsystematized and unverified, led to a better appreciation of the communicational significance of all human behavior.

In the 1930s, psychoanalysts began to place increasing emphasis on so-called ego psychology—which meant, among other things, emphasis on communicative behavior rather than on instinctual drives. At about the same time, Sullivan provided the impetus for an explicitly interpersonal—sociologic and communicational—approach to psychiatry and psychotherapy. He thus spearheaded a trend that soon became incorporated into psychoanalysis. I refer to the increasingly explicit recognition by psychoanalysts that human experiences and relationships—and especially human communications—are the most significant observables with which they actually deal.

Although I consider Sullivan's contribution to psychiatry impressive, many of his early theoretical formulations—especially those concerning so-called psychiatric syndromes—were modifications of, rather than improvements on, Freud's ideas. For example, in *Conceptions of Modern Psychiatry,* Sullivan proposes this definition of hysteria:

Hysteria, the mental disorder to which the self-absorbed are peculiarly liable, is the distortion of inter-personal relations which results from extensive amnesias.[10]

This statement of Sullivan's, though unencumbered by physiologizing about behavior, is open to the same criticisms as I have leveled against the traditional psychoanalytic concept. Sullivan, too, speaks of hysteria as if it were a disease entity, and as if amnesias caused it. But how could amnesia "cause" hysteria? Is this not like saying that fever "causes" pneumonia? Moreover, Sullivan's interpretation was only a modification of Freud's classic dictum that "hysterical patients suffer from reminiscences."[11]

There can be little doubt, of course, that both Freud and Sullivan were correct in identifying painful memories, their repression, and their persistent operation as significant antecedents in the personal and social behavior of hysterically disabled individuals. In his later work, Sullivan describes hysteria as a form of communication and lays the ground for viewing it as a special type of game-playing behavior. I will discuss his views on hysteria again in connection with the presentation of a game-model theory of this phenomenon.[12]

So far, Fairbairn has been one of the most successful exponents of a consistently psychological formulation of psychiatric problems. Emphasizing that psychoanalysis deals with observations of, and statements about, "object relationships" —that is, human relationships—he has reformulated much of psychoanalytic theory from the vantage point of this ego-psychological—and by implication communicational— approach. In his paper "Observations on the Nature of Hysterical States" he writes:

Hysterical conversion is, of course, a defensive technique—one designed to prevent the conscious emergence of emotional conflicts involving object-relationships. Its essential and distinctive feature *is the substitution of a bodily state for a personal problem;* and this substitution enables the personal problem as such to be ignored.[13]

I am in agreement with this simple yet precise statement. According to it, the distinctive feature of hysteria is the substitution of a "bodily state" for communications by means of ordinary language concerning personal problems. As a result of this transformation both the content and the form of the discourse change. The content changes from personal problems to bodily problems, while the form changes from verbal (linguistic) language to bodily (gestural) language.

Accordingly, hysterical conversion is best regarded as a process of translation—a conception first proposed by Freud. It was Sullivan and Fairbairn, however, who gave impetus to the fuller appreciation of the communicative aspects of all types of occurrences encountered in psychiatric and psychotherapeutic work.

Organic Theories

I shall make no attempt here to review the principal organic—that is, biochemical, genetic, neuropathological, etc.—theories of hysteria. I shall only state my position vis-à-vis organic theories of hysteria, and mental illness generally, and their relation to the present work.

To begin with, I do not contend that human relations, or mental events, take place in a neurophysiological vacuum. It is more than likely that if a person, say an Englishman, decides to study French, certain chemical (or other) changes will occur in his brain as he learns the language. Nevertheless, I think it would be a mistake to infer from this assumption that the most significant or useful statements about this learning process must be expressed in the language of physics. This, however, is exactly what the organicist claims.

Notwithstanding the widespread social acceptance of psychoanalysis in contemporary America, there remains a wide circle of physicians and allied scientists whose basic position concerning the problem of mental illness is essentially that expressed in Carl Wernicke's famous dictum: "Mental diseases are brain diseases." Because, in one sense, this is true of such conditions as paresis and the psychoses associated with systemic intoxications, it is argued that it is also true for all other things *called* mental diseases. It follows that it is only a matter of time until the correct physicochemical, including genetic, "bases" or "causes" of these disorders will be discovered.[14] It is conceivable, of course, that significant physicochemical disturbances will be found in some "mental patients" and in some "conditions" now labeled "mental illnesses." But this does not mean that all so-called mental diseases have biological "causes," for the simple reason that it has become customary to use the term "mental illness" to stigmatize, and thus control, those persons whose behavior offends society—or the psychiatrist making the "diagnosis."

Let us sharply distinguish here between two epistemological positions. The first, extreme physicalism, asserts that only physics and its branches can be considered sciences.[15] Hence, all observations must be formulated in the language of physics. The second position, a sort of liberal empiricism, recognizes a variety of legitimate methods and languages within the family of science.[16] Indeed, since different types of problems are considered to require different methods of analysis, a diversity of scientific methods and expressions is not merely tolerated, but is considered necessary. According to this position, the value, and hence the scientific legitimacy, of any particular method or language depends on its pragmatic utility, rather than on how closely it approximates the ideal model of theoretical physics.

It is well to recognize that both of these attitudes toward science rest on certain value judgments. Physicalism asserts that all of the sciences should, as far as possible, be like physics. If we adhere to this view, the physical bases of human performances will be regarded as most significant. In contrast, the second type of scientific attitude—which may be called empiricism, pragmatism, or operationism—focuses on the value of instrumental utility, that is, on the power to explain the observed and to influence it.

It seems to me that most of those who adhere to an organicist position in psychiatry espouse a system of values of which they are unaware. They imply that they recognize as scientific only physics (and its branches), but instead of asserting this, they say that they object to psychosocial theories only because they are false. Here is a typical example:

From the results of this investigation, it seems proper to suggest that the diagnosis of hysteria might be made by following the standard procedure used in the general field of diagnostic medicine: that is, determining the facts of the chief complaint, past history, physical examination and laboratory investigation. If the relevant symptoms of hysteria are known, this method can be applied by any physician without the use of special techniques, dream analysis or prolonged investigation of psychological conflicts. These studies give no information about the cause of hysteria or about the specific mechanisms of symptoms. It is believed that these are unknown. Further, it is believed that they will be discovered by scientific investigation, rather than by the use of non-scientific methods, such as pure discussion, speculation, further reasoning from the dictums of "authorities" or "schools of psychology" or by the use of such pretentious undefined words as "unconscious," "depth psychology," "psychodynamics," "psychosomatic," and "Oedipus complex," and that fundamental investigation must rest on a firm clinical basis.[17]

In short, we may conclude that the psychologically minded psychiatrist and his organicist colleague, though often members of the same professional organizations, do not speak the same language and do not have the same interests. It is not surprising, then, that they have nothing good to say to or about each other, and that when they do communicate, it is only to castigate each other's work and point of view.

Part Two

■

Foundations of a Theory of Personal Conduct

III

SEMIOTICAL

ANALYSIS OF

BEHAVIOR

■

7   Language and Protolanguage

The definitions of such terms as "language," "sign," and "symbol" will be indispensable for our further work. The concept of sign is the most basic of the three, and I shall start with it. Signs are, first of all, physical things: for example, chalk marks on a blackboard, pencil or ink marks on paper, sound waves produced in a human throat. According to Reichenbach, "What makes them signs is the intermediary position they occupy between an object and a sign user, i.e., a person."[1] For a sign to be a sign, or to function as such, it is necessary that the person take account of the object it designates. Thus, anything in nature may or may not be a sign, depending on a person's attitude toward it. A physical thing is a sign when it appears as a substitute for, or representation of, the object for which it stands with respect to the sign user. The three-place relation between sign, object, and sign user is called the *sign relation* or *relation of denotation*.

The Structure of Protolanguage

According to strict symbolic-logical usage, to use signs is not the same as to use language. What, then, are nonlinguistic signs? We may distinguish, still following Reichenbach, three classes of signs. In the first class may be placed signs that acquire their sign function through a causal connection between object and sign: smoke, for example, is a sign of fire. Signs of this type are called *indexical*. The second class is made up of signs that stand in a relation of similarity to the objects they designate: for example, the photograph of a man or the map of a terrain. These are called *iconic signs*. In the third class are placed signs whose relation to the object is purely conventional or arbitrary: for example, words or mathematical symbols. These are called *conventional signs* or *symbols*. Symbols usually do not exist in isolation, but are coordinated with each other by a set of rules, called the rules of language. The entire package, consisting of symbols, language rules, and social customs concerning language use, is sometimes referred to as the *language game*. In the technical idiom of the logician, we speak of language only when communication is mediated by means of systematically coordinated conventional signs.

According to this definition, there can be no such thing as a "body language." If we wish to express ourselves precisely, we must speak instead of communication by means of bodily signs. This is not mere pedantry. The expression "bodily sign" implies two significant characteristics. First, that we deal here with something other than conventional, linguistic symbols. Second, that the signs in question must be identified further as to their special characteristics. In speaking of bodily signs, I shall generally have in mind phenomena such as so-called hysterical paralyses, blindness, deafness, seizures, and so forth. These occurrences speak for themselves, as it were, and hence communication by means of such signs need not involve speech. In this, they are distinguished from certain other bodily signs, such as pain, which may be communicated either verbally or by pantomime—that is, by behavior suggesting to the observer that the sufferer is in pain. Finally, since speech itself makes use of bodily organs, it too could loosely be called a "bodily sign." This, however, would be a vague and non-technical use of this expression.

So much for initial definitions. Let us now take up the question posed earlier: What are the characteristic features of the signs employed in so-called body language?

The concept of iconic sign fits exactly the phenomena described as body signs. The relationship of iconic sign to denoted object is one of similarity. A photograph, for example, is an iconic sign of the person in the picture. Similarly, a hysterical seizure is an iconic sign of a genuine (organic) epileptic seizure; or, a hysterical paralysis or weakness of the lower extremities may be an iconic sign of weakness due to multiple sclerosis or tabes dorsalis. In brief, body signs are best conceptualized as iconic signs of bodily illness. This interpretation is consistent with the fact that communications of this type occur chiefly in interactions between a sufferer and his helper. The two participants may or may not be specifically defined as patient and physician. The point is that body signs, as iconic signs of bodily illness, form an integral part of what might best be called the *language of illness*. In other words, just as photographs as iconic signs have special relevance to the movie industry and its patrons, so iconic signs pertaining to the body have special relevance to the "healing industry" and its patrons.[2]

Philologists classify languages in accordance with their own interests and needs. They thus distinguish individual languages, such as English, German, French, Hungarian, and so forth; and families of languages, such as the Indo-European, Finno-Ugric, Indian, and others.

Logicians and philosophers, under the impetus of Whitehead and Russell,[3] have developed a completely different kind of language classification, distinguishing among languages according to the level of complexity of the logical descriptions or operations involved. The first, or lowest level, is called *object language*.* The signs of this language denote physical objects, for example, cat, dog, chair, table, and so on. We may next introduce signs referring to signs. The words "word," "sentence," "clause," and "phrase" are signs belonging to (the first-level) *metalanguage*. This iteration of the coordination of signs and referents may be repeated *ad infinitum*. Thus, progressively higher levels of metalanguages can be constructed, by forever introducing signs which denote signs at the next lower logical level. The distinction between object language and metalanguage (and metalanguages of increasingly higher orders) is the single most significant contribution of symbolic logic to the science of language. Only by means of this distinction did it become apparent that in order to speak about any object language, we need a metalanguage. It must be remembered, of course, that on both of these levels of language, the same linguistic stock may be used. As Jakobson remarked, "We may speak in English (as metalanguage) about English (as object language) and interpret English words and sentences by means of English synonyms, circumlocutions, and paraphrases."[4] So-called ordinary language consists of a mixture of object and metalanguages.

For our present purposes, it is especially important to note that, in this scheme, the lowest level of language is object language. There is no room here for what goes in psychiatry by the name of body language. This is because body language is composed of iconic signs. Hence, it constitutes a system

* The word "object" is used in several different senses in this book, depending on the context in which it appears. It is used in a technically specialized fashion in two situations. In connection with object relations, "object" usually means a person, less often a thing or idea. In connection with logical hierarchies, say of languages, the term "object" denotes a level of discourse about which one may speak only in a metalanguage. The logical relationship between object and meta levels is always a relative one. Thus a first-level metalanguage may be considered an object language with respect to a second-level metalanguage.

logically more primitive than the operations of object language.

Inasmuch as conventional signs (or symbols) make up the lowest level of language, and signs of signs the first-level metalanguage, and so on, a communication system employing signs that denote less, as it were, than do conventional signs may be regarded as forming a level of language below that of object language. I suggest, therefore, that we call this type of language a *protolanguage*. This seems fitting since the word "metalanguage" denotes that languages of this type are later, beyond, or higher than object languages. The prefix "proto," being the antonym of "meta," refers to something that is earlier or lower than something else (as in "prototype").

A hysterical symptom, say a seizure or paralysis, expresses and transmits a message, usually to a specific person. A paralyzed arm, for instance, may mean: "I have sinned with this arm and have been punished for it." It may also mean: "I wanted or needed to obtain some forbidden gratification (erotic, aggressive, etc.) by means of this arm." But what exactly is meant when it is stated that a symptom has such and such a meaning? This problem raises such related questions as: Does the patient—the sender of the message—know *that* he is communicating, and *what* he is communicating? Does the receiver of the message—physician, husband, wife, etc.— know *that* he or she is being communicated with, and *what* is being communicated to him or her? If they do not know these things, how can they be said to be communicating?

Although Freud never raised these questions, at least not as I have framed them, he gave some good answers to them. Perhaps precisely because they were so useful, his answers obscured the original questions which raised them but which were never explicitly stated. Freud suggested that we distinguish two basically different types of "mentation" and "knowledge," one conscious, the other unconscious. Unconscious activity is directed by so-called primary processes, while conscious mentation is logically organized and is governed by so-called secondary processes.[5]

Freud never clearly identified what he meant by the term "conscious," and used it in its conventional sense. He was much more concerned with defining what he meant by the term "unconscious," a concept he later differentiated from the "preconscious."[6] It is enough for us here that Freud spoke of the unconscious partly as if it were a region in or part of the mental apparatus, and partly as if it were a system of mental operations. He assumed the existence of such alleged phenomena as unconscious knowledge, unconscious conflicts, unconscious needs, and so forth, and used these expressions to describe them.

Unfortunately, this terminology obscures rather than clarifies some of the very problems that must be solved. It is a fundamental postulate of science as a social enterprise that we recognize as knowledge only that which can be made public. This is why the scientific idea of knowledge—as contrasted with mystical or religious versions of it—is so inextricably tied to the idea of representation by means of language or other conventional signs. What cannot be expressed in either object or metalanguage cannot, by definition, be scientific knowledge. It may, of course, be some other kind of "knowledge." For example, a painting may be interesting and beautiful, but its "meaning" is not "knowledge."

A further, related distinction that must be made here is that between knowledge and information. Cloudy skies or books contain information, as their messages may be read, deciphered, and understood by human beings. But only persons contain, and can communicate, knowledge.

If we accept and adhere to this more precise terminology, we must conclude that body languages of the type we have been considering convey not knowledge but information; persons who send such messages claim to send them not as agents but as bodies. This is why, both for a common-sense understanding of these phenomena and even more for any kind of "rational" psychotherapy with such persons, it is necessary to translate their protolanguage into ordinary language. Freud expressed a similar idea when he spoke of making the patient's unconscious conscious. However, he never conceptualized the "unconscious" as a language, and as *nothing but* a language: that is, not a mysterious mental landscape, but a form of communication. Hence, although the idea of translating protolanguage into ordinary language describes some of the same things Freud described as rendering the unconscious conscious, the two schemes are by no means identical.*

We may now reconsider the question concerning the connection between the use of protolanguage and the sender's "conscious knowledge" of the message he so communicates. The relationship here is an inverse one: while it is evidently impossible to speak about something one does not know, it is possible to express, by means of protolanguage, something which is not clearly understood, explicitly known, or socially acknowledged. The reason for this is that learning and knowledge on the one hand, and symbolic codification and communication on the other, are interdependent and develop together.[8] Since the use of iconic body signs is the simplest communicational device available to man, communication of this type varies inversely with knowledge and learning. The proposition that relatively less sophisticated persons are more likely to use protolanguage is consistent with our knowledge concerning the historical and social determinants of so-called hysterical symptoms. We may recall here the time when human beings tried literally to be the *icons* of Christ on the cross, exhibiting so-called hysterical stigmata. "Conversations" in this sort of protolanguage can occur only if the participants in the communicational process do not easily speak a higher

* There are also some similarities between what I call *protolanguage,* and what von Domarus and Arieti call *paleologic.*[7]

level of language. As a more skeptical attitude developed toward religion, this form of protolinguistic communication began to disappear, and was replaced by one making use of the imagery of illness and treatment.

The Function of Protolanguage

Thus far I have considered only two aspects of the body language characteristic of so-called hysterical symptoms. First, I identified the elements of this language as iconic signs and suggested that it be called protolanguage to set it apart from, and bring it into relation to, object and metalanguage. Second, I analyzed the relationship between the iconic signs of body language and the objects they denote. I was thus concerned with the cognitive uses of languages. The purpose of this type of inquiry is to clarify the meaning of signs by elucidating the relationship between them and the objects to which they refer.

In the science of signs, concern with the cognitive uses of language is designated *semantics*. Semantics refers therefore to the study of the relationship between signs and objects or denotata. Truth and falsehood are semantical indices of the relationship between sign and object. Semantics may now be contrasted with *pragmatics,* which adds the dimension of reference to persons. In pragmatics, one studies the threefold relationship of sign-object-person. The statement "This sentence is a law of physics" illustrates the pragmatic use of language (metalanguage), for it asserts that physicists consider the sentence true. Although the term "semantics" has a conventional, everyday meaning, designating all sorts of studies dealing with verbal communications, I shall use it here in its strict sense.

Let us, following Reichenbach, distinguish three functions, or instrumental uses, of language: the informative, the affective, and the promotive.

The questions in which we are here interested are: What kind of information is communicated by means of iconic body signs, and to whom? How effective is this mode of communication? What are its sources of error?

In order to answer these questions—that is, to identify the *pragmatics of protolanguage*—it is necessary to express our findings in ordinary language or in some logical refinement of it. Thus, we must translate our initial observations into a symbol system other, and logically higher, than that in which they are first articulated.

The principal informative use of a typical hysterical body sign—once again, let us take as our example a hysterically paralyzed arm—is to communicate the idea that the sender is disabled. This may be paraphrased as: "I am disabled," or "I am sick," or "I have been hurt," etc. The recipient for whom the message is intended may be an actual person or may be an internal object or parental image.

In everyday situations—and especially in medical practice—the pragmatic use of body language is regularly confused with its cognitive use. In other words, when we translate the nonverbal communication of a nonfunctioning arm into the form "I am sick" or "My body is disordered," we usually equate and confuse a nonspecific request for help with a request for a specific—that is to say, medical—type of assistance. But insofar as the patient's statement is promotive, it should be translated simply as "Do something for me!"

Although a purely cognitive analysis of this type of message may be irrelevant and misleading, when physicians perform a differential diagnosis for a hysterical symptom they address themselves to body signs as if they constituted cognitive communications. As a result, they come up with the answer "Yes or No," or "True or False." But to say to a patient with a so-called conversion symptom, "Yes, you are ill"—which is what Breuer and Freud said; or "No, you are not ill, you malinger"—which is what physicians before them said, are both incorrect. Only semantically can an utterance be said to be true or false. Pragmatically, the issue is whether or not the recipient of the message believes what he has been told. Hence, since psychiatry is concerned with sign users rather than with signs—herein lies one of the differences between it and, say, semiotic—a purely semantic analysis of communications will fail to take into account some of the most important aspects of the problems psychiatrists study and try to unravel.

From a pragmatic standpoint, then, viewing illness-imitation as malingering represents a disbelief in, and rejection of, the legitimacy of this sort of communication. It is as if the skeptical physician said to the malingerer: "You can't talk to me like that!" Conversely, viewing illness-imitation as hysteria represents a belief in, and acceptance of, the legitimacy of this sort of communication. It is as if the devout psychoanalyst said to the hysteric: "Tell me more!" To be sure, the analyst, if he is worth his salt, implies more than this; what he usually implies is something of this sort: "I believe that you believe that you are sick (in the sense that your body is ailing). Your belief, however, is probably false. Indeed, you probably believe that you are sick—and want me to believe it—so that we should not have to deal with your real troubles—which are personal, not physical." But as a rule none of this is actually said. And so both patient and analyst come to believe that the patient is somehow truly sick—though just how remains inexplicit.

To properly identify various communicational situations, we must know whether a particular pattern of communication is informative or noninformative. For example, persons making small talk participate in an easygoing, pleasant human relationship. To communicate significant messages is not a part of this situation. A person teaching a class, on the other hand, is expected to convey a certain amount of novel information to his students.

The same distinction must be made with respect to medicine and psychiatry. Each of these disciplines takes a different interest in and attitude toward body signs. Physicians, concerned with the functioning and breakdown of the human body as a machine, are committed to viewing body language as if it spoke in terms of indexical signs. For example, tightness in the chest with pain radiating into the left shoulder and arm in a middle-aged man is viewed as a message informing the physician of a coronary occlusion. Psychoanalysts, concerned with the functioning and breakdown of the human person as an agent, are committed to viewing body language as if it spoke in terms of iconic signs. For example, the same tightness in the chest and pain mentioned above might be viewed as a sign that the patient felt "oppressed" by his wife or employer. And, accordingly, while the physician's task is to diagnose and treat disease, the psychoanalyst's is to foster a self-reflective attitude in the patient toward his own body signs (and other "symptoms"), to facilitate their translation into ordinary language. This process of translation, although easy to describe in the abstract, is in practice often a very difficult undertaking. It constitutes, in my opinion, the core of what has been so mistakenly and misleadingly labeled "psychoanalytic treatment" and "cure."

Another function to which language may be put is to arouse certain emotions in the listener and so induce him to undertake certain actions. Reichenbach calls this the suggestive, and I shall designate it as the affective, use of language. Poetry and propaganda typically serve this function. Few utterances are entirely free of an affective and promotive component.

The significance of the affective use of body language—or generally, of the language of illness—can hardly be exaggerated. The impact of hysterical pantomime, to use Freud's felicitous metaphor, is a matter of everyday knowledge. It is part of our social ethic that we ought to feel sorry for sick people and should try to be helpful to them. Communications by means of body signs may therefore be intended mainly to induce the following sorts of feelings in the recipient: "Aren't you sorry for me now? You should be ashamed of yourself for having hurt me so! You should be sad seeing how I suffer. . . ." and so forth.

There are, of course, many other situations in which communications are used for a similar purpose. Among these are the ceremonial occasions during which the image of the crucified Christ is displayed. This spectacle affects the spectator as a mood-inducer, commanding him to feel humble, guilty, overawed, and in general mentally constricted—and, hence, receptive to the messages of those who claim to speak for the man and the deed of which the icon is an iconic sign. Similarly, the *grande hystérie* seen at the Salpêtrière, or the flamboyant "schizophrenic bodily feelings" encountered today, represent communications in the contexts of specific social situations. Their aim is to induce mood rather than to convey information. They thus make the recipient of the message feel as if he had been told: "Pay attention to me! Pity me! Scold me!" and so forth. It is indeed common knowledge that body language is much more effective in inducing mood than is ordinary language: children and women often can get their way with tears where their words would fall on deaf ears—and so can patients with symptoms.

The point is that when some persons in some situations cannot make themselves heard by means of ordinary language—for example, speech or writing—they may try to make themselves heard by means of protolanguage, for example, weeping or "symptoms." Others in other situations may try to overcome this obstacle in exactly the opposite way, that is, by shifting from ordinary language spoken in a normal tone of voice to ordinary language spoken in a shout or in a threatening tone. Obviously, the weak tend to use the former strategy, and the strong the latter. When a child cannot get his mother to listen, or a wife her husband, each might try tears; but when a mother cannot get her child to listen, or a husband his wife, each is likely to shout.

This, then, is the essential communicational dilemma in which many weak or oppressed persons find themselves vis-à-vis those who are stronger or who oppress them: if they speak softly, they will not receive a hearing; if they raise their voices literally, they will be considered impertinent; and if they raise their voices metaphorically, they will be diagnosed as insane.

But all this—familiar to ordinary people, poets, and playwrights long before "scientists" studied "psychology"—has apparently eluded psychiatrists, and even ordinary common sense. As a result when persons in authority, or so-called love objects, on whom others depend or feel entitled to make demands, fail or refuse to listen to those who depend or make demands on them; and when, in fear and frustration, rage and retaliation, the complainants then address them by means of iconic signs—the authorities, lay and legal, medical and psychiatric, all conclude that the complainants' communications are "psychiatric symptoms" and that the complainants are "psychiatric patients." We have thus come to speak of all these silent and not-so-silent cries and commands, pleas and reproaches—that is, of all these endlessly diverse "utterances"—as so many different mental illnesses! Evidently, in the modern world many people prefer to believe in various kinds of mental illnesses, such as hysteria, hypochondriasis, and schizophrenia—rather than admit that those so diagnosed resemble plaintiffs in courts more than they do patients in clinics, and are engaged in making various communications of an unpleasant sort, as might be expected of plaintiffs.

The informative use of language thus requires not only that the messages exchanged be cognitively significant but also that the participants be more or less equal or that the situation be free enough for them to act as they wish. Under such circumstances, information may produce the desired action or generate some sort of appropriate counterinformation. When, on the other hand, a weak person seeks aid from a strong one, he must usually resort to affective language. A direct request for help would only further expose his own weakness. Whereas an indirect request for it, say through the exhibition of suffering, may be effective in securing the sought-for help.[9]

The third function of language, the promotive, is to make the listener perform certain actions. Commands such as "Thou shalt not steal" or "Turn right" illustrate this usage. Employing the imperative form makes the promotive use of language explicit. However, indicative sentences may also be used promotively, as for example, in the sentence "All men are created equal." Although ostensibly a descriptive assertion, it is clear that the statement was intended to be, and can only be, prescriptive and promotive.

Only descriptive assertions or indicative sentences can be said to be true or false. The appropriate response to prescriptive assertions or imperative sentences is agreement and compliance, or disagreement and noncompliance. Having been asked to shut the door, we may either do so or refuse to do so.

Reichenbach has suggested a simple method for transforming imperative sentences into indicative ones—namely, by including the sign user in the statement: "Thus to the imperative 'Shut the door' we can coordinate the indicative sentence 'Mr. A. wishes the door to be shut.' This sentence is true or false."[10] The indicative sentence, however, does not have the promotive power which the prescriptive sentence has.

To be sure, seemingly descriptive sentences may actually play the role of prescriptive ones, and these often have the greatest promotive impact. It is a fundamental characteristic of the language of psychiatry that imperative sentences habitually masquerade in it as indicative ones. This is invariably the case when the communicative situation involves third parties—that is, persons other than the psychiatrist and his patient. For example, the statement "John Doe is psychotic" is ostensibly indicative and informative. Actually, however, it is promotive and prescriptive, and may be translated—by explicitly including the sign users—roughly as follows: "Mrs.

John Doe does not like the way her husband is acting. Dr. James Smith believes that men preoccupied by jealousy are mentally ill and potentially dangerous. Hence, both Mrs. Doe and Dr. Smith want Mr. Doe to be confined in a hospital." Clearly, however, these indicative sentences do not have nearly the same promotive impact as does the much shorter assertion that "John Doe is psychotic."

If language is used promotively and expresses neither truth nor falsehood, how does one respond to it? By offering another promotive communication. Words like "right" and "wrong," which are themselves imperatives, perform this function. The command "Thou shalt not steal" may thus be countered by saying either "right" or "wrong," depending on whether we agree or disagree with this rule.

The most obvious function of body language is its promotive use. By communicating through such "symptoms" as headache, backache, or menstrual pains a housewife who feels overburdened or dissatisfied with her life may be able to make her husband more attentive and helpful toward her. And if not her husband, then perhaps her physician. And if not her physician, then perhaps some specialist to whom he might refer her. And so forth. This action-inducing meaning of iconic body signs may be paraphrased as follows: ("I am sick, therefore . . .) Take care of me!—Be good to me!—Make my husband do such and such!—Tell my draft board to stop bothering me!—Tell the court and the judge that I was not responsible!" And so forth.

Symbolization in Hysteria: A Critical Example

I will now illustrate my thesis by means of an excerpt from Breuer and Freud's *Studies on Hysteria*. The following is from Freud's account of his treatment of Frau Cäcilie M.:

In this phase of the work we came at last to the reproduction of her facial neuralgia, which I myself had treated when it appeared in contemporary attacks. I was curious to discover whether this, too, would turn out to have a psychical cause. When I began to call up the traumatic scene, the patient saw herself back in a period of great mental irritability toward her husband. She described a conversation which she had with him and a remark of his which she had felt as a bitter insult. Suddenly she put her hand to her cheek, gave a loud cry of pain and said: "It was like a slap in the face." With this her pain and her attack were both at an end.

There is no doubt that what had happened had been a symbolization. She had felt as though she had actually been given a slap in the face. Everyone will immediately ask how it was that the sensation of a "slap in the face" came to take on the outward forms of a trigeminal neuralgia, why it was restricted to the second and third branches, and why it was made worse by opening the mouth and chewing—though, incidentally, not by talking.

Next day the neuralgia was back again. But this time it was cleared up by the reproduction of another scene, the content of which was once again a supposed insult. Things went on like this for nine days. It seemed to be the case that for years insults, and particularly spoken ones, had, through symbolization, brought on fresh attacks of her facial neuralgia.[11]

Here, as elsewhere, Freud speaks of a process of "symbolization" by means of which an insult is transformed into pain. And he calls this process "conversion," thus perpetuating the so-called riddle of the jump from the psychic into the organic. Freud could just as well have said that the patient spoke metaphorically and then mistook her own metaphor for a fact: the insult that was *like* a slap in the face thus became a *real* slap in the face. If so, all one needs to do is to reverse the process and translate literalized metaphor back into true metaphor—that is, facial pain back into humiliation; neurological disease or hysteria back into marital conflict or anger.

I assume that at least one of the reasons why Freud failed to carry through consistently with the model of translation was that he did not grasp exactly what type of symbolization he had identified. How can a slap on the face be "converted" to (what looks like) trigeminal neuralgia? How can the one be a symbol for the other? Freud did not answer these questions nor, in fact, did he raise them. Instead, he proceeded as follows. First, he assumed that the symbolization described above is essentially similar to that obtaining between verbal symbol and referent. Next, he proceeded as if this had been a fact instead of an unverified—and, as it turned out, incorrect—assumption. And finally, he interpreted hysterical symptoms as if the translation they required were no different from, say, rendering ancient Greek into modern English. Furthermore, he approached the reason for or motives behind the symbolization through the traditional model of medicine. The problem thus became: Why does "conversion" occur? Or, stated more generally: Why does a "patient" develop "hysteria"? In this way, Freud ended up with a classic medical problem: namely, with the problem of the "etiology of hysteria." However, if hysteria is a language, looking for its "etiology" is about as sensible as looking for the "etiology" of English. A language has a history, a geographic distribution, a system of rules for its use—but it does not have an "etiology."

We may now consider the type of symbol which Freud described in the case history cited. How can a facial pain represent a slap in the face? Why should an insult be so denoted? This symbolization is actually of two types.

The first is based on *similarity:* the pain of a slap in the face is similar to the pain of facial neuralgia (or, for that matter, of any other facial pain). Hence, Frau Cäcilie's facial pain is an iconic sign of the pain due to a certain kind of neurological illness affecting the face. Indeed, to some extent, every pain constitutes a potential iconic sign of every other pain. For as in a picture of an egg we recognize every egg we have ever seen, so in each pain we remember every pain we have ever had.

The second is based on *causation:* being slapped in the face and having facial pain stand in a cause-and-effect relationship to one another. Hence, the patient's facial pain is an indexical sign of facial injury. We know, or can infer, "slaps" from "pains," even though this may not be the only way in which such information can be obtained. Hence, a pain can be an indexical sign of being slapped in the face or of having trigeminal neuralgia—in the same way as having a fever can be an indexical sign of an infection. Both types of sign relations enter into the actual communicational patterns we are here considering. For example, a woman communicating facial pain to her husband may "sound" to him—especially if he has hurt her—as if she were saying: "Do you see now how you have injured me?" The same woman making the same communication to her physician may, on the other hand, "sound" to him as if she were saying: "I have trigeminal neuralgia." Although both husband and physician interpret the pain as a sign at once iconic and indexical, they read it quite differently depending on their specific position in the three-place relation holding between sign, object, and interpreter of sign. It is because of his special position in this three-place relation that the psychoanalyst tends to read the facial pain as an iconic sign— that is, as: "This looks like neuralgia but probably is not."

There remains the question of why a slap on the face should be denoted by facial pains. It should suffice to note here[12] that the use of this type of body language is fostered by circumstances that make direct verbal expression difficult or impossible. The custom of referring to sexual organs and activities by Latin words rather than in one's native tongue affords a typical illustration. Translation from what could be, or had been, ordinary language into protolanguage serves a similar purpose. It makes communication about an important but delicate subject possible, while at the same time it helps the speaker disown the disturbing implications of his message. The specific choice of body signs is generally determined by the unique personal and social circumstances of the sufferer, in accordance with the principles discovered by Freud.

8   Hysteria as Communication

In his Introduction to Wittgenstein's *Tractatus,* Russell declares that "the essential business of language is to assert or deny facts."[1] Only a logician, mathematician, or natural scientist, or someone having these enterprises in mind, could make such a statement. In ordinary life, language is used far more often for purposes other than to assert or deny facts than it is for it: in advertising, in friendly conversation, in religion, politics, psychiatry, and the so-called social sciences—in all these fields and situations and in many others language is used to express emotions, influence actions, and make some sort of verbal contact with other persons. These distinctions point to still another criterion for classifying languages, namely their *discursiveness.*

Discursive and Nondiscursive Languages

Discursiveness is a measure of the degree of arbitrariness in the symbolization. When a mathematician says "Let x stand for a bushel of apples," or "Let g stand for the force of gravity," he is using fully discursive symbols: that is, symbols at once completely arbitrary and completely conventional. Any symbol may be used to denote the force of gravity; its actual use depends on agreement among scientists on that particular symbol.

On the other hand, when a painter uses certain colors or forms to express his despair, or when a housewife uses certain bodily signs to express hers, the symbols they use are not conventional but idiosyncratic. In short, in art, dance, and ritual—and in so-called psychiatric illness—the characteristic symbols are lawful rather than arbitrary, and yet personal rather than social.

Many philosophers have contended, and continue to contend, that when communications do not convey facts, they are mere "noises" expressing the inner feelings of the speaker. In *Philosophy in a New Key,* Langer criticizes this view and asserts her belief in the necessity of "a genuine semantic beyond the limits of discursive language."[2] One of my aims in this book is to do just this: namely, to provide a systematic semiotical analysis of a language form hitherto regarded as purely expressive—that is, of the language of certain bodily signs.

In contrast to the arbitrariness of the symbols of discursive languages, one of the most important characteristics of the symbols of nondiscursive languages is their nonarbitrariness. This is best illustrated by means of the picture as a symbol: as Langer points out, the photograph of a man does not describe the person who posed for it but rather presents a replica of him.[3] Nondiscursive symbolism is hence often called *presentational.* Further, while discursive symbols are typically abstract, having general referents, nondiscursive symbols are characteristically concrete, having specific objects or persons as their referents. For example, the word "man" refers to every conceivable man—and even woman!—in the universe, but points to no specific person. On the other hand, the photograph of a man represents and identifies a particular person.

In the earliest forms of written language, representation was achieved by means of iconic signs—that is, by hieroglyphs, which are a form of picture writing. According to Schlauch,[4] the two simplest elements in written language are pictographs and ideographs. Both express their messages by means of pictures that *resemble* the object or idea to be conveyed. They are the earliest prototypes of what we now call the analogic type of codification. Psychoanalysis and "kinesics"[5] are modern attempts to explore and understand the hieroglyphics that a person writes, not on marble tablets, but on and with his own body.

The advantages of discursive symbolism for transmitting information are obvious. The question is whether nondiscursive symbolism has any function besides that of expressing emotions? As I shall now show, it has several such functions.

Since verbal symbols describe the objects they denote in a relatively general, abstract fashion, the identification of a specific object requires much circumlocution (unless it has a name, which is a very special kind of discursive sign). Because of this, Langer notes that

. . . the correspondence between a word-picture and a visible object can never be as close as that between the object and its photograph. Given all at once to the intelligent eye, an incredible wealth and detail of information is conveyed by the portrait, where we do not have to stop to construe verbal meanings. That is why we use a photograph rather than a description on a passport or in the Rogue's Gallery.[6]

Similarly, so-called hysterical body signs are pictures which bear a much greater similarity to the objects they depict than do words describing the same objects.* To exhibit, by means of bodily signs—say, by paralyses or convulsions—the idea

---

* Treating certain forms of behavior as pictures, used to communicate messages, also helps us to comprehend such everyday acts as wearing certain distinctive articles of clothing, such as caps or jackets. Uniforms are used deliberately to bestow a specific identity or role on a person. In all these situations we deal with the social uses of iconic signs.

and message that one is sick is at once more impressive and more informative than simply saying: "I am sick." Body signs portray—they literally present and represent—in exactly what way the sufferer considers himself sick. In the symbolism of his symptom, the patient could be said to present his own complaint and—albeit in a highly condensed form—even his autobiography. This is tacitly recognized by psychoanalysts who often treat the patient's presenting symptom—if he has one—as if it contained the whole history and structure of his "neurosis." When psychoanalysts say that even the simplest symptom can be understood fully only in retrospect, they mean that in order to understand the patient's "symptom" we must be acquainted with all the historically unique aspects of his personal development and social circumstances.

The situation in regard to cases of typical organic disease is quite different. The patient's symptom—say, chest pain due to coronary insufficiency—is not autobiographical. The symbolism is, in other words, not personal and idiosyncratic, but anatomical and physiologic. Chest pains cannot, for example, be the sign of, say, a fractured ankle. Knowledge of pathological anatomy and physiology thus makes it possible to interpret the medical "meaning" of certain bodily symptoms. To interpret iconic symbols, however, it is of no use to be familiar with the language of medicine. What is needed, instead, is familiarity with the personality of the sign user, including his personal history, religion, occupation, and so forth.

Because so-called psychiatric problems have to do with difficulties which are, by their very nature, concrete human experiences, presentational symbolism lends itself readily to the expression of such problems. Human beings do not suffer from Oedipus complexes, sexual frustration, or pent-up anger, as abstractions; they suffer from their specific relationships with parents, mates, children, employers, and so forth. The language of psychiatric symptoms fits this situation perfectly: iconic body signs point to particular persons or events.

The Nondiscursiveness of Hysteria

To better appreciate just why the communicative aspects of hysterical symptoms are incomprehensible in terms of the logic of everyday speech, let us reconsider some of Freud's clinical observations, cited earlier. Remarking on the differences between organic and hysterical pains, Freud states:

I was struck by the indefiniteness of all the descriptions of the character of her pains given me by the patient, who was nevertheless a highly intelligent person. A patient suffering from organic pains will, unless he is neurotic in addition, describe them definitely and calmly. He will say, for instance, that they are shooting pains, that they occur at certain intervals, that they seem to him to be brought on by one thing or another. Again, when a neurasthenic describes his pains, he gives an impression of being engaged in a difficult intellectual task to which his strength is quite unequal. He is clearly of the opinion that language is too poor to find words for his sensations and that these sensations are something unique and previously unknown, of which it would be quite impossible to give an exhaustive description.[7]

Freud's account shows how exceedingly difficult it is for the patient to find words for his so-called sensations. The same holds true for patients expressing bodily feelings associated with psychiatric syndromes other than hysteria. This loss for words by the psychiatric patient has been attributed either to the patient's having unusual experiences which are difficult to articulate precisely because of their peculiarity, or to the patient's being generally impoverished in the use of words. I would like to suggest still another possible reason for it—

namely, that the patient's experience—for example, a bodily feeling—is itself a symbol in, or a part of, a nondiscursive language.[8] The difficulty in expressing such a feeling in verbal language would then be due to the fact that nondiscursive languages do not lend themselves to translation into other idioms, least of all into discursive forms. The referents of nondiscursive symbols have meaning only if the communicants are attuned to each other. This is consistent with the actual operations of psychoanalysis: the analytic procedure rests on the tacit assumption that we cannot know—in fact, must not even expect to know—what troubles our patients until we have become attuned to them.

The Informative Function of Iconic Body Signs

In what way can nondiscursive languages be used to transmit information? This question has occupied philosophers and students of signs for a long time. The informative function of a particular nondiscursive language, namely, of so-called hysterical body signs, has been of special interest to psychiatrists. Although hysteria has been approached as if it were a language, it has never been systematically so codified. Let us therefore consider the informative uses of iconic body signs as a system of nondiscursive language. The following remarks will, of course, apply not only to hysteria but also hypochondriasis, schizophrenia, and many other "mental illnesses," insofar as the patient exhibiting them makes use of body signs. Where traditional psychiatric nosology emphasizes "diagnosis," I emphasize here the use of iconic symbols in a medical or psychiatric context.

The informative use of language depends generally on the referents of its symbols. The radical positivist view, rarely held any more, maintains that nondiscursive languages have no referents at all: messages framed in this idiom are considered to be meaningless. A more balanced and today more widely accepted philosophical position regards the difference between discursive and nondiscursive languages as a matter of degree rather than kind: nondiscursive languages, too, are considered to have referents and cognitive meaning.

Rapoport has suggested that the referents of nondiscursive symbols are the "inner states" of the communicants.[9] While acknowledging that nondiscursive languages have referents, he has continued to adhere to a traditional "out there–in here" distinction between them. Although nondiscursive communications tend to be simple and concrete, they are often not just expressions of the sender's inner experience. Let us consider, in this connection, the example of people fleeing a burning theater. The panicky behavior of some members of the audience may signify—even to someone who neither sees flames nor hears anyone shout "Fire!"—more than mere panic. At first, perhaps, one may respond to the purely affective function of body language: "People around me are panicky: I, too, feel panicky." But closely connected with this, there is also a communication of a quasi-cognitive message: "I am in danger! I must flee to save myself!"

I cite this case to show that the referent inside a communicant—say, his affect—cannot be completely severed from the experiencing person's relationship to the world about him. This is because affects are at once private—"inner referents"—and public—indices of relationships between ego and object(s), self and others.[10] Affects are thus the primary link between inner, private experiences and outer, publicly verifiable occurrences. Herein lies the ground for assigning more than only subjective, idiosyncratic meanings to the referents of nondiscursive languages. Accordingly, the limitation of iconic body signs does not lie only in the subjectiveness of the experience and its expression—that is, in the fact that no one can feel another's pain; it lies, also, in the fact that such signs present a picture—say, of a person writhing in pain—which, standing alone, has a very limited cognitive content.

The role of gestural communication is pertinent in this connection. Gesture is the earliest faculty of communication, the "elder brother of speech,"[11] which is consistent with the relatively primitive cognitive use to which it may be put, and with the equally primitive learning—by imitation or identification—which it subserves. In semiotical terms, gesture is a highly iconic system of signs, verbal speech is only slightly iconic, while mathematics is completely noniconic.

Hysteria, Translation, and Misinformation

When hysterical body signs are used to transmit information, they exhibit the same limitations as do nondiscursive languages generally. Weakly discursive languages cannot be readily translated into more strongly discursive ones. When such translation is attempted, the possibilities for error are enormous, since virtually any discursive rendition of the original message will, in a sense, be false. There are two basic reasons, then, why hysterical symptoms so often misinform: one is the linguistic difficulty, just noted, of rendering nondiscursive symbolism into discursive form; the other is that the message may actually be intended for an internal object and not for the recipient who actually receives and interprets it.

To be sure, misinformation—whether it be a mistake or a lie—may be communicated by means of ordinary language as well as by iconic body signs. We speak of a lie when the misinformation serves the speaker's interests and when we believe that he has sent the false message deliberately. And we speak of a mistake when the misinformation appears to be indifferent and when we believe that the speaker has not sent the false message deliberately. Hence, there can be no such thing as a "deliberate mistake," but mistakes out of accident, ignorance, or lack of skill are possible.

In formulating this distinction between lies and mistakes I have deliberately avoided the concept of consciousness. The traditional psychoanalytic idea that so-called conscious imitation of illness is "malingering" and hence "not illness," whereas its allegedly unconscious simulation is itself "illness," that is, "hysteria," creates more problems than it solves. I think it is more useful to distinguish between goal-directed and rule-following behavior on the one hand, and indifferent mistakes on the other. In psychoanalytic theory there is no room for indifferent mistakes—because it is tacitly assumed that all action is goal-directed. It then follows that a person's failure to perform adequately cannot be due to his ignorance of the rules of the game or to his lack of skills in playing it. Instead, the failure itself is regarded as a goal, albeit an unconscious one. This perspective is useful for the therapeutic attitude it inspires. But it is obvious that not all human error is of this purposive kind. To insist on this view is to deny the very possibility of genuine error.

Furthermore, when discovered, people caught in a lie usually utter more lies or say they were merely mistaken (which itself may be lie), whereas people caught in a mistake usually apologize for it. From a cognitive point of view, of course, both lies and mistakes are simply falsehood; from a pragmatic point of view, lies are acts for which we hold persons responsible, whereas mistakes are occurrences for which we do not hold them responsible. Accordingly, whether a particular communication is considered to be a lie or a mistake depends in part on the observer's attitude toward the speaker and his judgment of the speaker's character and conduct. In short, we have a choice between regarding hysteria as a lie or as a mistake. I believe it is cognitively more accurate, and morally more dignified, to regard it as a lie than as a mistake: empirical evidence favors this view as description or theory; and the desirability of treating persons as responsible agents rather than as inert things favors this view as prescription or strategy.

Language as a Means of Making Contact with Objects*

The study of hysteria, and of psychiatric problems generally, places Donne's famous utterance "No man is an island, entire of itself" in a fresh perspective. Human beings need other human beings. This need cannot be reduced to other, more elementary needs. Freud himself went far in elucidating the young child's immense need for and dependence on his parents, especially his mother or mother surrogate. The theory of object relationships—so central to contemporary psychoanalytic theory—presupposes the need for objects. The essential task of psychoanalysis may even be said to be the study and clarification of the kinds of objects people need, and the exact ways in which they need them. Indeed, much of recent psychoanalytic literature deals with the various mechanisms for seeking and maintaining object relationships. This perspective has made it possible to interpret such things as touching, caressing, cuddling, and, of course, sexual intercourse itself as various means of making contact with objects.

There is no reason to assume that what is true for gestural communications is not also true for verbal language. Since all communicative behavior is addressed to someone, it has, among other functions, also the aim of making contact with another human being. We may call this the object-seeking and relationship-maintaining function of language. The significance and success of this function varies with the discursiveness of the language used. If the principal aim of the com-

---

* I use the term "object" here in the psychoanalytic sense to refer to persons or to objects invested with personal qualities, such as dolls.

munication is to establish human contact, the language used to achieve it will be relatively nondiscursive—for example, small talk, dancing, "schizophrenic" bodily symptoms. Because of this, we are justified in treating relatively slightly discursive communications mainly as methods of making contact with people rather than as methods of communicating information to them.

This viewpoint is especially relevant to the interpretation of such things as the dance, music, religious ritual, and the representative arts. In all of these, one person can enter into a significant relationship with another by means of a nondiscursive sign system. Using a pharmaceutical analogy, it is as if the language—dance, art, etc.—were the vehicle in which the active ingredient—human contact—is suspended and contained. Many things that people do together have mainly this function, whether it be playing tennis, going hunting with a friend, or attending a scientific meeting.

The object-contacting function of language is most important during the early years of life. With psychological development, its significance is replaced by the informative function of communication. This transformation is shown in condensed form in Table 4. The foremost aim of the child's earliest communications is often to seek objects and to maintain contact with them. Gradually, this "grasping" function of language diminishes. Children then learn to use language abstractly. Serious psychological commitment to reading and writing implies an orientation to persons not physically present. While verbal language, as well as the special languages of science, retain an object-seeking aspect, this becomes increasingly less personal.

Abstract symbol systems, such as mathematics, are especially valuable for object-seeking for schizoid personalities. By means of such symbolizations, object contact may be sought and obtained, while at the same time a psychological distance

Table 4. Development of the Object-seeking Function of Language

Developmental Stage	Typical Communications and Their Effects on the Recipient	Linguistic Characteristics	What Is Gained and/or Learned?
The baby's cry	Crying, weeping, bodily manifestations of suffering and discomfort: "Feel like me!" "Come to me!"	Nonverbal, nondiscursive, high degree of iconicity	Early identifications; maintenance of the organism
The child's verbal complaint	"It hurts!" "I can't sleep!" "Take care of me!" "Don't leave me!"	Verbal, nondiscursive, reduced degree of iconicity	Internalization of objects and building of the self
The child's questioning	"What is it called?" "Where does it come from?" "Can we have some?"	Verbal, increasingly discursive, noniconic (conventional) signs	Internalization of objects; acquisition of information or knowledge
The adolescent's intelligent conversation	Intellectual curiosity: "Talk to me." "Be interested in me (my mind)." "Respect me for my thoughts and knowledge."	Verbal, increasingly discursive	Same as above; identification as adult by relating to adult objects; increasing emphasis on knowledge as a source of self-esteem
The (young) adult student's communicative attitude toward his teacher	The wish for personal instruction: "Teach me!"	Verbal or special discursive symbol systems	Symbols, skills, and knowledge. (Gradually diminishing interest in teacher as person)

| Communication with books | The wish to learn impersonally: "Teach me!" as a message addressed to a physically absent person | Same as above | Same as above in a context of individual achievement |
| Communication with others in a cooperative situation | The wish to learn in a cooperative enterprise; not "Teach me!" but rather "We shall participate together, exchange ideas and skills, and learn from each other." | Same as above | Same as above in a context of cooperative achievement |

137

may be maintained between self and other; it is virtually impossible to have a personal relationship and at the same time to maintain such distance.

Hysteria as Indirect Communication

Highly discursive languages, such as mathematics, permit only direct communications. Mathematical signs have clearly defined referents, accepted by the mutual agreement of all who engage in "conversation" in this idiom. Ambiguity and misunderstanding are thus reduced to a minimum.

The principal linguistic cause of misunderstanding is ambiguity. In ordinary language many signs are employed in several different senses, a circumstance that allows for much ambiguity and hence misunderstanding. At the same time, referential ambiguity allows one to make indirect communications intentionally, by employing expressions known to be interpretable in more than one way.

The difference between indirectness and nondiscursiveness may now be stated. A language is called nondiscursive not because its signs have a multiplicity of well-defined referents, but rather because the referents are idiosyncratic and, hence, poorly defined. Directness and discursiveness overlap at one end, in that highly discursive expressions are also direct. They do not overlap at the other end, for nondiscursiveness itself is no guarantee that the language is useful for indirect communications. For this purpose a language of some discursiveness, such as ordinary language, is more useful than one that is completely nondiscursive, such as music.

There are many terms for various kinds of indirect communications—such as hinting, alluding, speaking in metaphor, double talk, insinuation, implication, punning, and so forth. Significantly, while hinting is neutral in regard to what is being alluded to, insinuation refers only to depreciatory allusions. Moreover, insinuation has no antonym: there is no expression to describe insinuating something "good" about someone. Although flattery might at times be communicated by allusion, the fact that no special word exists for it provides linguistic support for the thesis that hinting serves mainly to protect a speaker who is afraid of offending.

When the relationship between two people is emotionally significant but uncertain—or when either one feels dependent on or threatened by the other—then the stage is set for the exchange of indirect messages between them. There is good reason for this—namely, that indirect messages serve two important functions—to transmit information and to explore and modify the relationship between the communicants. The exploratory function may include the aim of attempting, however subtly, to change the other person's attitude to make him more receptive to the speaker's needs and desires.

Dating and courtship provide many examples of indirect communications. The young man may want sexual intercourse. The young woman may want marriage. In the initial stages of the dating game neither knows just what the other wants. Hence, they do not know precisely what game they are going to play. Moreover, in our culture direct communications about sexual interests and activities are still felt to be discouraged, even prohibited. Hinting and alluding thus become indispensable methods of communication.

Indirect messages permit communicative contacts when, without them, the alternatives would be total inhibition, silence, and solitude on the one hand, or, on the other, communicative behavior that is direct, offensive, and hence forbidden. This is a painful choice. In actual practice, neither alternative is likely to result in the gratification of personal or sexual needs. In this dilemma, indirect communications provide a useful compromise. As an early move in the dating game, the young man might invite the young woman to dinner or to the movies. These communications are polyvalent: both the invitation and the response to it have several "levels" of meaning. One is the level of the overt message—that is, whether they will have dinner together, go to a movie, and so forth. Another, more covert, level pertains to the question of sexual activity: acceptance of the dinner invitation implies that sexual overtures might perhaps follow. Conversely, rejection of the invitation means not only refusal of companionship for dinner but also of the possibility of further sexual exploration. There may be still other levels of meaning. For example, acceptance of the dinner invitation may be interpreted as a sign of personal or sexual worth and hence grounds for increased self-esteem, whereas its rejection may mean the opposite and generate feelings of worthlessness.

Freud was a master at elucidating the psychological function of indirect communications. Speaking of the patient's associations to neurotic symptoms, he writes: "The idea occurring to the patient must be in the nature of an *allusion* to the repressed element, like a representation of it in indirect speech."[12] The concept of indirect communication occupies a central position in Freud's theory of dream work and neurotic symptom formation. He compared dream formation to the difficulty which confronts "the political writer who has disagreeable truths to tell those in authority."[13] The political writer, like the dreamer, cannot speak directly. The censor will not allow it. Each must avail himself of "indirect representations."[14]

Indirect communication is also a frequent source of jokes, cartoons, and humor of all sorts.[15] Why is the story of the rich playboy asking the aspiring actress to come to his apartment to view his etchings funny? It is evident that the man is not interested in showing his etchings, nor the woman in looking at them, but that both are interested in sex. The man is interested because it will give him pleasure, the woman perhaps because she will be rewarded in some material way. The same message conveyed in direct language—that is, telling of a man offering a woman, say, fifty dollars to go to bed with him—would be informative but not humorous.

A linguistic interpretation of humor would thus attribute its pleasurable effects to the successful mastery of a communicative task. If a joke is taken literally—as it often is by children, persons who do not speak the language well, or so-called schizophrenics—it is no longer funny.

The Protective Function of Indirect Communications

The protective function of indirect communications is especially important when they convey embarrassing or prohibited ideas or wishes, such as sexual and dependency needs and problems about money. Faced with such "delicate" matters, indirect communications permit the expression of a need and its simultaneous denial or disavowal. A classic example from medical practice is the physician's avoidance of discussing fees with patients and his assigning this task to a secretary or nurse. The physician communicating through his employee is simultaneously asking for money and not asking for it. The first message is contained *explicitly* in the secretary's request; the second is contained *implicitly* in the doctor's avoidance of the subject. Since the secretary acts as the physician's agent, the physician is, in effect, asking for money. However, by not discussing financial matters openly, the physician is implying that money is of no importance in his relationship with the patient. Much of what is called hypocrisy is this sort of indirect communication, serving, as a rule, the interests of the speaker and infringing correspondingly on the interests of the listener.

Whether a person considers bodily diseases and personal problems acceptable or unacceptable will depend on his particular problems as well as on his system of values. In today's

health-conscious atmosphere, most bodily diseases are acceptable, but most problems in living—lip service to the contrary
notwithstanding—are not. Indeed, they are especially unacceptable in a medical setting. Both patients and physicians are
thus inclined to deny personal problems and to communicate
in terms of bodily illnesses: for example, a man worried about
his job or marriage may seek medical attention for hyperacid-
ity and insomnia; and his physician is likely to treat him with
antacids and tranquilizers.

Dreaming and Hysteria as Hinting

The main advantage of hinting over more direct forms of
communication is the protection it affords the speaker by
enabling him to communicate without committing himself to
what he says. Should the message be ill received, hinting
leaves an escape route open. Indirect communications ensure
the speaker that he will be held responsible only for the explicit meaning of his message. The overt message is thus a sort
of vehicle for the covert message whose effect is feared.

Any reported dream may be regarded as an indirect communication or a hint. The manifest dream story is the overt
message, while the latent dream thoughts constitute the covert
message to which the dreamer alludes. This function of dreaming—and of dream communication—is best observed in the
psychoanalytic situation, since in it the recounting of dreams
is a fully acceptable form of social behavior. Analytic patients
often produce dreams that refer to the analyst. Frequently,
such dreams reveal that the analysand has some feelings or
knowledge about the analyst which he finds distressing and is
afraid to mention lest the analyst become angry. For example,
the analyst might have been late or might have greeted the
patient absentmindedly. The patient now finds himself in the
difficult position of wanting to talk about this, to restore a
more harmonious relationship with the analyst, yet being

afraid to do so, lest by mentioning it he alienate the analyst still more. In this dilemma, the patient may resort to a dream communication. He might then report a dream alluding to the distressing occurrence, omitting perhaps the person of the analyst from it. This makes it possible for the patient to make the dangerous communication while keeping himself protected, since the analyst can interpret the dream in many different ways.[16]

If the analyst is able and willing to accept the patient's reproach, he can so interpret the dream. Its covert communicative aim will then have been achieved: the embarrassing message was dispatched, the relationship to the analyst was not further endangered, and a more harmonious relationship between patient and analyst was established. On the other hand, if the analyst is upset, defensive, or otherwise unresponsive to the dream's hidden message, he might interpret the communication in some other way. Although this is clearly less desirable for the course of the analysis, it is preferable for the patient to making an overt accusation and being reprimanded for it. The misunderstanding at least does not place an additional burden on an already disharmonious relationship.

The idea that dreams are allusions is not new, Freud himself having suggested it.[17] However, he paid less attention to dream communications as interpersonal events than he did to the mental or intrapsychic aspects of dreaming. Ferenczi went further: in a short paper provocatively titled "To Whom Does One Relate One's Dreams?"[18] he dealt with dreams explicitly as indirect communications.

Just as any reported dream may be regarded as a hint, so may any reported hysterical symptom. Freud attributed the multiplicity of meanings characteristic of hysterical and other psychiatric symptoms and of dreams to a "motivational overdetermination"—that is, to the multiplicity of instinctual needs which the symptom satisfied. I approach the same phenomena here from a semiotical rather than from a motivational point of view: accordingly, instead of an "overdetermination of symptoms," I speak of a diversity of communicational meanings.

The hinting function of hysterical symptoms may be illustrated by the following example. Freud's patient Frau Cäcilie M. suffered from hysterical facial pain, which had at least two distinct meanings.

1. Its overt meaning, directed to the self, significant objects, physician, and others, might be stated as follows: "I am sick. You must help me! You must be good to me!"

2. Its covert meaning, directed principally to a specific person (who may have been either an actual person, or an internal object, or both), might be paraphrased as follows: "You have hurt me as if you had slapped my face. You should be sorry and make amends."

Such communicational interactions, common between husbands and wives and between parents and children, are fostered by situations which make people closely interdependent, requiring that each person curb some of his desires in order to satisfy any of them. Moreover, having curbed some of his needs, the person then demands that his partner(s) do likewise. Thus, the open, undistorted expression of needs is discouraged, and various types of indirect communications and need-satisfactions are encouraged. This sort of arrangement must be contrasted with those situations in which one person supplies the needs of another because of his special knowledge or skills, rather than because of a special relationship between them.

Institutionally based, restrictive relationships, such as those among family members or professional colleagues, must thus be contrasted with instrumentally based, nonrestrictive relationships serving the aims of practical pursuits, such as those between freely practicing experts and their clients or between sellers and buyers. In instrumentally structured situations it is not necessary for the participants to curb their needs, because the mere expression of needs in no way compels others to gratify them, as it tends to do in the family.[19] Indeed, not only is the frank expression of needs not inhibited, but it is often encouraged, since it helps to identify a problem or need for which someone might have a solution or satisfaction.

Two proverbs illustrate these principles. "Honesty is the best policy" is a familiar English saying. In Hungarian, an equally familiar saying is "Tell the truth and get your head bashed in." The contradiction between these two proverbs is more apparent than real. In fact, each refers to a different social situation; and each is valid in its own context. Honesty is the best policy in instrumentally oriented relationships, but is dangerous in institutional settings. Einstein was rewarded for telling the truth in the open society of science; Galileo was punished for it in the closed society of the Church.[20]

Hysteria: From Illness to Idiom

Although the idea that psychiatry deals with the analysis of communications is not new, the view that so-called mental illnesses are idioms rather than illnesses has not been adequately articulated, nor have its implications been fully appreciated.

I submit that hysteria—meaning communications by means of complaints about the body and bodily signs—constitutes a special form of sign-using behavior. This idiom has a twofold origin: first, the human body—subject to disease and disability, manifested by means of bodily signs (for example, paralysis, convulsion, etc.) and bodily feelings (for example, pain, fatigue, etc.); second, culture and society—in particular the seemingly universal custom of making life easier, at least temporarily, for those who are ill. These two basic factors account for the development and use of the special language of hysteria—which is nothing other than the "language of illness." People use this language because they have not learned to use any other, or because it is especially useful for them in their situation.

The implications of viewing and treating hysteria—and mental disorders generally—as confronting us with problems like those presented by persons speaking foreign languages rather than like those presented by persons suffering from bodily diseases are briefly as follows. We think and speak of diseases as having "causes," "treatments," and "cures." However, if a person speaks a language other than our own, we do not look for the "cause" of his peculiar linguistic behavior. It would be foolish—and fruitless—to search for the "etiology" of speaking French. To understand such behavior, we must think in terms of learning and meaning. Accordingly, we might conclude that speaking French is the result of living among people who speak French.

It follows, then, that if hysteria is an idiom rather than an illness, it is senseless to inquire into its "causes." As with languages, we shall be able to ask only how hysteria was learned and what it means. It also follows that we cannot meaningfully talk about the "treatment" of hysteria. Although it is obvious that under certain circumstances it may be desirable for a person to change from one language to another—for example, to discontinue speaking French and begin speaking English—we do not call this change a "cure." Thus, speaking in terms of learning rather than in terms of etiology permits one to acknowledge that among a diversity of communicative forms each has its own *raison d'être,* and that, because of the particular circumstances of the communicants, each may be as "valid" as any other.

Finally, while in treating a disease the physician does something to a patient, in teaching a language the instructor helps the student do something for himself. One may get cured of a disease, but one must learn a (foreign) language. The perennial frustration of psychiatrists and psychotherapists thus comes down to the simple fact that they often try to teach new languages to persons who have not the least interest in learning them. When his patients refused to profit from his "interpretations," Freud declared them to be "resistant" to "treatment." But when immigrants refuse to speak the language of the country in which they live and stick to their old habits of speech, we understand their behavior without recourse to such mysterious pseudomedical explanations.

9 The Rule-Following Model of Human Behavior

Psychoanalytic explanations are typically couched in terms of motives or wishes: people do one thing or another in order to satisfy the desire which, as we say, "motivates" their behavior. While this sort of explanation is of some value, its worth is easily exaggerated. For example, a psychoanalyst might say about a person who takes up parachute-jumping as a hobby that he is motivated by a suicidal impulse. Regardless of whether or not this account assigns the correct motive to the actor, it obviously fails to explain why he expresses his suicidal propensity through parachute-jumping rather than through some other dangerous and potentially self-destructive activity. In other words, motives explain actions in a general or abstract way; they do not tell us why a particular person acted in a particular way at a particular time. To explain specific actions in concrete ways, we must know other things besides what motivates the actor. The concepts of rule and role are indispensable in this connection.

Motives and Rules

The distinction between motives and rules as explanations of behavior is explored by Peters in his essay *The Concept of*

Motivation. He correctly remarks that in order to foresee and foretell what a person will do, it often is not necessary to know much about him as an individual. It is enough to know the role he is playing:

We know what the parson will do when he begins to walk toward the pulpit in the middle of the penultimate hymn or what the traveller will do when he enters the doors of the hotel because we know the conventions regulating church services and staying at hotels. And we can make such predictions without knowing anything about the causes of people's behaviour. Man in society is like a chessplayer writ large.[1]

From this, Peters concludes that the first things we must know about human actions are the norms and goals that regulate the actor's conduct. The basic sciences of human action are, therefore, anthropology and sociology, for it is these disciplines that are concerned with exhibiting, in a systematic manner, the framework of norms and goals which are necessary to classify actions as being of a certain sort. Psychiatry and psychoanalysis, too, deal with these problems, although they often do so inexplicitly. For example, in the psychoanalytic study of perversions—indeed in the very definition of what constitutes a "perversion"—the observer is concerned with norms and goals. However, by tacitly supporting the socially accepted norms, and by couching the discussion in the language of "psychosexual functions," the psychoanalyst makes it appear as if he were not concerned with norms at all, but only with "biological processes."[2] This is just what Freud did in his *Three Essays on the Theory of Sexuality*[3] and in much of his other work as well.

Another way of putting this matter is to say that psychoanalytic theory offers causal explanations of behavior, whereas role theory[4] offers conventional explanations of it. Causal explanations are, furthermore, mechanistic, often make use of "hidden factors," and frame their hypotheses in terms of antecedently acting events or forces, such as instincts, drives, or libido. In contrast, conventional explanations are vitalistic, often make use of concepts like choice and will, and frame their hypotheses in terms of behavior-regulating conventions and goals, such as are articulated in religious and professional codes of conduct.

Actually, Freud entertained both causal and conventional explanations, relying on the former for psychoanalytic theory and on the latter for psychoanalytic therapy. Hence the epistemologically and ethically confusing character of psychoanalysis as developed by Freud and his followers.

I have offered examples of Freud's use of causal and motivational explanations, and now want to remark briefly on his use of conventional explanations. Especially in his so-called clinical or therapeutic work, Freud was concerned mainly with a general class of activities—composed of such things as dreams, obsessions, phobias, and perversions— which, according to Peters, are characterized by the fact that they seem "to have no point or a very odd point. . . . By extending the model of purposive rule-following behaviour to cover the unconscious,"[5] Freud reclaimed these phenomena for the "scientific psychology" he called "psychoanalysis." However, because like others in his time and place, Freud equated "conscious" rule-following behavior with the notions of responsibility and punishability, and because he wanted to treat hysteria, and mental illnesses generally, in a nonjudgmental "scientific" fashion, he mystified the very discovery he had made—namely, that "symptomatic" behavior also obeys the principles of rule-following actions. His famous therapeutic dictum, "Where id was, ego shall be," could thus be translated into our present idiom to mean that "obscure and inexplicit rule-following shall be replaced by clear and explicit rule-following." In the following chapters I shall describe and comment on the precise rules which hysterical behavior follows, how such behavior originates, and why it persists.

Nature and Convention—Biology and Sociology

A fundamental principle of modern science is that there is a logical gulf between nature and convention.* As Peters puts it: "Movements *qua* movements are neither intelligent, efficient, nor correct. They only become so in the context of action."[6] It follows, then, that whether a given phenomenon involving human participation is regarded as *action* or *happening* will have the most profound consequences, because happenings "cannot be characterized as intelligent or unintelligent, correct or incorrect, efficient or inefficient. Prima facie they are just occurrences."[7] For happenings, causal explanations are appropriate and conventional ones are not; for actions, it is the other way around.

Further, Peters notes that when a person is asked to state the motives for his actions, it is often implied that he might be up to no good; and when it is said that his motives are unconscious, it is implied that he is not only up to no good but does not even know it. In other words, there is an important difference between giving a *reason* for one's action and giving a *justification* for it. We hear of causes and reasons in contexts which are ostensibly morally neutral; whereas we hear of motives and justifications in contexts in which moral considerations are essential ingredients. The psychoanalytic effort to supply a motivational analysis of mental illnesses has thus fulfilled more than just a need to offer a scientific explanation of behavior: it has also supplied a covert moral justification for the patient's deviant or offensive behavior, and for the

---

* This distinction is obscured—or perhaps one should say denied—in the essentially religious concept of "natural law."

psychiatrist's interest in the patient and his efforts to cure, rather than control, him.

Rules, Morals, and Psychoanalysis

Nontechnical terms such as "ethics" and "morals" refer to the rules which persons follow in the conduct of their lives, and sometimes also to the study of these rules. The psychoanalytic term "superego" refers to much the same things: it denotes both a set of rules which the person follows, and sometimes also the scanning and study of his own rules and the rules of others. Furthermore, as I have suggested already, the word "psychoanalysis" itself sometimes refers to the study, and the approval or disapproval, of certain rules of personal conduct. The upshot is that we face here a plethora of terms, some a part of ordinary language and others a part of the specialized language of psychoanalysis, all of which mean approximately the same things. To cut through this morass, I shall simply speak of rule-following and of the consciousness of rules.

The fundamental moral limitation of psychoanalytic theory stems from the fact that Freud was more interested in denouncing the defects inherent in a "morality of infantilism," which is often displayed by "neurotics," than he was in defining the sort of morality he considered appropriate for the "mentally healthy" adult.

Still, it would be an error to believe that psychoanalytic theory makes no contribution to describing and assessing different types of ethical conduct. The crucial notion in this connection is the relative rigidity or flexibility of the superego. The childish, immature, or neurotic superego is rigid; it is characterized by slavish adherence to rules which, moreover, may not be clearly understood. The mature or normal superego, on the other hand, is flexible; it can evaluate the situation at hand and modify the rules accordingly. Thus, in an early, classic paper, Strachey suggested that the basic aim of psycho-analytic treatment is to make such "mutative interpretations" as would help to render the patient's "rigid superego" more "flexible."[8] Like the psychoanalytic theory of the superego, on which it is based, this view suffers from the limitation of being silent on what sort of rigidity is considered bad or undesirable and what sort of flexibility is considered good or desirable. In short, Freud and other psychoanalysts have persistently dallied with normative systems without ever committing themselves on normative standards.

Indeed, when it came to confronting openly the issue of normative standards, Freud refused the challenge. He went so far as to reiterate the simple, common-sense belief which many people hold—namely, that what is right is what they do. "Many years ago," Jones tells us, "Freud conducted a private correspondence with Putnam on the subject of ethics. Putnam showed it to me and I remember these two sentences: Ich betrachte das Moralische als etwas Selbstverständliches. . . . Ich habe eigentlich nie etwas Gemeines getan."[9]

To assert that morality is self-evident and that one had never done a mean thing are strangely revealing statements to come from the lips of a person whose object of study was man, himself included. It reflects, I believe, Freud's unshakable determination to be a moralist in the guise of a scientist.[10] In this endeavor, he succeeded only too well: as a crypto-moralist, Freud became the founder of a sort of secular religion which has had immense influence on popular contemporary thought and life. As a philosopher, moralist, and psychologist, however, the source of Freud's success was also the source of his failure. Virtually all behavior with which the psychoanalyst and psychiatrist deal is learned behavior. Since such behavior cannot be properly described or analyzed without dealing explicitly with the norms and standards that regulate it, and with the goals it seeks to attain, psychoanalytic theory is foreordained to being unable to offer an adequate account of such conduct.

Rules and Responsibility

The distinction between happening and action is crucial to my argument, not only in this chapter but throughout this book. I have suggested that, in general, we view physicochemical disorders of the body—for example, cancer of the colon—as happenings; and that we view so-called mental illnesses or psychiatric disorders—for example, a hand-washing compulsion—as actions.

Sometimes the line of demarcation between happening and action is not clear. The point at which a passively incurred event becomes transformed into a role-playing situation, provided that the person affected is neurologically intact, will depend on his own attitude toward his human condition. By "attitude" I refer here to whether he is hopeful or dejected, oriented toward active mastery or passive endurance. To illustrate this, let us consider the hypothetical case of a man involved in a train collision on his way to work. He is injured, is rendered temporarily unconscious, and is taken to a hospital: all this happens to him. On regaining consciousness, he finds himself in the patient role: henceforth his behavior must be viewed in terms of rule following and role playing. Indeed, no other analysis could adequately account for his personal conduct once his total loss of control due to unconsciousness is replaced by a measure of self-control due to his recovery of consciousness. While this may be obvious, I emphasize it because people in quandaries so often regard themselves as utterly helpless, the "victims of circumstances."

Actually, people may or may not be victims of circumstances. Usually, unfavorable circumstances and personal "styles of life"[11] both play a role in shaping the fates of men. The point is that even though a person may experience and define his situation as if he played no part in bringing it about, this may in fact not be true. On the contrary, such a claim often serves a defensive purpose. In other words, when choices are made—either by specific action, or more often by inaction —and when these lead to unhappy consequences, people often feel that "it was not their fault" that things turned out as they did. In a purely conventional moral sense they might be correct. But this is simply because common sense assigns guilt or blame only to the specific commission of acts—much less often to omissions—and even among these usually only to acts whose deleterious effects are immediate or short-range. In any case, I would insist that, to some extent at least, all people do shape their own destinies, no matter how much they might bewail the superior forces of alien wills and powers.

Rules and Antirules

To assert that man follows rules implies more than that he is inclined to act on the basis of rules which he has been taught; it implies that he is also inclined to act in diametrical opposition to these rules.

In this connection, Freud's[12] observations concerning the antithetical meanings of so-called primal words are pertinent. He noted that certain basic words of a language may be used to express contrary meanings; in Latin, for example, *sacer* means holy and accursed. This antithetical meaning of certain symbols is an important characteristic of dream psychology. In a dream, a symbol may stand for itself or for its opposite— for example, tall may signify tall or short, or young may stand for young or old. I have suggested that this principle also applies to affects.[13] For example, feeling afraid may signify that one is afraid—or that one is vigilant and prepared for danger; feeling guilty, that one is guilty—or that one is conscientious; and so forth. This antithetical signification seems to be inherent in the nature of man's capacity to form and use symbols: it applies to affects, iconic signs, words, rules, and systems of rules (games), each of which may signify or, more often, suggest both the referent and its opposite.

Antirules are especially significant in the behavior of children or other psychosocially unsophisticated individuals. Such persons tend to perceive and order their world mainly in terms of the rules they have been given and their opposites. It must be noted, too, that while positive rule following tends to assure social harmony, it often fails to satisfy the human need for personal autonomy. To satisfy this latter need, it is necessary to follow one's own rules. The earliest and simplest rules which we experience as our own are antirules. Thus, as early as during the first year of life, when babies are urged to eat, they often protest by refusing to eat. The so-called negativism of young children probably constitutes the earliest instances of negative rule following—or the following of antirules. This is well understood by intuitive persons and is expressed by such remarks as "If I want him to do something, I must ask him to do the opposite." The proverbially stubborn mule can be made to advance only if his master acts as if he were trying to make him back up. And then there is the familiar rule about forbidden fruit tasting sweeter. The importance of this principle for antisocial and delinquent behavior is well known to psychologists and even to laymen. The notion of antirules which I suggest here is, however, of wider scope, as it includes both proscriptive and prescriptive rules.

Thus, some of the rules set forth in the Ten Commandments are prohibitions—for example, of murder and theft; others are prescriptions—for example, to honor one's father and mother. Clearly, each of these implies and suggests its opposite. To be told not to kill or steal creates the idea that one might. To be sure, people no doubt entertained such ideas even before the Ten Commandments were promulgated. It would be fair to assert, therefore, that most criminal laws are aimed at curbing propensities that exist prior to their legislative prohibition.

Still, this does not negate the fact that laws—especially many modern laws—also create and encourage propensities to engage in the very behaviors which they prohibit.

A Classification of Rules

We are ready now to examine the function and transmission of rules. Children growing up in contemporary Western cultures must learn a large variety of rules. These may be conveniently divided into three classes: (1) natural laws or biological rules; (2) prescriptive laws or social (religious, moral) rules; and (3) imitative or interpersonal rules.

Biological Rules

Biological rules form a special part of the larger category commonly called the Laws of Nature. These rules are concerned with the physics and chemistry of the human body in relation to its material or nonhuman environment. The implicit aims of biological rules—made explicit by man—are survival of the individual as a physicochemical machine and survival of the species as a biological system. Many basic biological rules are learned by direct experience, but some, at least in a rudimentary form, may be said to be inborn. More sophisticated knowledge concerning biological rules must be learned by the methods of science. The basic medical sciences could be said to serve this end.

In this connection, the question arises as to whether animals "know" certain basic biological rules. In one sense, the answer must be that they do, for without "obeying" them they would perish. It is important, however, to be clear about the sense in which animals "know" such rules. This knowledge consists of the appropriate responses to certain objects in their environment; it is automatic, conditioned, and not self-reflective. In a hierarchy of learning and knowing, this type of knowledge would have to be considered the simplest and most basic. It consists of responding to objects as objects, not as signs, and may be called object learning.

Animals do not know any other types of rules—that is, metarules. Although monkeys play games, and some other animals—for example, bears and seals—can readily be taught to follow rules by imitation and practice, it appears that the animal's limited capacity for symbolization restricts his use of rules to those which are nonreflective. In short, animals cannot use rules intelligently, with an awareness or knowledge that they are using rules: they cannot modify rules in accordance with the demands of a particular situation, nor can they learn metarules.[14]

Social, Religious, or Moral Rules

In the class of social, religious, and moral rules belong all prescriptive laws governing social relationships, whether these are said to originate from a single God, a multiplicity of deities, or culture and society. These laws differ from so-called natural laws with respect to geographical scope or distribution and also in the nature of the sanctions. Natural laws hold for all parts of the world, although, as it is now realized, they may not apply in situations outside of it, for example on another planet.

The term "social rules" designates all the rules that originate from the prevailing practices of a social group. If these are significantly disobeyed, the person will perish. The emphasis here is on the word "person," for our focus has shifted from biological to social survival—which depends on adapting to the social rules or changing them to suit one's needs, much as biological survival depends on adapting to biological rules.

Imitative or Interpersonal Rules

Imitative or interpersonal rules are learned, principally in childhood, by imitating someone else's example. In innumerable instances children look, literally as well as metaphorically, to their parents, siblings, or peers, to see how they should act. Their conduct is based on example, much as a mock-up model in engineering serves as an example after which a particular product to be manufactured is fashioned.

The boundary between imitative and social rules is not always sharp or clear. Some social rules are acquired by imitation. Moreover, since imitative rules are learned chiefly in the family, they form a subgroup of the larger class called "social rules." Nevertheless, it is useful—especially for our present purpose in regard to hysteria and mental illness—to draw as sharp a distinction as possible between these two types of rules. Let us therefore pay special attention to the differences between social and interpersonal rules.

Imitative rules usually refer to trivial, everyday matters, such as how to eat, dress, care for one's body, and so forth. Instead of being articulated in verbal form, these rules are displayed in the actual everyday behavior of the older members of the family or group. Children acquire these rules by "blind imitation." The "blind" quality of this sort of learning must be emphasized, because—in contrast to, say, attempting to forge another person's signature—this type of imitation is unconscious or unreflective. For example, in learning to speak one's mother tongue, one is not aware of imitating others.

In contrast to the trivial nature of many of the acts learned by imitative rule following, and to the inexplicit nature of these rules, social rules refer to the regulation, by explicit rules, of more complex behavioral situations. Imitative rules thus articulate customs, while social rules articulate moral-religious prescriptions or secular laws. The sanctions for each vary accordingly: failure to learn or comply with imitative rules leads merely to being thought of as eccentric, stupid, foolish, or naughty; deviance from social rules, however, brings serious consequences upon the offender, ranging from stigmatization to expulsion from the group, and even to death.

Table 5. A Classification of Rules: Biological, Social, and Interpersonal

	Biological Rules	*Social Rules*	*Interpersonal Rules*
Example	"You must eat to live; otherwise you will starve to death."	"You must worship God to live; otherwise you will be expelled from the group."	"If you are a male, you must grow up to be self-reliant, so that you can provide for your wife and children; otherwise you will not be able to consider yourself a grown man."
Subject matter studied by	Biological sciences	Anthropology, Sociology	Anthropology, Psychology, Psychoanalysis
Aims of the rules	Survival of physical body and/or species. Biological identity	Survival of (large) group as a social organization. Social (group) identity	Survival of small group (family) or individual, as social being. Individual identity
Sanctions for breaking the rules	1. Illness or disability of the body 2. Dissolution of the physical body: "biological death"	1. Socially deviant behavior and "punishment"; "crime," "sin" 2. Expulsion from the group; loss of social identity; "social death"	Interpersonal conflict; personal defeat, frustration, and unhappiness; "mental illness"; "human failure"
Sanctions codified as	Natural laws	Legal (or religious) "laws"	Customs, codes of personal conduct
Rewards for successfully modifying the rules	Extension of life span and increase in physical effectiveness and health	Enlarged scope of fraternity and cooperation (e.g., supranational versus national interests and identity)	Creative self-determination; enhanced sense of identity and freedom
Rate of change	Nil or very slow	Gradual	Most rapid

By and large, sociologists study social rules; psychologists and psychoanalysts study imitative or interpersonal rules; and anthropologists study both types. (See Table 5 for a schematic summary of the characteristics of these three classes of rules.)

The Need for Rules

The existence and durability of social rules—irrespective of the sources to which man may have attributed them—is evidence of the intensity of the human need to follow rules. Indeed, man's need for rules and his propensity to follow them is equaled only by his desire to reject rules and be free of them. As I will try to show later,[15] this antithetical disposition is a special instance of a more general human ambivalence— namely, the simultaneous needs for intimacy and solitude. Alternating attitudes of submission to and rebellion against people and rules may be best viewed as manifestations of this fundamental human paradox. One of the most useful methods for resolving this dilemma is our capacity for abstraction which makes it possible to construct progressively higher levels of symbolization; these constructs, in turn, lead to a lessening of the feeling of compulsion attached to rules explicitly understood as rules. Thus, for each set of rules we can, in principle, construct a set of metarules. The latter are made up of the specifications governing the formation of the rules at the next lower (logical) level. Explicit awareness of metarules implies an understanding of the origin, function, and scope of the (next lower level) rules. Acquiring such understanding constitutes a form of mastery. Only by practicing what may be called the metarule attitude—which is actually a special case of the scientific attitude applied to the domain of rules—can we acquire a secure yet flexible integration of rules as behavior-regulating agencies. Finally, the metarule attitude enables us to increase our range of choices about whether or not to comply with rules, and whether or not to try to change them.

10   The Ethics of Helplessness and Helpfulness

I have suggested that the concept of hysteria refers to the expression and communication—chiefly by means of nonverbal, bodily signs—of a state of disability or illness. The implicit aim of such communication is to secure help. If the problem of hysteria is framed in this way, it becomes logical to ask where the idea originates that the rules of the game of life ought to be such that those who are weak, disabled, or ill should be helped? One answer is obvious: this is the game typically played in childhood. Every one of us was, at one time, a weak and helpless child, cared for by adults; without such help we would not have survived and become adults.

Another, almost equally obvious answer is that the prescription of a help-giving attitude toward the weak is embodied in the dominant religions of Western man. Judaism, and especially Christianity, teach these rules by means of parable and prohibition, example and exhortation, and by every other means available to their representatives.

In this chapter I shall try to present a systematic exposition of these two general systems of rules. The first might be regarded as the rules of the family game; the second, those of the religious game. I have singled out these rules because they provide much of the historical basis and continuing rationale for the strategies of so-called hysterical behavior as well as for those of many other mental illnesses. In short, men and women learn how to be mentally ill by following the rules of these two games.

Childhood and the Rules of Helplessness

The belief that human beings want to remain children and that becoming an adult is always and inescapably painful is at the very heart of the psychoanalytic theory of human development and personality. Freud himself was inordinately fond of this idea and never ceased to make use of it in his speculations. He thus claimed that the human inclination toward immaturity and childishness is innate or biologically "given," but that the inclination toward maturity and adulthood is reactive to frustration and is not biologically "given." In Freud's view, personal and cultural development is the result of instinctual—principally sexual—frustration imposed by "external" reality: hence the irreconcilable conflict between "selfish" instinctual satisfaction and the satisfaction of "social" interests or needs.[1] One of the important implications of this theory is that the human disposition to resume immature or childish patterns of behavior, which Freud called "regression," is regarded as satisfying a biological need similar to other biological needs, such as that for food or water. This makes it unnecessary to look for, or to attribute, regressive behavior to learning and to certain particular social influences. This whole scheme is, I think, quite absurd: according to it, only those things which Freud categorizes as mature or progressive are learned; all other things, categorized as immature or regressive, are the results of a quasi-automatic biological process called "regression."

Moreover, not only is this psychoanalytic account not scientific, it is also not new: Freud's view of the man-child being driven out of his immature state by "frustration" is a thinly disguised restatement of the Biblical account of the Fall. The story of Genesis implies that Adam and Eve liked living in the Garden; why else would they have had to be "expelled" from it? Similarly, Freud's story implies that human beings like to be children; why else would they have to be "frustrated" out of childishness? In both the religious and the psychoanalytic accounts, regressive goals are primary. This, it seems to me, flies squarely in the face of the most elementary observations about how children usually feel about being children and about growing up.

I submit that Paradise Lost is still another myth. The pleasures of childhood and regression are vastly overrated in psychoanalysis, and those of adulthood and competence vastly underrated. Many observers of the human condition have offered quite different accounts of how people develop, giving much greater weight to innate drives toward maturation.[2] Susanne Langer has emphasized especially the human drive toward symbolization, a view with which I am in full agreement.[3] I believe, moreover, that human beings have maturational drives not only with respect to symbolization but also with respect to object contact or human relationships.[4]

All this is not to deny that learning is often difficult and painful: it requires diligence, self-discipline, and perseverance. Since being childish is, in a sense, a habit, it must, like all habits one wants to change, be overcome. Nor must the labor-saving aspects of being childish be minimized. At the same time, it is important to keep in mind that saving effort is attractive only for those who are lazy or lethargic, sick or stupid. A healthy and energetic person, especially when young, has an urge to expend effort, not to conserve it; and, depending on how he expends it, he is likely to enjoy the effort.

In short, I submit that the significance of religious, cultural, legal, and familial prohibitions against learning and competence have been astonishingly neglected in most scientific theories of human development. I offer the following brief examples not to document but only to illustrate this contention.

1. The Jewish and Christian religions attribute man's fall from divine grace to the partaking of the fruit of the "tree of knowledge."

2. For centuries, the Roman Catholic Church maintained an Index of prohibited books. Secular authorities in most countries continue to prohibit the printing or distribution of certain books, pictures, and films.

3. Countless more subtle but equally powerful social forces prevent people from learning elementary facts about birth and death, medicine and law, religion and history. National narcissisms and religious, racial, and sexual prejudice all encourage and reward various kinds of overt or covert ignorance and infantilism.

4. In the family, and in other small groups, individuals often foster stupidity and dependency in others—for example, parents in children, husbands in wives or vice versa—in order to enhance their own self-esteem and security.

Biblical Rules Fostering Disability and Illness

Jewish and Christian religious teachings abound in rules that reward sickness and stupidity, poverty and timidity—in short, disabilities of all sorts. Moreover, these rules or their corollaries threaten penalties for self-reliance and competence, and for pride in health and well-being. This is a bold assertion, although not a particularly novel one. I shall try to support it by citing adequate evidence. I do not argue, of course, that prescriptions fostering disability constitute the whole or the essence of the Bible, which is a complex and heterogeneous work from which countless rules of conduct may be inferred. Indeed, the religious history of the West illustrates how, by taking one or another part of this work, it is possible to support or oppose a wide variety of human behaviors—from slavery to witch burning, and from celibacy to polygamy.

Personally, I support respect for the autonomy and integrity of one's self and others, but shall not make any attempt to justify these values here. I believe, however, that in a work of this kind it is necessary to make one's moral preferences explicit, to enable the reader to better judge and compensate for the author's biases.

My approach to religious rules and rule following is socio-psychological, not theological. Whether my interpretations of religious rules are "theologically correct" is, I believe, somewhat irrelevant. What is relevant is whether I have inferred correctly or falsely from the actual behavior of persons professing to be religious the rules that govern and explain their conduct.

In addressing myself to Scriptural passages as written statements, I try to assume the role of a critical interpreter. I shall scrutinize certain Biblical rules, not to praise or condemn them, which has been done enough—but rather to make explicit the values they approve or disapprove, endorse or reject. Naturally, some of my interpretations will conflict with the interpretations of modern clergymen trying to make Scriptural texts fit for modern consumption. Contemporary "liberal" interpretations of religious documents, whether Christian or Jewish, serve mainly one aim, namely to sell religion to modern man—an unenviable task if ever there was one. It is only right for vendors to wrap their merchandise so as to make it attractive for the buyer—in this case, to make these religions as compatible as possible with the political and scientific ideas and institutions of modern Western nations.

The motif that God loves the humble, the meek, the needy, and those who fear Him is a thread running through both the Old and New Testaments. Man's fear of being too well off lest he offend God and make Him envious is deeply ingrained in the Jewish religion as well as in ancient Greek pantheism. It is an element common to most primitive religions—that is, religions in which man conceives of God in his own image: God is like man, only more so. The deity is a kind of superman with his own needs for self-esteem and status which mortal men are enjoined to threaten at their own peril. The legend of Polycrates, the overly lucky king of Samos, illustrates this theme.[5]

This attitude, which is basically a dread of happiness generated by a powerful fear of envy, is fundamental to the psychology of the person seriously committed to the Judaeo-Christian ethic. The defensive, self-protective character of this maneuver is evident. For such a tactic to be effective, it is necessary to assume, first, the presence of another person (or persons) and, second, the operation of certain rules by which this person conducts himself.

Who is man's partner-opponent in this game of "I-am-not-happy"? What are the specific rules of this game that make this a good tactic? As to the identity of the opponent, we may say, without going into unnecessary details, that it is God and a succession of other powerful figures vis-à-vis whom the player occupies a subservient position. The power differential between the two players is crucial, for it alone can account for the fear of envy. In a dominant-submissive relationship, only the submissive member of the pair needs to fear arousing the envy of his partner. The dominant player has no such fears, because he knows that the other is powerless to injure him seriously.

In general, then, the open acknowledgment of satisfaction is feared only in oppressive situations—for example, by the much-suffering wife married to a domineering husband. The experience and expression of satisfaction (joy, contentment) are inhibited lest they lead to an augmentation of one's burden. This dilemma must be faced, for example, by persons who come from large, poor families and do moderately well financially while the other family members remain poor. If such a person manages to become very wealthy, he will be able to take care of all the other family members who want to be dependent on him. However, if he is only moderately well off, he will be faced with the threat that, irrespective of how hard he works, the demands of his poor relatives will prevent him from enjoying the fruits of his own labor, thrift, and perhaps good luck. Their needs will always be greater than his assets.* If our hypothetical moderately successful man wants to prevent antagonizing his poor relatives, he will be prompted to "malinger" in regard to his financial situation. He will pretend to be less well off than he really is.

There is thus a close similarity between misrepresenting health as illness on the one hand, and wealth as poverty on the other. Although, on the surface, both maneuvers seem painful and self-damaging, closer inspection of the social context in which they occur reveals that they are defensive operations. Their purpose is to sacrifice a part to save the whole. For example, in wartime, bodily survival may be safeguarded by simulating ill-health. Or financial possessions may be safeguarded by pretending to be poor.

The fear of acknowledging satisfaction is a characteristic feature of slave psychology. The "well-worked" slave is forced to labor until he is exhausted. To complete his task does not mean that his duties are finished and that he may rest. On the contrary, it only invites further demands. Conversely, although his task may be unfinished, he might be able to influence his master to stop driving him—and to let him rest—if he exhibits the appropriate signs of imminent collapse, whether genuine or contrived. However, displaying signs of exhaustion—irrespective of whether they are genuine or contrived—is, especially if it is habitual, likely to induce a feeling of fatigue or exhaustion in the actor. I believe that this explains many of the so-called chronic fatigue states of which harassed people complain: such persons are unconsciously "on strike"

* Progressive taxation may create similar feelings in people.

against individuals (actual or internal) to whom they relate subserviently and against whom they wage an unceasing and unsuccessful covert rebellion. In contrast to the slave, a free man can, depending on his circumstances, set his own pace: he can work although tired, and rest though rested—and can enjoy both his labor and its fruits.

Let us now consider some specific rules which make disability or illness potential or actual advantages. In certain situations, these rules prescribe that when man (subject, son, patient) is healthy, independent, rich, and proud, then God (king, father, physician) shall be strict with him and punish him. But should man be sick, dependent, poor, and humble, then God shall care for him and protect him. It might seem that I have exaggerated this rule. I do not believe so. Rather, this impression reflects our spontaneous antagonism to such a rule when it is clearly and forcefully stated.

Many Biblical passages could be cited to support this thesis. For example, in Luke we read:

> Now when Jesus heard these things, he said unto him, Yet lackest thou one thing: sell all that thou hast, and distribute unto the poor, and thou shall have treasure in heaven: and come, follow me. And when he heard this, he was very sorrowful: for he was very rich. And when Jesus saw that he was very sorrowful, He said, How hardly shall they that have riches enter into the kingdom of God! For it is easier for a camel to go through a needle's eye, than for a rich man to enter into the kingdom of God.[6]

The Sermon on the Mount[7] is probably the best-known illustration of Biblical rules fostering dependency and disability. Here, Jesus blesses the poor in spirit, the meek, the mourner, and so forth. This passage articulates most clearly the basic rules by which the Christian God plays His game with Man. What does God pledge Himself to do? And what type of behavior does He demand of Man? To frame my answers properly, I have paraphrased the Beatitudes by translating the Biblical phrasing "blessed are" into "should," and by supplementing each prescription so obtained by the corresponding proscription. The Beatitudes then read, in part, as follows:

The Biblical text (Matthew 5:3, 5, 8)	Its logical corollary (My interpretation)
Blessed are the poor in spirit: for theirs is the kingdom of heaven.	Man should be "poor in spirit"—i.e., stupid, submissive: Do not be smart, well-informed, or assertive!
Blessed are the meek: for they shall inherit the earth.	Man should be "meek"—i.e., passive, weak, submissive: Do not be self-reliant!
Blessed are the pure in heart: for they shall see God.	Man should be "pure in heart"—i.e., naïve, unquestioningly loyal: Do not entertain doubt (about God)!

Stated in this form, it is evident that these rules constitute a simple reversal of rules generally governing rewards and punishments for man on earth. As a result, defects and deficiencies are codified as positive values. Elsewhere man is explicitly enjoined to "take no thought for the morrow."[8] In other words, man should not plan for the future, should not try to provide for himself and for those who depend on him; instead, he should trust and have faith in God.

Rules rewarding "negative possessions"—that is, not having foresight, happiness, or wisdom—pervade the whole Christian ethic. The rewards of being poor,[9] hungry,[10] and emasculated are specifically emphasized, the latter in the following famous passage: "For there are some eunuchs, which were so born from their mother's womb: and there are some eunuchs, which were made eunuchs of men: and there be eunuchs, which have made themselves eunuchs for the kingdom of heaven's sake."[11]

Man's emasculation is here codified as one of the ways of courting God's love. The themes of self-castration and impotence—or, more generally, of lust and its vicissitudes—are the dominant images, first, in many parts of the Bible; second, in the documents dealing with witchcraft and justifying the persecution of witches;[12] and third, in the case histories and speculations of the early psychoanalysts.[13]

It is implicit in these Biblical rules of helplessness that the disabled may regard their weakened status as *prima facie* evidence of merit, which must be rewarded by the appropriate theological, medical, or psychiatric interventions. In the hysterical transaction, disability is used as a coercive tactic to force others to provide for one's needs. It is as if the patient were saying: "You have told me to be disabled—to be stupid, weak, and timid. You have promised that you would then love me and take care of me. Here I am, doing just as you have told me, it is your turn now to fulfill your promise!" Much of psychoanalytic psychotherapy may revolve around the theme of uncovering exactly who taught the patient to behave in this way, and why he accepted such teachings. It may then be discovered that religion, society, and parents have conspired, as it were, to inculcate this code of conduct, even though it is so tragically ill-suited to the requirements of our present social conditions.

Some Historical Comments on Rule Reversal

As I have implied earlier, the beliefs and practices of Christianity are best suited for children and slaves; this is hardly surprising when we recall the social circumstances in which this creed emerged.

Taken as a whole, I would offer the following generalization about the Bible: although some of its rules aim at the mitigation of oppression, their general sense nevertheless fosters the same oppressive spirit from which these rules arose and with which their creators must inevitably have been imbued. Moreover, since oppressed and oppressor form a

functional pair, their respective orientations to human relationships tend to be similar. This effect is further enhanced by
the basic human tendency for persons to identify with those
with whom they interact. Hence, each slave is a potential
master, and each master a potential slave. It is extremely
important to keep this in mind and to avoid the misleading
contrast between the psychology of the oppressed and that of
the oppressor. Instead, the similar orientation of each should
be contrasted with the orientation of the person who wants to
be neither slave nor master—but only his fellowman's equal.
Abraham Lincoln has put this with memorable perfection:
"As I would not be a slave, so I would not be a master. This
expresses my idea of democracy. Whatever differs from this, to
the extent of the difference, is not democracy."[14] If we define
a free, self-governing person as Lincoln saw him, then we
have an individual into whose scheme of life the Biblical rules
do not fit at all.

How are new social rules created and enforced? Forceful
subjugation is one obvious method for enforcing new rules. It
is available, however, only for the strong. The weak must rely
on more subtle methods of persuasion. The early as against
the later histories of many groups—Christianity and psychoanalysis among them—illustrate the uses of these methods.
When Christianity arose, its supporters were weak; hence,
they had to depend on noncoercive methods to spread their
views. However, after they gained power, they did not hesitate
to use coercive measures. The persecuted became the per-
secutors.

Another method, which oppressed individuals and groups
characteristically use, is rule change of the type "the first shall
be the last, and the last shall be the first."[15] On the face of it,
such a proposal often seems to be merely a modest effort to
improve the lot of the oppressed; but if it is successful, it often
turns out to be an effort to reverse positions, making the
oppressed the oppressors, and vice versa.

The historical model of the rule reversals advocated by Jesus was that used by Moses and the Jews. Dissatisfied with their real-life situation, the Jews apparently seized upon the inspired idea that, although they were having a poor time of it in their everyday life, they were actually God's Chosen People. Now, to be a chosen or preferred person implies that something especially good will happen to one, even if it is only to receive the love of an unseen God. If it works, this is a psychologically excellent maneuver: it helps to bolster the believer's weakened sense of self-esteem; and he may thus reject his degraded status as slave and rise to a more fully human stature.

The general usefulness of this maneuver was, however, seriously hampered by its unavailability: Judaism was not a proselytizing religion. The Jews thus imitated the slaveholder group: they, too, formed an essentially exclusive club.

Resting on this historical base, Jesus democratized the spirit of emancipation from slavery. In democratic societies, social status is based on achievement, not on ancestry. Early Christianity represents a forerunner of this modern arrangement: Jesus proclaimed that the New Rules shall apply to all who wish to embrace them. This far-reaching democratization of Judaism no doubt contributed heavily to the immense social success of Christianity over the next two millennia.

By New Rules I refer, of course, to some of the rules set forth in the New Testament. The New Testament must not be contrasted with the Old Testament, for the New Rules reversed not those of Judaism but rather those of the social order which prevailed at that time. What were these rules? That it was better to be a free citizen of Rome and a believer in Roman polytheism than not to be; that it was better to be healthy than sick, wealthy than poor, admired and beloved rather than persecuted and hated, and so forth. The New Rules, as set forth by Jesus and Saint Paul, consisted of a radical reversal of these real-life rules. Henceforth the "last" shall be "first"—the "loser" shall be the "winner": faithful Christians will be the winners, pagan Romans the losers; healthy, wealthy, and admired people will be punished, while the sick, poor, and persecuted will be rewarded.

The New Rules possessed several features that helped to make them popular and successful. In the early days of Christianity, there were, of course, many more slaves, sick, poor, and unhappy people than free, healthy, and satisfied ones. This remains true even today. Accordingly, while the rules of the earthly game, as practiced in Roman society, held out a promise of opportunity to only a few men, the rules of Christianity held out the promise of bountiful rewards in a life hereafter to many. In this sense, too, Christianity constituted a move toward democracy and populism.

We know only too well by now, however, that a social rule useful at one time and for one purpose may be useless and harmful at another time and for another purpose. Although Biblical rules once had a largely liberating influence, their effect has long since become both psychologically and politically oppressive. Alas, this transformation has characterized the course of most revolutions, the initial phase of liberation being quickly succeeded by a new phase of oppression.[16]

The general principle that a liberating rule may, in due time, become another method of oppression has broad validity for rule-changing maneuvers of all types. This is the reason why it is so dangerous today wholeheartedly to espouse new social schemes that offer merely another set of new rules. Although, if social life is to continue as a dynamic process tending toward ever-increasing human complexity and self-determination, new rules are constantly needed; but much more than mere rule changing is necessary to attain this goal. In addition to exchanging new rules for old, we must be aware of the rationale of the old rules and guard against their persistent effects. One such effect is to form new rules that are covert reaction-formations against the old ones. Christianity, the French Revolution, Marxism, and even psychoanalysis—as a revolution in medicine against the so-called organic tradition—all succumbed to the inescapable fate of all revolutions, the setting up of new tyrannies.

The effects of religious teachings on contemporary Western man is still a delicate subject. Psychiatrists, psychologists, and social scientists tend to avoid it. I have tried to reopen this subject by re-examining some of the values and rules of the Judaeo-Christian religions. If we sincerely desire a scientifically respectable psychosocial theory of man, we shall have to pay far more attention to religious—and perhaps even more to professional—rules and values than we have heretofore.

The Ethics of Paternalism and Therapeutism

As the infant's cry galvanizes his parent into succoring action,[17] so the adult's metaphoric cry for help, expressed in the verbal or nonverbal claim of illness, mobilizes the physician into therapeutic action. Revealingly, physicians, following in the footsteps of their predecessors, the priests, often refer to their occupation as a "calling"—implying, perhaps, that not only are the sick calling them, but so is God. The helpers thus hasten to the side of the helpless—the ill, the injured, and the disabled—and minister to him to restore him to health. In this imagery, the sick person is entitled to help simply because he is sick; if we don't help him, especially if we could, we incur moral blame for our neglect. To the extent that these principles are considered to be applicable to patients, they encourage malingering and the exploitation of physicians. And to the extent that they are considered to be binding on physicians, they encourage resentment of and retaliation against patients.

It is clear that the foregoing arrangement represents the same sort of emotional blackmail in a medical setting as that with which we are familiar in the family: the parent must take care of the child because the child is small and helpless; the physician must take care of the patient because the patient is sick and helpless. Therapeutism recapitulates paternalism.

To be sure, this parallel between children and patients is quite incomplete. Traditionally, patients have paid doctors for their services. But this exchange of money for medical services has always been treated as if it were a source of embarrassment for both parties. Today, it is being obscured as perhaps never before. Realizing that such a hypocritical stance toward the medical contract was incompatible with the practice of psychotherapy, Freud addressed himself to this problem much more frankly than did his predecessors, colleagues, or followers.[18] He deserves much credit for recognizing that patients cannot act autonomously so long as they are treated paternalistically; that their autonomy requires a frank discussion of the fee-arrangement between them and their doctors; and for constructing the psychoanalytic situation in such a way as to free the patient at least from this restraint.[19]

We must continue to scrutinize all therapeutic attitudes and arrangements attributed to benevolence, keeping in mind that, until proven otherwise, such arrangements serve to debase the patient and elevate the physician. We should recall here the traditional relationship between the slaveowner and his Negro slave: the good master treated his servant kindly—often more kindly than the Negro might have been treated in a northern industrial jungle—his benevolence being part and parcel of the paternalistic code of slaveholding.

I submit that in much the same way most of what now passes for "medical ethics" is nothing but a set of paternalistic rules whose aim is to diminish the patient while aggrandizing the physician. Genuine improvement in medical, and especially psychiatric, care requires the liberation and full enfranchisement of the patient—a change that can be accomplished only at the cost of full commitment to the ethic of autonomy and reciprocity. This means that all persons—whether sick or wicked, bad or mad—must be treated with dignity and respect—and that they must also be responsible for their conduct. If such a change in medical perspective were instituted, what patients would gain in dignity and control over the medical situation, they would lose in no longer being able to use illness as an excuse.

One of the thinkers who first recognized the moral implications of illness and treatment which we have been considering, and who noted especially the problems which rules favoring disability might pose for a society, was Herbert Spencer. A brief review of his relevant views will amplify this presentation of the ethics of helplessness and helpfulness.

Spencer, often considered one of the founders of modern sociology, was profoundly concerned with the problem of helping the helpless. Influenced by Darwin's evolutionary biological ideas, he noted that in the case of every higher species of animal, "the early lives of its members and the adult lives of its members, have to be dealt with in contrary ways."[20] Animals of "superior types" are comparatively slow in reaching maturity; having matured, however, they are able "to give more aid to their offspring than animals of inferior types."[21] He then formulated the general law that "during immaturity, benefits received must be inversely as the power or ability of the receiver. Clearly, if during his first part of life benefits were proportioned to merits, or rewards to deserts, the species would disappear in a generation."[22]

Next, Spencer contrasted the *"régime* of the family group" with the *"régime* of that larger group formed by the adult members of the species."[23] At some point in their lives, mature animals are left to themselves—to fulfill the requirements of life or to perish:

Now there comes into play a principle just the reverse of that above described. Throughout the rest of its life, each adult gets benefit in proportion to merit, reward in proportion to desert: merit and desert in each case being understood as ability to fulfill all the requirements of life—to get food, to secure shelter, or to escape enemies. Placed in competition with members of its own species and in antagonism with members of other species, it dwindles and gets killed off or thrives and propagates, according as it is ill-endowed or well-endowed. . . . The broad fact then, here to be noted, is that Nature's modes of treatment inside the family-group and outside the family-group are diametrically opposed to one another; and that the intrusion of either mode into the sphere of the other, would be fatal to the species either immediately or remotely.[24]

Spencer insisted that men can no more flout this Law of Nature than can animals. While he thought it necessary, and therefore proper, that children should be sheltered by their families, he felt strongly that a similar arrangement with respect to adults would bring disaster on the human species. In the true spirit of rugged individualism, Spencer pleaded for the self-reliant responsibility of man as opposed to the ministrations of the paternalistic State:

Surely none can fail to see that were the principle of family life to be adopted and fully carried out in social life—were reward always great in proportion as desert was small, fatal results to the society would quickly follow; and if so, then even a partial intrusion of the family *régime* into the *régime* of the State, will be slowly followed by fatal results. Society, in its corporate capacity, cannot without immediate or remoter disaster interfere with the play of these opposed principles under which every species has reached such fitness for its mode of life as it possesses, and under which it maintains that fitness.[25]

I do not believe that quite such a direct application of biological principles to the social—and hence inherently ethical—affairs of man is ever justified. I cite Spencer's views not so much for their political implications as for their historical significance. Spencer was a senior contemporary of Freud's. His thesis concerning the significance, especially for social organization, of the basic biological relationship between parent and young became a cornerstone of psychoanalytic theory. Roheim built an elaborate anthropological theory of man on essentially nothing more than a Spencerian notion of prolonged fetalization.[26]

Although Spencer's argument is plausible, we must be careful lest we use it to explain too much. Emphasizing the human infant's biologically determined dependence on its parents in order to explain "neurosis" may be a reversal of cause and effect. It seems more probable that the human child remains dependent for so long not because his prolonged childhood is biologically determined, but because it takes him a long time to learn all the symbols, rules, roles, and games which he must master before he can be considered a fully grown human being—and not just a biologically mature organism.

Let us now reconsider the similarities between being young (or immature) and being disabled (by illness or otherwise). For practical tasks, such as gathering food, building shelter, fighting off enemies, and so forth, children are useless. In fact, they are liabilities. The physically disabled, or those who, for whatever reason, refuse to play the game are similarly useless to society, and constitute a liability for it. Why, then, do human societies tolerate persons with such disabilities? Evidently because societies have concerns other than those for which disabled individuals are useless.

Because disabled adults are functionally similar to children, they fall readily into the same type of relationship to the able as children do to their parents. The disabled need help and will not survive without it. The able are capable of providing help and are motivated to do so. Besides the biological tendencies which parents and adults have to provide for their children and for others in need, there are often practical incentives promoting succoring behavior. In primitive social groups, for example, children could be counted on to assist, as soon as they were able, with the physical labor necessary for survival. Thus, caring for them when they were weak meant gaining helpers and allies when they were stronger.

The weakest link in Spencer's argument is his failure to make allowance for the fundamental change in man from biological organism to social being. With respect to rule-following behavior, this transformation means a change from acting automatically to acting self-reflectively. Rules may be "followed" regardless of which of these attitudes is maintained toward them: in the first case, they are followed in an obligatory manner, for the person or animal has no opportunity to deviate from them; in the second, they are followed self-consciously, with an opportunity to make a choice—that is, whether to obey or disobey the rule. Furthermore, rule-awareness leads to a fresh condition—namely, to the deliberate creation of occurrences designed for the purpose of bringing the operation of certain rules into play. Thus, as soon as men became intelligent, sign-using animals and hence aware of the kinds of relationships that invariably obtain between children and parents, the stage was set to imitate childishness to gain certain ends. The stage for the genesis of hysteria, too, was set at this early phase of human social development. The necessary conditions for the development of hysteria are, first, the biologically determined but socially implemented rule that parents (or well-functioning individuals) care for their children (or for ill-functioning individuals); and second, man's growth to self-reflection and awareness, made possible by the development of speech and symbolization. From this point of view, hysteria is a creative achievement or "progression," rather than a mere disability or "regression."

11 Theology, Witchcraft, and Hysteria

Educators, especially those concerned with inculcating religious teachings, have always endeavored to get hold of their pupils in early childhood. The idea that indoctrination during this period will have a lasting effect on the child's personality antedates psychoanalysis by many centuries. Freud reasserted this opinion when he claimed that a person's character is firmly fixed during the first five or six years of life. Although I do not share Freud's view, it is undoubtedly true that the rules on which a human being is fed, as it were, in the early years of life, profoundly affect his later behavior. This is especially true if a person's "rule diet" in later years does not differ markedly from that of his childhood. It seems to me that a great deal of a person's later education—say, between the ages of six and early adulthood—is often composed of an educational pabulum containing many of the same nonsensical rules he had been fed earlier. It is foolish to draw far-reaching conclusions about the effects of early learning experiences if these experiences are reinforced, rather than modified or corrected, by later influences. Among these reinforcing influences, I refer here specifically to the values and rules inherent in religious, national, and professional myths which foster the perpetuation of childish games and mutually coercive strategies of human behavior.

What I have called religious, national, and professional myths are games the main purpose of which is to glorify the group to which the individual belongs (or to membership in which he aspires). Such "closed" games must be contrasted with "open" games in which all who are capable of adhering to the rules can participate. Game rules based on such a suprareligious and supranational morality would seriously conflict with many of our current habits in living. Nevertheless, I believe that a social trend toward worldwide human equality—in the sense of equal rights and obligations, or of participating in all games according to one's abilities—need not be a threat to men and women. On the contrary, it represents one of the few values still deserving our admiration and support.

In this chapter, I shall try to show that, today, the notion of mental illness is used chiefly to obscure and explain away problems in personal and social relationships; and that the notion of witchcraft had been used in the same way during the declining Middle Ages. We now deny moral, personal, political, and social controversies by pretending that they are psychiatric problems: in short, by playing the medical game. During the witch hunts, people denied these controversies by pretending that they were theological problems: in short, by playing the religious game. The religious rules of life and their effects on man in the late Middle Ages thus not only illustrate the principles of rule-following behavior, but also display the belief in witchcraft as a historical precursor of the modern belief in mental illness.

The Medical Theory of Witchcraft

It is often asserted that the medieval women accused of witchcraft actually suffered from what we now know to be hysteria.

Numerous medical and psychiatric authors advocate such a psychiatric view of witchcraft.

For example, Zilboorg[1] maintains that witches were misdiagnosed mental patients, a view he bases largely on his interpretation of Krämer and Sprenger's *Malleus Maleficarum.*[2] It is clear, however, that Zilboorg is determined to prove that witches were mentally sick persons, and that he disregards all evidence suggesting other interpretations. He thus ignores the fact that the *Malleus* shows a much greater resemblance to a legal than to a medical document. The ferreting out of witches and the proving of witchcraft were preliminary to their sentencing. Although Zilboorg notes that a large part of the *Malleus* deals with the legal examination and sentencing of witches, he fails to draw the logical inference that witches were criminals or, to put it more neutrally, offenders against the prevailing social (theological) order. On the contrary, he suggests that "the *Malleus Maleficarum* might, with a little editing, serve as an excellent modern textbook of descriptive clinical psychiatry of the fifteenth century, if the word *witch* were substituted by the word *patient,* and the devil eliminated."[3]

A hundred pages later, however, Zilboorg offers another opinion, partly contradicting his earlier assertion: "Not all accused of being witches and sorcerers were mentally sick, but almost all mentally sick were considered witches, or sorcerers, or bewitched."[4]

Furthermore, although Zilboorg notes that medieval man was engaged in playing a game quite different from that we now play, he proceeds to cast Krämer and Sprenger's observations into a medical and psychiatric mold. He writes:

This passage from the *Malleus* is perhaps the most significant statement to come out of the fifteenth century. Here, in a concise and succinct paragraph, two monks brush aside the whole mass of psychiatric knowledge which had been so carefully collected and preserved by almost two thousand years of medical and philosophic investigation; they brush it aside almost casually and with such stunning simplicity that no room is left for argument. How can one raise objections to the assertion, "but this is contrary to true faith"? The fusion of insanity, witchcraft, and heresy into one concept and the exclusion of even the suspicion that the problem is a medical one are now complete.[5]

Further on, he adds:

The belief in the free will of man is here brought to its most terrifying, although most preposterous, conclusion. Man, whatever he does, even if he succumbs to an illness which perverts his perceptions, imagination, and intellectual functions, does it of his own free will; he voluntarily bows to the wishes of the Evil One. The devil does not lure and trap man; man chooses to succumb to the devil and he must be held responsible for this free choice. He must be punished; he must be eliminated from the community.[6]

Following Zilboorg, it has become popular for psychiatrists to assume—indeed, to insist—that witches were unfortunate women who "fell ill" with "mental illness." This interpretation must be challenged. The notion that so-called witches were mentally ill persons discredits the entire theological world view underlying the belief in witchcraft and enthrones the concept of mental illness as an explanatory theory of wide scope and unchallenged power.

Zilboorg asserts that the authors of the *Malleus* had brushed aside two thousand years of medical and psychiatric knowledge. But what medical and psychiatric knowledge was there in the fifteenth century that would have been relevant to the problems to which the theologians addressed themselves? Surely, the ideas of Galenic medicine would have been irrelevant. In fact, medieval man possessed no "medical" knowledge relevant to the problem of witchcraft. Nor was any such knowledge needed, for there was abundant evidence that charges of witchcraft were commonly trumped up for the purpose of eliminating certain people, and that confessions were extorted by means of cruel tortures.[7] Finally, if the belief in witchcraft was a "medical mistake"—codifying the mis-diagnosis of hysterics as witches—why was this mistake not made more often prior to the thirteenth century?

To explain witchcraft, Zilboorg offers what seems like a medical explanation, but without specifying how it is to be understood or used. To what sort of illness did the witches now said to be "mentally ill" succumb? Did they succumb to diseases such as paresis or brain tumor, or to problems in living, arising from or precipitated by family and social pressures, conflicting goals, and so forth? No such questions are raised, much less answered, by the proponents of the medical theory of witchcraft. Zilboorg's interpretation that the imputation of witchcraft signified a fanatical belief in free will is simply false. It contradicts the most obvious fact—namely, that the majority of witches were women, and especially old, poor, and socially readily expendable women. Moreover, when people were con-sidered to be possessed by the devil, this was generally not attributed to their free will, but was viewed rather as having occurred against their own "better judgment." Accordingly, the witch hunters were regarded as the agents of their unfortu-nate clients, and executing witches was defined as "thera-peutic." This totalitarian definition of what constitutes "therapy" and of who is a "therapist" has persisted to our day with respect to all involuntary psychiatric interventions.[8]

The medical theory of witchcraft ignores two obvious social determinants of the belief in witches and its corollary, witch hunts. First, a preoccupation with God, Jesus, and Christian theology cannot be arbitrarily separated from a belief in bad deities and their cohorts, devils, witches, sorcerers. Second, concern with the sexual activities of witches and devils was a counterpart, a mirror image, of the officially antisexual atti-tude of the Catholic church. The torturing and burning of witches must be viewed in the light of medieval man's theological world view, according to which the body is weak and sinful, and the only goal worthy of man is the eternal salvation of his soul.[9] Burning human bodies at the stake was a symbolic act which expressed adherence to the official rules of the game. This dramatic, ritualized affirmation of the faith insured the continued existence of an important social fiction or myth.[10] Burning accused witches during the witch hunts may thus be compared to destroying confiscated whisky during Prohibition. Both acts gave official recognition to a rule which few people followed in their actual conduct. During the Middle Ages, sexual conduct was, actually, exceedingly promiscuous, if measured by our current standards.[11] In both instances, then, the law expressed high ethical ideals to which most people had no intention to adhere. Their goal became, instead, to evade the laws, to appear as if they were law-abiding, and to make sure that there were suitable scapegoats available to be caught and punished. In situations of this sort, it is the scapegoat's social function to play the role of the person who violates, or is said to violate, the rules, is caught, and is duly punished.[12] We might thus view bootleggers and the entire class of so-called organized gangsters—all of whom came into being during Prohibition—as the scapegoats who were sacrificed at the altar of the false god of abstinence. The greater the actual discrepancy between prescribed rules of conduct and actual social behavior, the greater the need for scapegoat sacrifices as a means of maintaining the social myth that man lives according to his officially declared ethical beliefs.

The Scapegoat Theory of Witchcraft

I submit that witchcraft represents the expression of a particular method by means of which men have sought to explain and master various ills of nature. Unable to admit ignorance and helplessness, yet equally unable to achieve understanding and mastery of diverse physical, biological, and social problems, men have sought refuge in scapegoat explanations. The specific identities of the scapegoats are legion: witches, women, Jews, Negroes, the mentally ill, and so forth. All scapegoat theories postulate that if only the offending person, race, illness, or what-not could be dominated, subjugated, or eliminated, all manner of problems would be solved.

While medical men subscribe enthusiastically to the idea that witches were hysterical women who had been misdiagnosed, social scientists lean toward the view that they were society's scapegoats.[13] I am in substantial agreement with this latter interpretation and shall try to show exactly in what ways the scapegoat theory is superior to the medical one. In addition, I shall argue that not only is it misleading to consider witches misdiagnosed hysterics, but it is also misleading to regard people currently "ill" with hysteria or other mental illnesses as belonging in the same category as those ill with bodily ailments.

With respect to the scapegoat theory of witchcraft, we might raise the following questions: Who were considered to be witches? How were they tried and who profited from their conviction? What did those people who did not believe in the reality of witches think of witchcraft? Did they think that witches were ill? Or did they believe that the problem was not one of witchcraft at all, but that it was a matter of trumped-up charges? In discussing these questions, I shall try to develop the similarities between the medieval belief in witchcraft and the contemporary belief in mental illness; and I shall try to show that both are false explanations that conceal certain difficult moral problems. Moreover, both serve the interests of a special group—the one, the interests of the clergy, the other, those of the medical profession. Finally, both fulfill their function by sacrificing a special group of persons on the altar of social expediency: in the Middle Ages the scapegoats were the witches; today, they are the involuntary mental patients, and the mentally ill generally.

In comparing witchcraft with mental illness, it is important to bear in mind that the traditional concept of illness rests on the simple facts of pain, suffering, and disability. Hence, the sufferer, the patient himself, first considers himself ill and is then usually so considered by others. In sociological terms, the sick role in medicine is typically self-defined.[14]

The traditional concept of mental illness, or insanity, rests on precisely the opposite criteria. The alleged sufferer (especially the "psychotic") considers himself neither sick nor disabled; but others insist that he is both. The role of mental patient is thus often imposed on persons against their will. In short, the sick role in psychiatry is typically other-defined.

This distinction between assuming the role of patient voluntarily and being placed in it against one's will is all-important: the mentally sick role is self-defined usually in the expectation that doing so will help to secure certain types of help, for example private psychotherapy; in contrast, when this role is imposed on a person against his will, it serves the interests of those who define him as mentally ill. In other words, whereas the patient role is assumed in the hope of a personal cure, it is ascribed in the hope of social control.

How did people ascertain, during the Middle Ages, that someone was a witch? Of course, individuals rarely "discovered" that they themselves were witches. Rather, some persons or groups claimed—and it was subsequently ascertained by the methods then prescribed—that someone else was a witch. In short, the witch role was characteristically other-defined: in this crucial respect it was identical to the contemporary role of involuntary mental patient.

Most people accused of witchcraft were women. The word "witch" implies "woman," as did the word "hysteric." Janet and Freud, it will be remembered, were pioneers in asserting that there were "male hysterics."* In this respect, the parallels between being a witch and being a hysteric are striking. According to Parrinder, out of two hundred convicted witches in England, only fifteen were men.[15] He interprets this as a sign that women were a persecuted minority in a world ruled by men.

In addition to the high incidence of women, most persons accused of witchcraft were members of the lower classes. They were poor, stupid, socially helpless, and often old and feeble. Making a "diagnosis" of witchcraft then—much as calling someone mentally ill today—was an insult and an accusation. Obviously, it is safer to accuse socially unimportant persons than those who are socially prominent. When highly placed persons were accused of witchcraft, as happened occasionally, it was safer as well as more effective if the charge was made by large groups, as for instance a whole nunnery, rather than by a single person. Then, as now, there was safety in numbers— the assumption being that if many people claimed something, it had to be true. Nevertheless, the educated and the well-to-do could better protect themselves from being branded witches, and being treated for it by burning at the stake, much as well-informed and wealthy persons today can better protect themselves from being diagnosed as mentally ill against their will, and being treated for it with lobotomy.

Actually, the medieval inquisitors themselves were impressed by the discrepancy between the patently feeble and harmless character of the women accused of witchcraft and

* The discovery of "male hysteria," like Charcot's conversion of malingerers to hysterics, was another step in the democratization of misery. Freud was obviously more eager to acknowledge equality between the sexes in regard to their susceptibility to neurosis than in regard to their potentialities for creative performance. His assertion that men, too, may suffer from hysteria must be contrasted with his equally firm conviction that women are incapable of the same "sublimations" and "mental development" as men.

their allegedly diabolical and potent actions. Parrinder remarks:

The explanation was given that their evil deeds had been performed by the help of the devil, but that, like the deceiver he is, he had abandoned his disciples in their moment of need. . . . This was very convenient for the inquisitors, for it meant that they could handle these dangerous women without risk to themselves.[16]

Although Parrinder calls these antifeminine beliefs and actions "ridiculous," this should not distract us from the fact that similar attitudes were prevalent in Europe well into the twentieth century. In fact, such prejudices are by no means extinct today, even in so-called civilized countries. In the economically underdeveloped areas of the world, the systematic oppression and exploitation of women—much like slavery and the exploitation of alien races—are still the dominant customs and rules of life.

While these historical and cultural considerations are of momentous importance insofar as any progress toward an internationally meaningful science of human behavior is contemplated, what is even more significant, especially in relation to hysteria, is the cultural attitude toward women in Central Europe at the turn of the century. This was the time and place of the origin of psychoanalysis, and through it, of the entire body of what is now known as "dynamic psychiatry." That the status of women in that social situation was still one of profound oppression, while well known, is easily forgotten or relegated to a position of unimportance. Generally, women were then economically dependent on their parents or spouses, had few educational and occupational opportunities, and were regarded—perhaps not quite explicitly—as the mere bearers of uteri. Their "proper" roles were marriage and motherhood. Accordingly, they were considered biologically inferior to men in regard to such traits as intellectual ability and finer ethical feelings. Some of Freud's opinions about women were not unlike those of Krämer and Sprenger, as the following passage illustrates:

It must be admitted that women have but little sense of justice, and this is no doubt connected with the preponderance of envy in their mental life; for the demands of justice are a modification of envy; they lay down the conditions under which one is willing to part with it. We also say of women that their social interests are weaker than those of men, and that their capacity for the sublimation of their instincts is less.[17]

I cite this opinion of Freud's about women not so much to criticize it—that has been adequately done by others[18]—but to emphasize the significance of scapegoating in the phenomena called witchcraft, hysteria, and mental illness.

The belief in witches, devils, and their cohorts was, of course, more than just a matter of metaphysics or theological theory. It affected public behavior—most glaringly in the form of witch hunts and witch trials. In a way, these were the opposites or mirror images of saintly miracles. Alleged acts of witchcraft or miracle-working could be officially recognized only after they had been passed on and approved as valid by the holders of appropriate social power—in this case, the high-ranking clergy of the Roman Catholic church. Hence the expression "witch-trials." Clearly, a trial is neither a medical nor a scientific affair.

The distinction between legal and scientific disputes was recognized by medieval man, no less than by the ancients. Yet, this important distinction was obscured by the medical theory of hysteria. Legal contests serve to settle disputes of conflicting interests. Medical procedures serve to settle the nature of the patient's illness and the measures that might restore him to health. In such a situation, there are no obvious conflicts of interest between opposing parties. The patient is ill and wants to recover; his family and society also want him to recover; and so does his physician.

The situation is different in a legal dispute where the problem is a conflict of interests between two or more parties. What is good ("therapeutic") for one party is likely to be bad ("noxious") for the other. Instead of a situation of cooperation between patient and physician, we have one of conflict or conciliation between two contending parties, with the judge serving as arbitrator of the dispute.

In European witch-trials it was customary for the judge to receive a portion of the convicted heretic's worldly possessions.[19] Today, we take it for granted that, in free societies, the judge is impartial. His task is to uphold the law. Hence, he must occupy a position outside of the socio-economic interests of the litigants. While all this may seem dreadfully obvious, it needs to be said because, even today, the impartiality of the judge toward the litigants is often an unrealized ideal. In totalitarian countries, for example, so-called crimes against the state fall in the same class as witch-trials: the judge is an employee of one of the contesting parties. Even in free societies, in crimes violating cardinal moral and social beliefs—such as treason or subversion—judicial impartiality is often thrown to the wind—and we have "political justice." This is why "political criminals" may become "revolutionary heroes," and should the revolution fail, revert once more to the status of "criminals."

In witch-trials the conflict was officially defined as between the accused and God, or between the accused and the Catholic (later Protestant) church, as God's earthly representative. There was no attempt to make this an even match. The distribution of power between accuser and accused mirrored the relations between king and serf—one had all the power and the other none of it. Once again, we encounter the theme of domination and submission. Significantly, only in England—where, beginning in the thirteenth century with the granting of the Magna Charta, there gradually developed an appreciation of the rights and dignities of those less powerful than the king—was the fury of witch hunting mitigated by legal safe-guards and social sensibilities.

Behind the ostensible conflict of the witch-trial lay the usual conflicts of social class, values, and human relationships. Fur-thermore, there was strife within the Catholic church itself which later became accentuated by the antagonisms between Catholics and Protestants. It was in this context, then, that witches and sorcerers, recruited from the ranks of the poor and oppressed, played the role of scapegoats. They thus ful-filled the socially useful function of acting as social tranquil-izers.[20] By participating in an important public drama, they contributed to maintaining the stability of the existing social order.

Games of Life: Theological and Medical

Life in the Middle Ages was a colossal religious game. The dominant value was salvation in a life hereafter. Emphasizing that "to divorce medieval hysteria from its time and place is not possible,"[21] Gallinek observes:

It was the aim of man to leave all things worldly as far behind as possible, and already during lifetime to approach the kingdom of heaven. The aim was salvation. Salvation was the Christian master motive.—The ideal man of the Middle Ages was free of all fear because he was sure of salvation, certain of eternal bliss. He was the saint, and the saint, not the knight nor the troubadour, is the veritable ideal of the Middle Ages.[22]

However, if sainthood and salvation formed one part of the Christian game of life, witchcraft and damnation formed another. The two belong together in a single system of beliefs and rules, just as, say, military decorations for bravery and punishments for desertion belong together. Positive and nega-tive sanctions, or rewards and penalties, form a complemen-tary pair and share equally in giving form and substance to the game. A game is composed of the totality of its rules. If any of the rules is changed, the game itself is changed. It is important to keep this clearly in mind to avoid the sentimental belief that the essential identity of a game may be preserved by retaining only what is desirable (the rewards) and eliminating all that is undesirable (the penalties).

On the contrary, if preservation of the game—that is, maintenance of the social (religious) status quo—is desired, this can be best achieved by enthusiastically playing the game as it is. Thus, searching for and finding witches constituted an important maneuver in the religious game of life, much as looking for and finding mental illness is an important tactic in the contemporary medical-therapeutic game. The extent to which belief in and preoccupation with witchcraft constituted a part of the theological game of life may be gleaned from Parrinder's description of "Pacts with the Devil."[23]

It is significant that the criteria for "diagnosing" witchcraft and heresy were of the same type as the criteria for establishing the possession of genuine belief. Both were inferred from what the person said. As evidential proof, *claims* were thus raised over *deeds*. This was true equally of claims that aggrandized and flattered, and of those that accused and injured. Claims of having seen the Holy Virgin thus counted for more than decent behavior and honest work; and claims of having seen one's neighbor fly off on a broomstick counted for more than common sense and respect for others.

The importance of confession, even if extracted under torture, was an integral part of this reliance on words instead of on acts, which characterized the inquisitorial mentality. Moreover, the witch hunts and witch-trials took place in a social setting in which brutal behavior—especially by noblemen toward serfs, men toward women, adults toward children —was an everyday matter. Its very ordinariness thus dulled men's sensibilities and turned their attention from it. It is not easy to remain interested in what is commonplace—such as man's everyday brutality vis-à-vis his fellow man. Oh, but the dastardly behavior of persons in the grip of the devil: that was another, more interesting matter! Since this could not be directly observed, the "diagnosticians" of sorcery and witchcraft had to rely heavily on verbal communications. These were of two kinds: accusations against persons concerning the commission of evil deeds or peculiar acts, and confessions of misdeeds.

Let us now examine the values of a social system that encourages the "diagnosis" of hysteria. Clearly, one of the principal values of our culture is science. Medicine, regarded as a science, is thus an integral part of this value system. The notions of health, illness, and treatment are thus the cornerstones of an all-embracing modern medical-therapeutic world view.[24]

In speaking of science as a widely shared social value, I do not refer to any particular scientific method, nor have I in mind such things as the search for truth, understanding, or explanation. I refer rather to science as an institution, similar to organized theology in the past. It is to this aspect of science, sometimes called "scientism," that increasing numbers of people turn in their search for practical guidance in living. According to this scheme of values, one of the most important things for man to achieve is to have a strong and healthy body—a wish that is the true heir to medieval man's wish for a virtuous soul. A healthy body is regarded as useful, not, it is true, for salvation, but for comfort, sex appeal, happiness, and a long life. Great efforts and vast sums are expended in pursuit of this goal of having a healthy—and this has of late included an attractive—body. Finally, having a healthy mind has been added to this value scheme by regarding the mind as if it were simply another part of the human organism or body. In this view, the human being is endowed with a skeletal system, digestive system, circulatory system, nervous system, etc.— *and* a "mind." As the Romans had put it, *Mens sana in corpora sano:* "In a healthy body, a healthy mind." Curiously enough, much of modern psychiatry has been devoted to this ancient proposition. Psychiatrists who search for biochemical or genetic defects as the causes of mental illness are, whether they know it or not, committed to this perspective on human misery.

Even if we do not believe in reducing psychiatry to biochemistry, the notion of mental illness implies, first, that mental health is a "good thing"; and second, that there are certain criteria according to which mental health and illness can be diagnosed. In the name of this value, then, the same sorts of actions may be justified as were justified by medieval man marching under the banner of God and Christ. What are some of these actions?

Those who are considered especially strong and healthy—or who contribute to these values—are rewarded. The athletes, the beauty queens, and the movie stars are the modern-day "saints"—and the cosmetics manufacturers, doctors, and psychiatrists are their assistants. They are honored, admired, and rewarded. All this is well-known and should occasion little surprise. Who are the people who fall in the class of the witches and sorcerers; the people persecuted and victimized in the name of "health" and "happiness"? They are legion. In their front ranks are the mentally ill, and especially those who are so defined by others rather than by themselves. The involuntarily hospitalized mentally ill are regarded as "bad" and valiant efforts are made to make them "better." Words like "good" and "bad" are used here in accordance with the dominant value system of society. In addition to the mentally ill, elderly persons and people who are ugly or deformed find themselves in a class analogous to the now defunct category of witches and sorcerers.

The reason why individuals displaying such characteristics are considered "bad" is inherent in the rules of the medical game. Just as witchcraft was an inverted theological game, so much of general psychiatry—especially the so-called care of the involuntary mental patient—is a kind of inverted medical game. The rules of the medical game define health—which includes such things as a well-functioning body and happiness—as a positive value; and they define illness—which includes such things as a badly functioning body and unhappiness—as a negative value. It follows, then, that insofar as people play the medical game, they will, at least to some extent, dislike and demean sick persons. This penalty, which is an integral part of the sick role and cannot be severed from it without altering the basic rules of the medical game—is, in practice, mitigated by the sick person's submission to those who attempt to make him well and by his own efforts to recover from the illness. However, patients with hysteria and with most so-called mental illnesses do not make "appropriate" efforts to get well. Indeed, they usually make no such efforts at all, and try, instead, to be authenticated as "sick" in the particular ways in which they want to be, or see themselves as being, sick. In hysteria, as we have seen, the patient offers the dramatized representation of the message "My body is not functioning well." In depression, he offers the dramatized proposition "I am unhappy." To the extent to which such persons want to assume sick roles of such sorts and reject efforts to dislodge them from these roles, they forfeit the ordinary person's and the physician's disposition to treat them well as patients and invite instead their latent disposition to treat them badly as deviants.

In the framework of traditional medical ethics, the patient deserves humane attention only insofar as he is potentially healthy and is willing to be healthy—just as in the framework of traditional Christian ethics, the heretic deserved humane attention only insofar as he was potentially a true believer and was willing to become one. In the one case, people are accepted as human beings only because they might be healthy citizens; in the other, only because they might be faithful

Christians. In short, neither was heresy formerly, nor is sickness now, given the kind of humane recognition which, from the point of view of an ethic of respect and tolerance, they deserve.

It is easy, of course, to be skeptical of a belief that is no longer fashionable; but it is not easy at all to be skeptical of one that is. This is why contemporary intellectuals find it so easy to scoff at religion and witchcraft and find it so difficult to scoff at medicine and mental illness. In the Middle Ages, the suggestion to regard heresy as just another way of life would have seemed absurd, or worse. Today the suggestion to regard mental illness as just another way of life seems equally absurd, or worse.

GAME-MODEL

ANALYSIS OF

BEHAVIOR

■

12 The Game-Playing Model of Human Behavior

Much of what I have said so far has utilized a game model of human behavior, first clearly articulated by George Herbert Mead.[1] In Mead's view, mind and self are generated in a social process, with linguistic communication as the capacity most responsible for the differences between the behavior of animals and men.

Human Actions as Games

Mead considered games as paradigmatic of social situations. Playing a game presupposes that each player is able to take the role of all the other players. Mead also noted that children are intensely interested in game rules and that their increasing sophistication in playing games is crucial to the social development of the human being.

The social situation in which a person lives constitutes the team on which he plays and is, therefore, important in determining who he is and how he acts. Man's so-called instinctual needs are actually shaped—and this may include inhibiting, fostering, or even creating "needs"—by the social games prevalent in his milieu. The view of a dual, biosocial determination of behavior has become incorporated into psychoanalytic theory through increasing emphasis on ego psychology and object relationships. Useful as these modifications of classical psychoanalytic theory have been, explanations in terms of ego functions are not as satisfactory for either theory or therapy as those couched in terms of rules, roles, and games.

In this connection, let us briefly reconsider a problem that clarifies the connections between psychoanalysis and game theory (in the sense used here)—namely, the problem of primary and secondary gains. In psychoanalysis, gains derived from playing a game profitably—say, by being protectively treated for a hysterical illness—are regarded as secondary. As the term betrays, these gains are considered less significant as motives for the behavior in question than primary gains, which are derived from the gratification of unconscious instinctual needs.

If we reinterpret these phenomena in terms of a consistently game-playing model of behavior, the need to distinguish between primary and secondary gains disappears. The correlative necessity to estimate the relative significance of physiological needs and dammed-up impulses on the one hand, and of social and interpersonal factors on the other, also vanishes. Since needs and impulses cannot be said to exist in human social life without specified rules for dealing with them, instinctual needs cannot be considered solely in terms of biological rules, but must also be viewed in terms of their psychosocial significance—that is, as parts of the game.

It follows that what we call "hysteria" or "mental illness" can be properly understood only in the context of a specified social setting. While diseases such as syphilis and tuberculosis are in the nature of *events* and hence can be described without taking cognizance of how men conduct themselves in their social affairs, hysteria and all the other so-called mental illnesses are in the nature of *actions*. They are made to happen by sentient, intelligent human beings and can be understood best, in my opinion, in the framework of games. Mental illnesses thus differ fundamentally from bodily diseases, and resemble, rather, certain moves or tactics in playing games.

I have used the notion of games so far as if it were familiar to most people. I think this is justified as everyone knows how to play some games. Accordingly, games serve admirably as models for the clarification of other, less well-understood, social-psychological phenomena. Yet the ability to follow rules, play games, and construct new games is a faculty not equally shared by all persons. It will be helpful now to review briefly the child's development in regard to his ability to play games.

Piaget[2] has conducted many careful studies on the evolution of games during childhood, and has suggested that moral behavior be viewed as a type of rule following. He writes: "All morality consists in a system of rules, and the essence of all morality is to be sought for in the respect which the individual acquires for these rules."[3] Piaget thus equates morality, or ethical feeling and conduct, with the individual's attitude toward and practice of various rules. This perspective provides a rational basis for the analysis of moral schemes as games, and of moral behavior as the players' actual conduct.

Piaget distinguishes two distinct features of rule-following behavior: one, the practice of rules, that is, the ways in which children of different ages apply rules; the other, the consciousness of rules, that is, self-reflection about the rules and role-taking behavior. Children of different ages have quite different ideas about the character of game rules: young children regard them as obligatory, externally imposed, and "sacred," whereas older children regard rules as socially defined and, in a sense, self-imposed. Piaget traces rule-following and game-playing behavior from early childhood stages of egocentrism, imitation, and heteronomy, to the later, mature stage of co-operation, rational rule following, and autonomy.[4]

Piaget identifies four discrete stages in the practice or *application of rules*. The earliest stage is characterized by the automatic imitation by the preverbal child of certain behavior patterns he observes in others. Piaget calls these motor rules, which later become habits.

The second stage begins some time after the second year of life, "when the child receives from the outside the example of codified rules."[5] His play during this phase is purely egocentric: he plays in the presence of others, but not with them. This type of rule application is characterized by a combination of imitation of others with an idiosyncratic use of the examples received. For example, everyone can win at once. This stage usually ends at about the age of seven or eight years.

During the third stage, which Piaget calls "the stage of incipient cooperation," children "begin to concern themselves with the question of mutual control and of the unification of rules."[6] Nevertheless, play remains relatively idiosyncratic. When, during this period, children are questioned about the rules of the game in which they are engaged, they often give entirely contradictory accounts of them.

The fourth stage appears between the ages of eleven and twelve years and is characterized by the codification of rules. The rules of the game are now clearly understood, with a correspondingly high consensus among the children about what they are. The game rules are now explicit, public, and conventional.

This scheme may be supplemented by the development of the *consciousness of rules*—that is, the person's experience in regard to the origin and nature of the rules, and especially his feeling and conception about how they obligate him to obey the rules. Piaget identifies three stages in the development of rule consciousness. During the first stage "rules are not yet coercive in character, either because they are purely motor, or else (at the beginning of the egocentric stage) because they are received, as it were, unconsciously, and as interesting examples rather than as obligatory realities."[7] During the second stage, which begins at about the age of five years, rules are regarded as sacred and untouchable. Games composed of such rules are called heteronomous. The rules emanate from the adults and are experienced as lasting forever: "Every suggested alteration strikes the child as a transgression."[8] The third and final stage begins when the child regards rules as acquiring their obligatory character from mutual consent. Such rules must be obeyed because loyalty to the group, or to the game, demands it. Undesirable rules, however, can be altered. It is this attitude toward games that we usually associate with and expect of an adult in a free society. Such a person is expected to know and feel that just as the rules of a game are man-made, so are the laws of a nation. This may be contrasted with the rules of the game of a theocratic society, in which the citizen is expected to believe that the laws are God-given. So-called autonomous games, in contrast to heteronomous ones, can be played only by individuals who have reached the last stages in the foregoing developmental sequences.

The evolution of the child's concept of games and rules parallels the development of his intelligence. The ability to distinguish biological from social rules thus depends on a certain degree of intellectual and moral development. This makes it easy to understand why it is during adolescence that children begin to have doubts concerning the rationality of Biblical rules. It seems to me, therefore, that much of what has been labeled "adolescent rebelliousness" may be attributed to the fact that it is only at this time that children have enough sense to be able intelligently to scrutinize parental, religious, and social demands as systems of rules. The Bible lends itself especially well to criticism by the developing logical sense of the adolescent, for in it biological and social rules are often undifferentiated, or deliberately confused. In Piaget's terms, all rules are treated as if they were parts of heteronomous games. This type of game fits best into the world of a less than ten-year-old child.

Since children, especially very young children, are completely dependent on their parents, their relative inability to comprehend other than externally imposed, coercive rules is not surprising. In the same way, to the extent that adults depend, or are made to depend, on others rather than on themselves, their game-playing aptitudes and attitudes will be like those of children.

A Logical Hierarchy of Games

I have treated games so far as if they were all more or less of the same kind. This point of view will no longer suffice. Since games consist, among other things, of bits of communicative action, it is not surprising that a hierarchy of games analogous to a hierarchy of languages is easily constructed. Linguistic signs point to referents, such as physical objects, other words, or more complex systems of signs. Similarly, games consist of systems of rules which point to certain acts—the rules standing in the same relation to the acts as the words to their referents. Accordingly, games with rules that point to the simplest possible set of patterned acts will be called "object games." Games composed of rules which themselves point to other rules will be called "metagames." Typical examples of object games are patterns of instinctive behavior. Their goals are physical survival, release of urinary, anal, or sexual tension, and so forth. Hence, playing object games is not limited to human beings. In the medical setting, the reflex immobilization of an injured extremity would be an example of a "move" in an object game.

Clearly, the learned and distinctively human elements of behavior are wholly on the level of metagames. For example, first-level metagames would be the rules determining where to urinate and where not to, when to eat and when not to, and so forth. Ordinary or conventional games—such as bridge, tennis, or chess—all consist of mixtures of complex metagames.

Let us apply the concepts of game hierarchy to the analysis of an ordinary game, say tennis. Like any game of skill and strategy, tennis is characterized, first, by a set of basic rules which specify such things as the number of players, the layout of the court, the nature and use of rackets and balls, and so forth. Actually, although these rules are object rules to tennis, they are metarules with respect to such logically anterior games as the proper laying out of courts or the manufacturing of rackets. When we play tennis, however, we are not usually concerned with games lying on levels lower than the basic game of tennis itself. These infra-tennis games might, however, be important for those who want to play tennis but are prevented from doing so by insufficient funds to purchase the necessary equipment.

Beginning at the level of the basic rules—assuming, that is, the presence of players, equipment, and so forth—it is evident that there is much more to an actual, true-to-life tennis game than could be subsumed under the basic rules. This is because there is more than one way to play tennis, while still adhering to these rules. For example, one player might aspire at winning at any cost; another at playing fairly. Each of these goals implies rules specifying, first, that in order to play tennis one must follow rules A, B, and C, and second, how one should conduct oneself while following these rules. The latter prescriptions constitute the rules of "metatennis." In everyday language, the term "tennis" is used, of course, to denote all of the rules of this game. The fact that ordinary games may be played in more than one way—that is, that they contain games at different logical levels—leads to conflict whenever different types of players meet.

When two wildly competitive youngsters play tennis, the game is so constituted that both players regard winning as their sole aim. Style, fair play, one's state of health, and everything else may become subordinated to this goal. In other words, the players play to win at any cost—adhering only to the minimal basic rules of the game.

A next higher level of tennis may be distinguished—a "metatennis game," as it were—which, in addition to the basic rules, contains a new set of rules which refer to the basic rules. These might include prescriptions about style, the tempo of the game, courteous behavior, etc. Playing according to these higher-level rules, or metarules, implies, first, that the players will orient themselves to and follow a new set of rules, these being additional to, rather than substitutes for, the old set; and second, that the players will adopt as their own the new goals implicit in the new rules. In tennis, this might mean to play fairly or perhaps elegantly, rather than to win at any cost. It is important to note now that the goals of the object game and of the metagame may come into conflict, although they need not necessarily do so. Adherence to the rules and aims (ethics) of the higher-level game usually implies that its rules and goals take precedence over those of the basic game. In other words, for a properly socialized Englishman, it is better—that is, more rewarding in relation to both the spectators and his own self-image—to be a "fair loser" than an "ugly winner." But if this is true, as indeed it is, then our everyday use of the words "loser" and "winner" no longer do justice to what we want to say. For when we speak of James as a "fair loser," especially if he is contrasted with an opponent considered an "ugly winner," what we mean is that James lost the basic game but has won the metagame. But we cannot say anything like this in ordinary language—except by circumlocution—for example, by saying that "James played a good game but lost."

Everyday life is full of situations similar to the example sketched above. Men are constantly engaged in behavior involving complicated mixtures of various logical levels of games. Unless the precise games which men play are clarified—and also, whether they play them well, badly, or indifferently—there is little chance of understanding what "is actually going on" or of altering it.

If we ask, What rules do men actually follow in their daily lives? the metaphorical net we cast is so wide that we catch more than we can handle. Let us, therefore, narrow our question to the case of a "simple man." We seek to understand only the basic rules of living, and only one version of them— for example, the Biblical rules of life. The Ten Commandments may then be likened to the directions one receives when purchasing a new appliance. The buyer is told that he must follow certain rules if he wants to derive the benefits the machine has to offer. If he fails to follow the directions, he will have to suffer the consequences. Thus, in case of a breakdown, the manufacturer's warranty is honored only if the machine has not been misused. Here is a fitting analogy for legitimate illness (manufacturing defect), as contrasted to sin or other types of illegitimate illness (misuse of the machine). The Ten Commandments—and Biblical teachings generally —are the rules man must follow if he expects to obtain the benefits which the manufacturer of the game of life (God) offers the purchaser (man).

However, in the case of real-life games, the situation is more complicated. It often happens that the game rules instruct the player that in order to "win" he must "lose." Let us recall here some of the Biblical rules discussed in Chapter 9; for example, the following two prescriptions for "good living": (1) "Blessed are the meek: for they shall inherit the earth";[9] (2) "Blessed are they which are persecuted for righteousness' sake: for theirs is the kingdom of heaven."[10] There is a tacit premise behind these rules—namely, that it happens that some people are meek and that others are persecuted. Being meek and persecuted are assumed to be occurrences not deliberately sought. But are they not? And might they not be?

In the days of early Christianity, much as today, aggressive men often tended to get the better of their less aggressive neighbors. Apparently, ethical rules came into being in an effort to provide for the sort of things which the British call fair play. This complicated matters considerably, for games of increasingly higher orders were thus generated.

Looking at problems in living from this point of view, it seems apparent that much of what goes by the names of "growing up," "becoming sophisticated," "getting treated by psychoanalysis" (and by other methods as well) are all processes having one significant characteristic in common: the person learns that the rules of the game—and the very game itself—by which he has been playing are not necessarily the same as those used by others around him. For example, he learns that others are not interested in playing the game which he has been so avidly pursuing; or, if they are, that they prefer some modifications of the game rules. All this, however, applies only to more or less ordinary persons in ordinary circumstances, and does not apply to persons of extraordinary influence. Individuals who wield vast powers can persuade, seduce, or coerce others to play their own games. This explains why such persons never consult psychiatrists and are never defined as "mentally ill"; and why, after they have lost their power—in particular, after they have died—they are often declared to have been "obviously mad."[11]

In short, then, unless a person finds others to play his own game, according to his own rules—or can coerce others to accept life on his terms—he has a choice among three options.

First, he may submit to the other person's coercive rules and accept the submissive role offered.

Second, he may renounce, and withdraw from, many socially shared activities and cultivate solitary pursuits. These may be considered and labeled artistic, religious, scientific, neurotic, or psychotic according to various—often poorly defined—criteria. While we cannot consider here what these criteria are, it may be noted that the issues of social utility and the power to define what constitutes such utility play important roles in articulating these standards.

Third, he may become increasingly aware of the precise character of the games he and others play, and may try to accommodate and shape each to fit the other. This is an arduous and unceasing undertaking which, moreover, can never be wholly successful. Its main attraction lies in the protection it affords for the freedom and dignity of all concerned. However, because of the burdens it places on those who so try to conduct themselves, it need not surprise us if many persons prefer easier means leading to what they consider more important ends.

Personality Development and Moral Values

I submit that the concept of a distinctively human, normal, or well-functioning personality is rooted in psychosocial and ethical criteria. It is not biologically given, nor are biological determinants especially significant for it. I do not deny, of course, that man is an animal with a genetically determined biological equipment which sets the upper and lower limits within which he must function. I accept the limits, or the general range, and focus on the development of specific patterns of operation within them. Hence, I eschew biological considerations as explanations, and instead try to construct a consistently moral and psychosocial explanatory scheme.

Clearly, different societies exhibit different values. And even within a single society, especially if it is composed of many individuals, adults and growing children have certain choices about which values to teach and which to accept or reject. In contemporary Western societies, one of the principal alternatives is between autonomy and heteronomy, between "risky" freedom and "secure" slavery.

The French Revolution, for example, was waged in the names of *Liberté, égalité, et fraternité.* Two of these values—

equality and fraternity—imply cooperation rather than oppression. Yet the cooperative value ideals of the philosophers
who provided the original impetus for the revolution soon
gave way to the pragmatically held values of the masses. These
values, in turn, did not differ greatly from the values by which
the oppressed masses had been ruled by sovereign royalty.
Power, coercion, and oppression thus soon replaced equality,
fraternity, and cooperation.

In the next major European revolution, the moral values of
the lower classes received a more unconcealed expression. The
Marxist revolution promised a dictatorship of the proletariat:
the oppressed shall become the oppressors! This was rather
similar to the Scriptural program which promised that "the
last shall be the first." The main difference between the two
lay in their respective means of implementation.

Piaget, as we have seen, describes the evolution of children's games and, through it, of the human moral sense, as a
developmental sequence that starts with heteronomy and proceeds toward autonomy. If we rephrase this in terms of interpersonal rules or strategies, we could say that as children
develop, they move from regulation by external controls toward regulation by self-control, from coercion toward cooperation. Although Piaget has well described the psychological
and social dimensions of this process of personal development,
he has completely neglected its ethical dimensions. For
whether one speaks of psychosexual development, as Freud
did, or of the development of games, as Piaget does, one deals
with what is at bottom moral behavior: coercion and cooperation, autonomy and heteronomy, and all the other concepts
and criteria which Piaget uses to describe various styles of
game-playing behavior, are moral criteria.

In particular, it seems to me that what Piaget identifies as
the "normal" development of the child is actually the sort of
development which he considers desirable; and which many
members of the middle and upper classes of contemporary

Western societies would also consider desirable. He thus declares:

In our societies the child, as he grows up, frees himself more and more from adult authority; whereas in the lower grades of civilization puberty marks the beginning of an increasingly marked subjection of the individual to the elders and to the traditions of his tribe.[12]

As I have shown, however, this endorsement of the value of autonomy is by no means as unqualified even today as Piaget's foregoing statement would make it seem. Indeed, Piaget himself remarks on some of the forces that foster coercive, power-dependent, heteronomous conduct:

It looks as though, in many ways, the adult did everything in his power to encourage the child to persevere in its specific tendencies, and to do so precisely in so far as these tendencies stand in the way of social development. Whereas, given sufficient liberty of action, the child will spontaneously emerge from his egocentrism and tend with his whole being towards cooperation, the adult most of the time acts in such a way as to strengthen egocentrism in its double aspect, intellectual and moral.[13]

Although I agree with Piaget that some types of adult behavior foster the child's egocentrism, I doubt that the child would emerge from this stage and move toward autonomy spontaneously. Autonomy and reciprocity are complex values which must be taught and learned. Naturally, they cannot be taught coercively, but must be practiced and displayed as examples for the child to imitate.

Piaget singled out the adult's coercive or autocratic attitude toward the child as a cause for his persistent subservience in later life. But such rules abound in religious, medical, and educational codes and situations. Consequently, those exposed to them—for example, patients committed to state hospitals, candidates in psychoanalytic institutes, etc.—are subjected to pressures to adapt by assuming the required postures of helplessness.[14] This leads to behavior judged appropriate or "normal" within the system, but not necessarily outside of it. Resistance to the rules may be tolerated to varying degrees in different systems, but in any event tends to bring the individual into conflict with the group. Hence, most persons seek to conform rather than to rebel. Others try to adapt by becoming aware of the rules and of their limited, situational relevancy; this may make it possible to get along in the system, while also allowing the actor to maintain a measure of inner freedom.

What are the specific connections between these considerations and the problems posed by hysteria and mental illness? If we regard psychiatry as the study of human behavior, it is evident that it is intimately related to both ethics and politics. This relationship was already illustrated by means of several examples. With respect to hysteria, the connections between ethics and psychiatry may be highlighted by asking: What kinds of human relationships and patterns of mastery does the so-called hysteric value? Or, phrased somewhat differently: What kind of game does such a person want to play? And what sort of behavior does he regard as playing the game well and winning? I shall try to answer these questions in the next chapter.

13 Hysteria as a Game

Interpersonal Strategies in Hysteria

By slightly modifying Piaget's scheme of the development of the capacity to follow and be aware of rules,[1] I propose to distinguish three stages, or types, of mastery of interpersonal processes: coercion, self-help, and cooperation. Coercion is the simplest rule to follow, self-help is the next most difficult, and cooperation is the most demanding of them all.

The hysteric plays a game consisting of an unequal mixture of these three strategies. While coercive maneuvers predominate, elements of self-help and cooperation are also present. A distinct achievement of this type of behavior is a synthesis of sorts among three separate and to some extent conflicting games, values, and styles of life. In this lies its strength as well as its weakness.

Because of an intense internal contradiction in the hysteric's life style, he fails to play well at any one of the three games. To begin with, the hysteric places a high value on coercive strategies. True, he may not be aware that he has made a choice between coercive and other tactics. His wish to coerce others may be unconscious—or at least inexplicit. In psychotherapy, it is generally easily recognized by the therapist and readily acknowledged by the patient. The point I want to emphasize here is that although the hysteric tacitly espouses the value of coercion and domination, he cannot play this game in a skillful and uninhibited manner. To do so requires two qualities he lacks: a relatively indiscriminating identification with the aggressor, and a large measure of insensitivity to the needs and feelings of others. The hysteric has too much compassion to play the game of domination openly and successfully. He can coerce and dominate with suffering, but not with "selfish" will.

To play the game of self-help well requires committing one's self to it. This often leads to isolation from others: religious, artistic, or other work investments tend to displace interest in personal relationships. Preoccupation with one's body or with suffering and helplessness interfere, of course, with one's ability to concentrate on the practical tasks that must be mastered to play such games well. Moreover, the tactic of dominating others by displaying helplessness cannot be maintained unaltered in the face of a high degree of demonstrable competence in important areas of life. The aim of coercing others by exhibiting helplessness may still be maintained, but the tactics by which this goal is pursued must be modified. The proverbial absentminded professor is a case in point: here is a person who is highly competent in his specialized work but who is, at the same time, virtually helpless when it comes to feeding himself, putting on his galoshes, or paying his income tax. Exhibitions of incompetence in these areas invite help in exactly the same way as bodily complaints invite medical attention.

Finally, the game of cooperation implies and requires a value which the hysteric may not share at all. I believe that, in hysteria, we are confronted with a genuine clash of values—namely, between equality and cooperativeness on the one hand, and inequality and domination-submission on the other. This conflict of values actually takes place in two distinct spheres: in the intrapersonal system of the patient, and in the interpersonal system of therapy.

In psychiatry, the problem of hysteria is not formulated or seen in this way. Psychiatrists prefer to operate with the tacit assumption that whatever their own values are, their patients and colleagues share them—or should share them! Of course, this cannot always be the case. If, however, value conflicts of this sort are indeed as important in psychiatry as I am suggesting, why are they not made explicit? The answer is simple: because doing so would threaten the cohesion of the group— that is, the prestige and the power of the psychiatric profession.

Actually, the idea that hysterical—and other neurotic— symptoms are "compromises" is a cornerstone of psychoanalytic theory. At first, Freud thought in terms of compromise formations between instinctual drives and social defenses, or between selfish needs and the requirements of social living. Later, he asserted that neuroses were due to conflicts and compromises between id and ego, or id and superego. I now want to describe hysteria as still another kind of compromise, this time among three different types of games.

Typical of the coercive game we call "hysteria" is the powerful promotive impact of iconic body signs on those to whom they are directed. The patient's relatives tend to be deeply impressed by such communications, often much more deeply than they would be by similar statements framed in ordinary language. The display of sickness or suffering is thus useful for coercing others. This aspect of hysteria, perhaps more than any other, accounts for its immediate and immense practical value for the patient.

The game of self-help is also discernible in most cases of hysteria. Traditionally, hysterical patients were said to exhibit an attitude of indifference toward their suffering. I suggest that this manifest indifference signifies, first, a denial that the patient has in fact made a coercive communication and, second, an affirmation that the patient aspires to a measure of self-sufficiency. Hysterics are thus not wholly coercive in their relationship to others. However, they attend to their self-helping strategies only halfheartedly, being ready to coerce by means of symptoms should other methods of mastery fail. Also, they feel that learning new tactics of self-help or cooperation is very difficult; moreover, such learning is often not encouraged in the social setting in which they live.

Hysterics play the cooperative game imperfectly. This is to be expected, as this game requires and presupposes a feeling of relative equality among the players. Persons employing hysterical methods of communication feel—and often are—inferior and oppressed. In turn they aspire to feeling superior to others and to oppressing them. But they also seek equality of sorts and some measure of cooperation as potential remedies for their oppressed status.

Hysteria is thus mainly a coercive game, with small elements of self-help and still smaller elements of cooperation blended in. This view implies that the hysteric is unclear about his values and their connection with his behavior.

We might again note here that several of the patients reported in the early psychoanalytic literature were young women who became "ill" with hysteria while caring for a sick, usually older, relative. This was true in the case of Breuer's famous patient Anna O.:

In July, 1880, the patient's father, of whom she was passionately fond, fell ill of a peripleuritic abscess which failed to clear up and to which he succumbed in April, 1881. During the first months of the illness Anna devoted her whole energy to nursing her father, and no one was much surprised when by degrees her own health greatly deteriorated. No one, perhaps not even the patient herself, knew what was happening to her; but eventually the state of weakness, anaemia and distaste for food became so bad that to her great sorrow she was no longer allowed to continue nursing the patient.[2]

Anna O. thus started to play the hysterical game from a position of distasteful submission: she functioned as an oppressed, unpaid, sick-nurse, who was coerced to be helpful by the very helplessness of a sick person and by her particular relationship to him. The women in Anna O.'s position were— as are their counterparts today, who feel similarly entrapped by their small children—insufficiently aware of what they valued in life and of how their own ideas of what they valued affected their conduct. For example, young middle-class women in Freud's day considered it their duty to take care of their sick fathers. Hiring a professional servant or nurse for this job would have created a moral conflict for them, because it would have symbolized to them as well as to others that they did not love their fathers. Similarly, many contemporary American women find themselves enslaved by their young children. Today, married women are generally expected to take care of their own children; they feel that they are not supposed to delegate this task to others. The "old folks" can be placed in a home; it is all right to delegate their care to hired help. This is a complete reversal of the social situation which prevailed in upper- and middle-class European circles until the First World War and even after it. Then, children were often cared for by hired help, while parents were taken care of by their adult children.

In both situations, the obligatory nature of the care required generates a feeling of helplessness in the person from whom help is sought. If a person cannot, in good conscience, refuse to provide help—and cannot even stipulate the terms on which he will supply it—then truly he becomes the help-seeker's slave. Similar considerations apply to the relationship between patients and physicians. If physicians cannot define their own rules—that is, when to help and in what ways—then they, too, are threatened with becoming the hostages of patients.

The typical cases of hysteria cited by Freud thus involved a moral conflict—a conflict about what the young women in question wanted to do with themselves. Did they want to prove that they were good daughters by taking care of their sick fathers? Or did they want to become independent of their parents, by having a family of their own, or in some other way? I believe it was the tension between these conflicting aspirations that was the crucial issue in these cases. The sexual problem—say, of the daughter's incestuous cravings for her father—was secondary (if that important); it was stimulated, perhaps, by the interpersonal situation in which the one had to attend to the other's body. Moreover, it was probably easier to admit the sexual problem to consciousness and to worry about it than to raise the ethical problem indicated.[3] In the final analysis, the latter is a vastly difficult problem in living. It cannot be "solved" by any particular maneuver but requires rather decision making about basic goals, and, having made the decisions, dedicated efforts to attain them.

An Illustration of the Hysterical Game: Sullivan's "Hysterical Dynamism"

Although Harry Stack Sullivan persisted in using many traditional psychiatric concepts, he used the game model in one of his actual descriptions of hysteria:

The hysteric might be said in principle to be a person who has a happy thought as to a way by which he can be respectable even though not living up to his standards. That way of describing the hysteric, however, is very misleading, for of course the hysteric never does have that thought. At least, it is practically impossible to prove that he has had that thought.[4]

Sullivan here asserts that the hysteric is a person who impersonates respectability—in short, someone who cheats. In the tradition of psychoanalysis, he hastens to add that the hysteric does not do this consciously. While it does not seem that the hysteric carefully plans his strategy, it is a mistake to emphasize the unwitting quality of his behavior. The question of precisely "how conscious" a given mental act is has plagued psychoanalysis from its earliest days. I think this is largely a pseudo-problem, for consciousness—or, self-reflective awareness—depends partly on the situation in which a person finds himself. In other words, it is partly a social characteristic rather than simply a personal one.

In the following passage Sullivan provides an explicitly game-playing account of hysteria:

To illustrate how the hysteric dynamism comes into operation, let us say that a man with a strong hysterical predisposition has married, perhaps for money, and that his wife, thanks to his rather dramatic and exaggerated way of doing and saying things, cannot long remain in doubt that there was a very practical consideration in this marriage and cannot completely blind herself to a certain lack of importance that she has in her husband's eyes. So she begins to get even. She may, for example, like someone I recently saw, develop a neverfailing vaginismus, so that there is no more intercourse for him. And he will not ruminate on whether this vaginismus that is cutting off his satisfaction is directed against him, for the very simple reason that if you view interpersonal phenomena with that degree of objectivity, you can't use an hysterical process to get rid of your own troubles. So he won't consider that; but he will suffer terribly from privation and will go to rather extravagant lengths to overcome the vaginismus that is depriving him of satisfaction, the lengths being characterized by a certain rather theatrical attention to detail rather than deep scrutiny of his wife. But he fails again and again. Then one night when he is worn out, and perhaps has had a precocious ejaculation in his newest adventure in practical psychotherapy, he has the idea, "My God, this thing is driving me crazy," and goes to sleep. . . .

Now the idea, "This thing is driving me crazy," is the happy idea that I say the hysteric has. He wakes up at some early hour in the morning, probably at the time when his wife is notoriously most soundly asleep, and he has a frightful attack of some kind. It could be literally almost anything, but it will be very impressive to anyone around. His wife will be awakened, very much frightened, and will call the doctor. But before the doctor gets there, the husband, with a fine sense of dramatic values, will let her know, in some indirect way, that he's terribly afraid he is losing his mind. She is reduced to a really agitated state by that. So when the doctor comes, the wife is in enough distress—in part because of whatever led to her vaginismus—to wonder if she might lose her own mind, and the husband is showing a good many odd symptoms.[5]

Sullivan's gift for portraying psychiatric diseases as problems in living is beautifully demonstrated here. The mutually coercive relationship between husband and wife is especially noteworthy; and so is the patient's impersonating or taking the role of the mentally ill person.

Sullivan then proceeds to describe the "hysterical dynamism" as a form of unconscious or inexplicit malingering without, however, using this term. He calls hysteria a form of "inverted sublimation"—meaning that the patient "finds a way of satisfying unacceptable impulses in a personally satisfactory way which exempts him from social blame and which thereby approaches sublimation. But the activity, if recognized, would not receive anything but social condemnation."[6] These remarks illustrate once again the use and function of nonverbal or indirect communications in hysteria, and also the close connection between hysteria and malingering. Phrased in terms of game playing, the hysteric is here described as someone who would gladly take advantage of cheating if he believed he could get away with it. His cheating is so staged, moreover, as to lead those around him to interpret it not as a selfish stratagem but as unavoidable suffering.

Another aspect of the game the hysteric plays—or of the sort of player he is, which, after all, determines the game he plays—may be discerned from the following passage:

The hysteric has a rather deep contempt for other people. I mean by this that he regards other people as comparatively shadowy figures that move around, I sometimes think, as audience for his own performance. How does this show? Well—hysterics may be said to be the greatest liars to no purpose in the whole range of human personalities—nothing is good enough as it is. It always undergoes improvement in the telling; the hysteric simply has to exaggerate everything a little. . . . When they talk about their living—their interests, their fun, their sorrows and so on—only superlative terms will suffice them. And that, in a way, is a statement of the inadequacy of reality—which is what I mean when I say that hysterics are rather contemptuous of mere events and mere people. They act as if they were accustomed to something better, and they are.[7]

Sullivan here touches on the fact that the hysterical game is relatively unsophisticated. It is well suited to children, uneducated people, the oppressed, and the fearful; in brief, to those who feel that their chances for self-realization and success on their own are poor. Hence, they resort to impersonation and lying as strategies of self-advancement.

Most of the "dynamisms" mentioned by Sullivan thus far illustrate the use of coercive maneuvers. This is consistent with my thesis that hysteria is predominantly a coercive type of game.

Concerning hysterical conversion—that is, the use of iconic body signs—Sullivan writes:

Now, when there is this conversion, it performs a useful function; and that function occurs principally within the self-system. . . . There one discovers sometimes the almost juvenilely simple type of operation set up to profit from the disabling system. The patient will often tell you in the most transparent fashion: "If it were not for this malady then I could do—" and what follows is really quite a grandiose appraisal of one's possibilities. The disability functions as a convenient tool of security operations.[8]

This, of course, is only one aspect of conversion, albeit a significant one. Sullivan's formulation is another way of saying that the hysteric plays at being sick because he is afraid that, if he tried to participate competently in certain real-life activities, he would fail. At the same time, by adopting this strategy, the hysteric invites and assures his own defeat.

Sullivan's concluding remarks concerning hysteria strongly support the thesis that persons who tend to play this sort of game do so because they are impoverished in their game repertoire:

The presence of the hysteric dynamism as the outstanding way of meeting difficulties in living seems to me to imply that the patient has missed a good deal of life which should have been undergone if he was to have a well-rounded personality with a rather impressively good prospect for the future. Because hysterics learn so early to get out of awkwardnesses and difficulties with a minimum of elaborate process, life has been just as they sound: singularly, extravagantly simple. And so, even if one could brush aside the pathogenic or pathologic mechanisms, one would have persons who are not at all well-suited to a complex interpersonal environment. There they just haven't had the experience; they have missed out on an education that many other people have undergone.[9]

All this highlights the moral underpinnings of psychological and psychoanalytic theories and therapies. What a person considers worth doing or living for, or not worth it, will depend on what he has learned or taught himself to value. In this respect, especially, mental illnesses are much like religions: one man's devotion is another man's delusion. It is quite obvious, although psychiatrists have almost succeeded in obscuring it, that there are many persons for whom playing hysterical—or other so-called psychopathological—games is a perfectly acceptable and reasonable thing to do. Psychiatric theories now deny this fact, and psychiatric therapies view the game-playing habits of patients less as habits patients want to keep than as happenings they want to lose. I think psychiatric theories ought to recognize the moral choices inherent in psychiatric symptoms and syndromes, and psychiatric therapies ought to view the game-playing habits of patients more as habits the patients want to keep than as happenings they want to lose.

Lying: A Specific Strategy in Hysteria

It is unfashionable nowadays for psychiatrists to speak of lying. Once a person is called a "patient," psychiatrists cease to consider the possibility that he might be deceptive or mendacious; if in fact he is, they regard the lies as symptoms of a mental illness which they call hysteria, hypochondriasis, schizophrenia, or some other "psychopathology." As a result, anyone who continues to speak of lies and deceptions in connection with psychiatric problems is immediately regarded as "antipsychiatric" and "antihumanitarian": in other words, he is dismissed as both mistaken and malevolent.

I have long considered lying as one of the most important phenomena in psychiatry, a view I have formed partly by taking some of Freud's earliest observations seriously. Let us recall here how emphatically Freud condemned certain social and medical hypocrisies, which are, after all, simply lies of a certain kind. Freud was especially critical of the deceitful habits of both physicians and patients with respect to sex and money. This is the gist of Freud's recollection of his encounter, early in his medical career, with the Viennese obstetrician-gynecologist Chrobak. Chrobak had referred a patient to Freud, a woman who, because her husband was impotent, was still a virgin after eighteen years of marriage.[10] The physician's moral obligation in such cases, so Chrobak told Freud, was to shield the husband's reputation by lying about the patient's condition. I mention this case only to show that lying—on the parts of both patients and physicians—was an important issue in psychoanalysis from its very inception. Indeed, I believe that certain psychoanalytic concepts came into being in order to deal with the *idea of lies,* for example, the unconscious and hysterical conversion; and that certain psychoanalytic arrangements came into being in order to deal with the *management of lies,* for example, free association and the psychoanalytic contract.

The medical situation, like the family situation which it often imitates, is, of course, a traditionally rich source of lies. The patients, like children, lie to the doctor. And the physicians, like parents, lie to the patients.[11] The former lie because they are weak and helpless and cannot get their way by direct demands; the latter lie because they want their wards to know only what is "good" for them. Infantilism and paternalism are thus the sources of and models for deception in the medical and psychiatric situations.

The following illustration, based on the psychoanalysis of a young woman, may be useful in forming a fuller picture of hysteria as a game. I shall say nothing about why this woman came for help or what sort of person she was, but shall concentrate on only one aspect of her behavior—namely, her lying. That she lied—in the sense that she communicated statement A to someone when she knew perfectly well that statement B was the truth—became apparent early in the analysis and remained a prominent theme throughout it. She felt, and said, that the main reason she lied was because she saw herself as a trapped child confronted by an oppressive and unreasonable mother. As a child, she discovered that the simplest and most effective way she could cope with her mother was by lying. Her mother's acceptance of her lies encouraged her use of this strategy and firmly established lying as a habitual pattern in her life. When I saw her, many of her friends and especially her husband apparently or ostensibly accepted her lies, much as her mother had done before. Her expectation in regard to her own untruthful communications was revealing. On the one hand, she hoped that her lies would be accepted as truthful statements; on the other hand, she wished that they would be challenged and unmasked. She realized that the price she paid for lying successfully was a persistent psychological dependence on those to whom she lied. I might add that this woman led a socially perfectly normal life and did not lie indiscriminately. She was inclined to lie only to people on whom she felt dependent or toward whom she felt angry. The more she valued a relationship, the more convinced she was that she could not risk any open expression of personal differences; she then felt trapped and lied.

Lying thus became for this patient an indirect communication similar to hysterical conversion or dreaming. As we familiarized ourselves with the type of game she was playing, it became increasingly evident that, much of the time, the people to whom she lied knew that she was lying. And, of course, she did too. None of this diminished the usefulness of the maneuver whose main value lay in controlling the behavior or response of the other player(s). In terms of game playing, it was as if she could not afford to take the chance to play honestly. Doing so would have meant that she would have had to make her move and then wait until her partner-opponent made his or hers. The very thought of this made her unbearably anxious, especially when she felt at conflict with someone close to her. Instead of playing honestly and exposing herself to the uncertainties and anxieties this entailed for her, she preferred to play dishonestly: that is, she lied, making communications whose effects she could predict with a high degree of confidence. Her whole marriage was thus a complicated and ceaseless game of lies, her husband ostensibly accepting her falsehoods as truths, only the better to manipulate her with them. This, then, gave her fresh ground for feeling oppressed and for lying to him. The result was a highly predictable series of exchanges between them, and a quite secure marriage for them.

Uncertainty and Control in Game-Playing Behavior

One of the important psychological characteristics of playing games honestly is the absolute freedom of each player to make his moves as he sees fit, and hence the relative unpredictability of the behavior of each by the other. For example, in chess each player is free to make whatever move the game rules allow. Unless the players are extremely unevenly matched—in which case one can hardly speak of a real chess game at all—neither player can foretell with any great certainty what the other's moves will be. This, indeed, is the very point of certain games: the players are presented with risks and uncertainties which they must bear and master. And this, too, is why games are either pleasurably exciting or painfully disturbing.

To play a game, and especially to play it well, it is necessary, therefore, to be able to tolerate a measure—often a very large measure—of uncertainty. This is true no less for the metaphorical games of human relationships than it is for literal games such as chess or roulette. In social relations, too, if a person conducts himself honestly, he will often be unable to predict how others will react to him and to his behavior. Suppose, then, that for some reason a person wants to control and predict the behavior of those with whom he interacts: he will then be tempted to lie and cheat. Such a person may even be said to be playing a different game than he would be playing if he were playing honestly, even though, formally, the two games are the same. An example will make this clear: in playing chess honestly, the player's aim is to master the rules of chess; in playing it dishonestly, his aim is to beat his opponent. In one case, winning is secondary to playing well and learning to play better; in the other, winning is primary and all that counts. Honest game playing thus implies that the players value the skills that go into playing the game well; whereas dishonest game playing implies that they do not value these skills. It is evident, then, that honest and dishonest game playing represent two quite different enterprises: in the one, the player's aim is successful mastery of a task—that is, playing the game well; in the other, his aim is control of the other player—that is, coercing or manipulating him to make certain specific moves. The former task requires knowledge and skills; the latter—especially in the metaphorical games of human relations—information about the other player's personality.

These considerations have the most far-reaching implications for social situations in which those in authority are concerned not with their subordinate's performance, but with their personality. Characteristically, in such situations, superiors not only tolerate but often subtly encourage inadequate task performance by their subordinates; what they want is not a competent subordinate but a subordinate they can dominate, control, and "treat." One of the most ironic examples of this is the psychoanalytic training system, in which the trainers are avowedly more concerned with the personality of the trainees than with their competence as psychoanalysts.[12] The workings of countless other bureaucratic and educational organizations, in which superiors seek and secure psychological profiles and psychiatric reports on their subordinates, illustrate and support this interpretation: in these situations, the superiors have replaced the task of doing their job competently, with the task of managing their personnel "compassionately."

Lying, as in the marriage game described earlier, serves this function of relationship management well, especially if it is mutual. This value of lying derives not so much from its direct, communicative meanings as it does from its indirect, metacommunicative ones. By telling a lie, the liar in effect informs his partner that he fears and depends on him and wishes to please him: this reassures the recipient of the lie that he has some control over the liar and therefore need not fear losing him. At the same time, by accepting the lie without challenging it, the person lied to informs the liar that he, too, needs the relationship and wants to preserve it. In this way, each participant exchanges truth for control, dignity for security. Marriages and other "intimate" human relationships often endure on this basis.

As against such secure though often humiliating arrangements, relationships based on truthful communications tend to be much more vulnerable to dissolution. This accounts for the ironic but intuitively widely understood fact that bad marriages are often much more stable than good ones. I use the words "good" and "bad" here to refer to such values as dignity, honesty, and trustworthiness, and their opposites. The continuation of a marriage or its dissolution by divorce, as mere facts, codifies only the legal status of a complex human relationship; it conveys no information whatever about the true character of the relationship. This is one reason why it is so hopelessly naïve and foolish to regard—as psychiatrists often do—contracting or sustaining a marriage as a sign of successful game playing—that is, as a sign of maturity or mental health; and dissolving a marriage by separation or divorce as a sign of unsuccessful game playing—that is, as a sign of immaturity or mental illness.

On Changing the Hysterical Game

As an illness, hysteria is characterized by conversion symptoms. As a game, it is characterized by the goal of domination and interpersonal control; the typical strategies by which this goal is pursued are coercion by disability and illness, and by deceitful gambits of various kinds, especially lies.

Diseases may be treated. Game-playing behavior can only be changed. Accordingly, if we wish to address ourselves to the problem of the "treatment" of hysteria (or of any other mental illness), we must first come to grips with the patient's life goals and values and with the physician's "therapeutic" goals and values. In what directions, toward what sorts of game-playing behavior, does the patient want to change? In what direction does the therapist want him to change? As against the word "change," the word "treatment" implies that the patient's present behavior is bad—because it is "sick"; and that the direction in which the therapist wants him to change is better or good—because it is "healthier." In this, the traditional psychiatric view, the physician defines what is good or bad, sick or healthy. In the individualistic, autonomous "psychotherapy" which I prefer, the patient himself defines what is good or bad, sick or healthy. With this arrangement, the patient might set himself goals in conflict with the therapist's values: if the therapist does not accept this, he becomes "resistant" to helping the patient—instead of the patient being "resistant" because he fails to submit to the therapist. It seems to me that any sensible description of psychotherapy ought to accommodate both of these possibilities.

In short, accounts of therapeutic interventions with so-called mental patients, and of modifications in their life activities, should be couched in the language of changes in the patient's game orientations rather than in the language of symptoms and cures. Thus, in the case of hysterical patients, changes which might be categorized as "improvements" or "cures" by some might occur in any of the following directions: more effective and ruthless coercion and domination of others; more passive and masochistic submission to others; withdrawal from the struggle over interpersonal control and increasing isolation from human relationships; and, finally, learning to play other games and acquiring interest and competence in some of them.

A Summing Up

"When one psycho-analyses a patient subject to hysterical attacks," wrote Freud in 1909, "one soon gains the conviction that these attacks are nothing but phantasies projected and translated into motor activity and represented in pantomime."[13] In suggesting that the hysterical symptom is in effect a type of pantomime or dumb-show—the patient expressing a message by means of nonverbal, bodily signs—Freud himself acknowledged that hysteria is not an illness but an idiom or language, not a disease but a dramatization or game. For example, pseudocyesis, or false pregnancy, is the pictorial representation and dramatization of the patient's belief that she is pregnant even though she is not.

In short, hysteria is a type of language in which communication is effected by means of pictures (or iconic signs), instead of by means of words (or conventional signs). Hysterical language thus resembles other picture languages, such as charades. Those who want to deal with so-called hysterical patients must therefore learn not how to diagnose or treat them, but how to understand their special idiom and how to translate it into ordinary language. In a game of charades, one member of a team enacts an idea or proverb, and his teammates try to translate his pantomime into ordinary, spoken language. Similarly, in a game of hysteria, the "patient" enacts a belief or complaint—which is what makes him the "patient"; and his teammates—family members, physicians, or psychiatrists—try to translate his pantomime—now called "hysterical conversion"—into ordinary language.

14　Impersonation and Illness

Impersonation and Role-Taking

The concept of impersonation refers to the assumption or imitation of someone else's appearance, character, condition, or social role. Impersonation is a ubiquitous phenomenon and is not, as such, considered to constitute a psychiatric problem. Indeed, everyday speech offers numerous terms for a variety of impersonations or, more precisely, impersonators; for example, charlatan, confidence man, counterfeiter, forger, impostor, quack, spy, traitor, and so forth. Two impersonators, the malingerer and the hysteric, have been of special interest to psychiatrists. I have remarked on them both in the previous chapters of this book.

A definition of impersonation is now in order. According to Webster, to impersonate is "to assume or act the person or character of. . . ." This definition provokes some interesting difficulties: if role-taking behavior is universal, as Mead and others have suggested,[1] how do we distinguish ordinary role-taking from impersonation? I suggest the following answer: role-taking refers to consistent or honest role-playing, in the context of a specific game—whereas impersonation refers to inconsistent or dishonest role-playing, in the context of everyday life. For example, taking the role of a vendor and approaching another person as a prospective customer implies that the seller either owns the goods offered for sale or is authorized to act in the owner's name. When a person sells something he does not own, he impersonates the role of an honest vendor and is called a "swindler."

Since role-taking is a permanent and universal characteristic of human behavior, it is evident that practically any action can be interpreted as a type of impersonation. The so-called Don Juan may thus be said to impersonate a man of acrobatic virility; the transvestite, the social role and sexual functions of a member of the opposite sex; and so forth. Simone de Beauvoir offers this account of role-taking as impersonation:

Even if each woman dresses in conformity with her status, a game is still being played: artifice, like art, belongs to the realm of the imaginary. It is not only that girdle, brassiere, hair-dye, make-up disguise body and face; but that the least sophisticated of women, once she is 'dressed,' does not present herself to observation; she is, like the picture or the statue, or the actor on the stage, an agent through whom is suggested someone not there—that is, the character she represents, but is not.[2]

If what de Beauvoir says is true about women, it is even more true about children, who spend much of their time impersonating others. They play at being fireman, doctor, nurse, mother, father. Since the child's identity is defined in predominantly negative terms—that is, in terms of what he cannot do, because he is not allowed to do it or is incapable of doing it—it is not surprising that he should seek role fulfillment through impersonation. A child's real identity or social role is, of course, to be a child. But in an achievement-oriented culture, as opposed to a tradition- and kinship-oriented one, being a child tends to mean mostly that one is unable or unfit to act in certain ways. Thus, childhood itself may be viewed as a form of disability.*

* Similar considerations hold for old age. As old persons become unemployed and unproductive, and particularly if they are economically and physically disabled, their principal role becomes being old.

Let us now briefly reconsider the impersonations which children, say between five and ten, characteristically engage in. From the adult's point of view, what is perhaps most striking about these play-acts is their transparency as impersonations. How could anyone possibly mistake a child playing doctor or nurse for a real doctor or nurse? The question itself is ludicrous—because the task of distinguishing impersonated role from genuine role is here nonexistent. A blank sheet of typewriter paper is not an imitation of a twenty-dollar bill; nor is a five-year-old playing doctor an impostor. In part, it is of course the child's size that stamps a clear identity on him, and vitiates his effort at any credible imitation of an adult role: he is simply too small and looks too unlike an adult to be able to assume an adult role. He may, of course, possess the skills of an adult, and more—as, for example, a musical prodigy does; but he cannot possess the social role of an adult.

Although the child's impersonations are so obvious as to present no problem at all for adults to recognize, there are others which are so subtle, or require such specialized informations and skills, that most adults are quite incapable of recognizing them. Many people cannot tell a quack from a licensed physician, or an art forger from a recognized artist. Similarly, most people cannot readily distinguish between a clinical psychologist and a psychiatrist, or a psychiatrist and a "regular" physician: to make these distinctions—that is, to see how psychologists impersonate psychiatrists, and psychiatrists regular physicians—requires that one possess certain kinds of specialized information not generally available.[3]

Impersonation, then, is an integral part of childhood. Another way of saying this is by asserting that children learn how to grow up by imitating adults and by identifying with them. For the reasons I have just noted, the problem of distinguishing between successful and unsuccessful impersonation does not arise until after the person has attained physiological and social maturity. Only an adult can fake another.

Nevertheless, psychiatrists and psychoanalysts have systematically failed to distinguish between impersonation, which is the general class, and imposturing, which is but one type of impersonation. Helene Deutsch, who has written extensively on this subject, actually equates, and thus confuses, these two concepts and phenomena.[4] Some of her observations apply to impersonating, and others to imposturing, as the following passage illustrates:

The world is crowded with "as-if" personalities, and even more so with impostors and pretenders. Ever since I became interested in the impostor, he pursues me everywhere. I find him among my friends and acquaintances, as well as in myself. Little Nancy, a fine three-and-a-half-year-old daughter of one of my friends, goes around with an air of dignity, holding her hands together tightly. Asked about this attitude she explains: "I am Nancy's guardian angel, and I'm taking care of little Nancy." Her father asked her about the angel's name. "Nancy" was the proud answer of this little impostor.[5]

Deutsch is correct that the world is full of people who act "as if" they were someone else. Alfred Adler noted the same phenomenon and called it the "life-lie."[6] In this connection, we might also recall Vaihinger's important work, *The Philosophy of "As If,"*[7] which influenced both Freud and Adler.

The point is that not all impersonators are impostors, but all impostors are impersonators. In illustrating impersonation, which she erroneously calls imposturing, Deutsch cites examples of the behavior of children. But, as we saw, children must impersonate others because they are nobodies. Deutsch concludes that the essence of imposturing lies in "pretending that we actually are what we would like to be."[8] But this is merely a restatement of the common human desire to appear better than one actually is. It is not a correct formulation of imposturing, which implies deceitful role-taking for personal gain. Impersonation is a morally more neutral name for a class that contains role pretensions which are both objectionable and unobjectionable, blameworthy and praiseworthy.

The desire to be better or more important than one is is likely to be strongest, of course, among children, or among persons who are, or consider themselves to be, in inferior, oppressed, or frustrating circumstances.* These are the same persons who are most likely to resort to various methods of impersonation. Conversely, those who have been successful in realizing their aspirations—who, in other words, are relatively well satisfied with their actual role achievements and definitions—will be unlikely to pretend to be anyone but themselves. They are satisfied with who they are and can afford the luxury of telling the truth about themselves.

Varieties of Impersonations

Since, in principle at least, every human activity or role can be imitated, there are as many types of impersonations as there are human performances. From this rich variety of impersonations, I shall select and briefly comment here on a few which seem to me especially relevant to psychiatry and to the present study of it.

Lying is the logical example to begin with. The liar impersonates the truth-teller. We speak of lying usually in relation to verbal or written communications; and then only when there is an expectation that the communicants are supposed to be truthful. Poets speak in metaphor, and politicians in rhetoric, and we do not call their utterances lies. Witnesses in courts of law, on the other hand, are explicitly enjoined to tell the truth, and are guilty of perjury if they do not.

Cheating is like lying, but in the context of games. The cheat impersonates the honest player, to unfairly enhance his chances of winning. We speak of cheating only when the rules of the game are clearly codified and generally known. For

* I do not wish to imply that children are always oppressed, or that their lack of a firm inner identity is due to oppression. Indeed, the role of being oppressed can itself be the core of one's identity. The lack of firm personal identity in childhood is a reflection mainly of the child's incomplete social and psychological development.

example, a person may be cheated in a business venture, or a husband by his wife or vice versa. When the game rules are uncertain or unknown to the players, we give other names to rule breaking. In psychiatry, for example, instead of saying that persons cheat in the medical game, we say that they suffer from hysteria or hypochondriasis; in politics, instead of saying that office holders cheat, we say that they are patriotic or protect the general welfare.

Malingering, which I have discussed in detail earlier and elsewhere,[9] is impersonating the socially legitimatized sick role. What constitutes being correctly sick depends, of course, on the rules of the illness game. If the medical game recognizes the legitimacy of the sick role only for persons who are bodily ill, then those who assume this role without being bodily ill will be considered to be malingerers; whereas if it also recognizes the legitimacy of the sick role for persons who are not bodily ill, then those who assume the sick role without being bodily ill will be considered to be mentally ill.

Although it may be obvious and a truism, I want to emphasize that a person who did not know the rules of the illness game could not malinger. This is like asserting that a person who did not know that a canvas by Picasso was valuable could not, and hence would not, try to sell a painting which he believes to be a fake Picasso for a large sum. This, then, lets us deal more clearly with the problem of error and self-deception in impersonation. In the case of illness, a person might sincerely believe that he is bodily ill when in fact he is not; and he might then represent himself as sick. Such an individual is like a person who has unknowingly purchased a fake Picasso, who sincerely believes that it is an original, and who then represents and tries to sell it as a genuine Picasso. Clearly, there is a difference between what this man is doing and what the forger is doing. In psychiatry and psychoanalysis, malingering has traditionally been seen as similar to a forgery, and hysteria as similar to the unwitting possession and sale of a forgery. It is, I think, helpful to see both as impersonations—of possessing a genuine Picasso in the one case, and of possessing a genuine illness in the other. Whether the impersonation is conscious and deliberate, or otherwise, is usually easily ascertained—by communicating with the potential impersonator and by investigating his claims and possessions.

So-called mental illnesses are best conceptualized as special instances of impersonation. In hysteria, for example, the patient impersonates the role of a person sick with the particular disease or disability which he displays. Many psychiatrists more or less recognize and admit that this is what the hysteric does, but hasten to add that the hysteric does not know what he is doing. This belief flatters the psychiatrists, for it means that they know more about their patients than the patients know about themselves—which is usually not true. The hysteric's seeming ignorance of what he is doing may also be interpreted as his not being able to afford to know it, for if he knew it he could no longer do it; in short, that the patient cannot bear to tell himself the truth about his own life or some particular aspect of it. He must therefore lie both to himself and others. As I have indicated already, I consider this to be the correct view.

The so-called hypochondriac and schizophrenic also impersonate: the former takes the role of certain medical patients, whereas the latter often takes the role of other, invariably famous, personalities. The hypochondriac may thus claim that he has cancer, just as a quack may claim that he is a doctor. And the schizophrenic may assert that he is Jesus, just as a child may assert that he is a daddy. These examples also show why and when psychiatrists, and the public, resort to labeling persons crazy or psychotic: the more publicly unsupported a person's impersonation is, and the more stubbornly he clings to it despite the attempts of others to reject it, the more he courts being defined and treated as a madman or psychotic.

Another type of impersonation is that exemplified by the

confidence man who pretends to be trustworthy only to de-fraud his victim.[10] This sort of impersonation is conscious, is frankly acknowledged to self and friends, and is concealed only from intended victims. In confidence games, the swindler's gains and the victim's losses are obvious, at least in retrospect.

There remains one particular type of impersonation which deserves special attention—namely, acting, or impersonation in the theater. In this setting, role-taking is explicitly identified as impersonation by the context in which it occurs. The actor who plays Lear or Lincoln is not Lear or Lincoln, and both actors and audiences know this. Theatrical impersonation is, in many ways, the model of all impersonations. Although such impersonation is characteristically confined to the theater, the actor being himself when he is offstage, the actor's real life, or at least the public's image of it, is often profoundly affected by his theatrical roles, especially if these are consistently of the same sort. I refer here to what in the theater and movies is known as "typecasting" and "being typed," phenomena which, as we shall presently see, are of considerable importance for psychiatry and ordinary social relations as well. If actors or actresses appear in the same sorts of roles over and over again, they are likely to create the impression in the public that they are "really" like the characters they are portraying. One immediately thinks in this connection of the actors who are always the gangsters, or the actresses who are the sex bombs. To many Americans, Boris Karloff *was* Frankenstein, Raymond Massey *was* Lincoln, and Ralph Bellamy *was* Franklin Roosevelt. Moreover, the actors' assumed identities may prove convincing not only to their audiences but to themselves as well. They may then begin to act offstage as if they were on it. Roles can and do become habits. In many chronic cases of mental illness, we witness the consequences of playing hysterical, hypochondriacal, schizophrenic, or other games over years and decades, until they have become deeply ingrained habits.

The Ganser Syndrome

A type of impersonation of special interest and importance to psychiatrists is the so-called Ganser syndrome, which, simply put, is the strategic impersonation of madness by a prisoner. Yet for decades psychiatrists have argued about whether this alleged illness is a form of malingering, a form of hysteria, a form of psychosis, or whether it is an illness at all.[11] I suggest that we regard the Ganser syndrome as a special kind of impersonation of the sick role, occurring under the conditions of prison life as defined by judges, wardens, and prison psychiatrists.

The Ganser syndrome was first described, or perhaps I should say was created, by a German psychiatrist of that name in 1898.[12] He called it a "specific hysterical twilight state," the chief symptom of which he identified as *vorbeireden.* Other psychiatrists subsequently named it "paralogia," or the "syndrome of approximate answers," or the Ganser syndrome. Here is the description of this alleged illness from a standard American text, Noyes's *Modern Clinical Psychiatry:*

An interesting type of mental disorder sometimes occurring in the case of prisoners under detention awaiting trial was described by Ganser. It develops only after commission of a crime and, therefore, tells nothing about the patient's mental state when he committed the offense. In this syndrome, the patient, being under charges from which he would be exonerated were he irresponsible, begins, without being aware of the fact, to appear irresponsible. He appears stupid and unable to comprehend questions or instructions accurately. His replies are vaguely relevant to the query but absurd in content. He performs various uncomplicated, familiar tasks in an absurd manner, or gives approximate replies to simple questions.

The patient, for example, may attempt to write with the blunt end of his pencil, or will give 11 as the product of 4 × 3. The purpose of the patient's behavior is so obviously to appear irresponsible that the inexperienced observer frequently believes that he is malingering. The dynamics is probably that of a dissociative process.[13]

It should be noted that, in this account, the person exhibiting such conduct is labeled a "patient," and his behavior a "mental disorder." But how has it been shown that he is "sick"?

Here is another interpretation of the Ganser syndrome— this one by Fredric Wertham:

A Ganser reaction is a hysterical pseudo-stupidity which occurs almost exclusively in jails and in old-fashioned German textbooks. It is now known to be almost always due more to conscious malingering than to unconscious stupefaction.[14]

If the Ganser "patient" impersonates what he thinks is the behavior of the mentally sick person—to plead irresponsibility and avoid punishment—how does his behavior differ from that of a person who cheats on his income tax return? One feigns insanity, the other poverty. Nevertheless, psychiatrists continue to view this sort of behavior as a manifestation of illness and to speculate about its nature, causes, and cures.

This fact is itself significant and points to the parallels between the impersonations of the Ganser patient and of the actor who has been typecast. Persons diagnosed as suffering from the Ganser syndrome have succeeded, to an astonishing degree, in convincing both themselves and their significant audience that they are, in fact, sick—disabled, not responsible for their "symptomatic" behavior, perhaps even suffering from some obscure physicochemical disorder of their body. Their success in this respect is exactly like that of the actor who comes to believe that he is, say, irresistible to women, and about whom others come to share the same belief.

Roles: Assumed, Impersonated, and Genuine

When an actor has been typecast, he has succeeded in making his assumed role so believable and accepted that people will think he no longer "acts" but "plays himself." Similarly, if a person diagnosed as suffering from malingering, hysteria, or the Ganser syndrome has been accepted as truly ill, as a sick patient (even if the sickness is mental sickness), then he too has succeeded in making his assumed role so believable that people will think he no longer "acts" but "is sick." This phenomenon is actually encountered in all walks of life, and there is nothing mysterious about it. Our image of the world about us is constructed on the basis of our actual experiences. How else could it be constructed? The proverbs tell us that "Seeing is believing" and that "Four eyes can see better than two." In other words, we build our world on the basis of what we see and what other people tell us they see. Complementary channels of information thus form an exceedingly important corrective of and support for our own impressions and experiences. For example, by listening only, we may not be able to distinguish a person's voice from a recording of it; by looking at the source of the sound we can easily resolve this problem. When the complementary channel of information is another person, his agreement or disagreement with us can be similarly decisive in shaping our own experience and judgment.

We may state this more generally by asserting that the concept of impersonated role has meaning only in contrast with the concept of genuine role. The method for differentiating impersonated or false roles from genuine or real ones is the familiar process of verification. This may be a social process, consisting of the comparison of opinions from various observers. Or it may be a scientifically more distinctive operation, consisting of testing assertions or hypotheses against observations or experiments. In its simplest forms, verification involves no more than the use, as mentioned above, of complementary channels of information—for example, sight and hearing, checking the patient's statements against certain official documents, etc. Let us consider the case of a person who claims to be Jesus. If we ask such a person for evidence to support his claim, he may say that he suffers and soon expects to die or that his mother is the Virgin Mary. Of course, we don't believe him.

This, however, is perhaps too crude an example. It fails to confront us with the more subtle and difficult problems in validating the sick role, such as occur characteristically with persons who complain of pain. Here the question becomes: Does the patient "really" have pain—that is, is he a genuine occupant of the sick role? Or is his pain "hysterical"—that is, does he impersonate the sick role? In this sort of case we cannot rely on asking other people whether they think that the patient is "sick" or "malingering." The criterion for differentiating between the two roles must be scientific rather than social. In other words, it will be necessary to perform certain "operations" or "tests" to secure more information on which to base further inferences. In the case of differentiating bodily from mental illness, the principal method for gathering further information is the physical, laboratory, and psychological examination of the patient.

Viewing impersonation and genuine role-playing in terms of games, they could be said to represent two fundamentally different games.[15] In genuine role-playing, the actor commits himself to the game with the goal of playing as well as he can: for example, the surgeon tries to cure the sick person by the proper removal of the diseased organ. In impersonated role-playing, the actor commits himself to imitating the well-playing person: for example, the man who impersonates a physician tries to convince people that he is one so that he can enjoy the economic and social rewards of the physician's role.

In impersonation, then, the goal is to look like the imitated person: that is, to effect an outward, or "superficial," similarity between self and other. This may be achieved by dress, manner of speech, symptom, making certain claims, and so forth. Why some persons seek role imitation rather than competence and task mastery need not concern us here.

The desire for unnecessary surgical operations—"unnecessary," that is, from the point of view of pathophysiology—is often a part of the strategy of impersonation. In this situation, the impersonator plays the illness game and tries to validate his claim to the sick role. The surgeon who consents to operate on such a person performs a useful function for him, albeit his usefulness cannot be justified on surgical grounds. His intervention legitimizes the patient's claim to the sick role. The surgical scar is official proof of illness: it is the diploma that proves the genuineness of patienthood.

In genuine role-playing, on the other hand, the individual's purpose, usually consciously entertained, is to acquire certain skills or knowledge. The desire for a certain kind of similarity to another person—say, to a surgeon or scientist—may be operative here also. But the goals as well as the rules of this game require that the similarity be substantive rather than superficial. The goal is learning, and hence an alteration of the "inner personality" rather than a mere "outer change" such as occurs in impersonation.

The Psychiatric Authentication of Impersonated Roles as Genuine

In the case of malingering, hysteria, and the Ganser syndrome—and, indeed, in all cases of so-called mental illness—psychiatrists actually confirm the patient's self-definition as ill and so help to shape his illness. This psychiatric authentication and legitimization of the sick role for those who claim to be ill, or about whom others make such claims, has the most profound implications for the whole field of psychiatry, and beyond it, for all of society. When physicians and psychiatrists began to treat those who impersonated the sick role as genuinely ill patients, they acted much as an audience would if it treated Raymond Massey or Ralph Bellamy as Presidents of the United States. This sort of feedback to the actor means not only that he can no longer rely on his audience for a corrective definition of reality and his own identity in it, but also that, because of the audience's response, he must doubt his own perceptions about who he really is. In this way, he is encouraged to acquiesce in the role which in part he wants to play, and which his audience wants him to play. While actors are sophisticated about the risks of typecasting, persons playing on the metaphorical stage of real life are usually quite unsuspecting of this danger. Hence, few persons who launch themselves on a career of impersonating the sick role reckon with the danger of being authenticated in this role by their families and by the medical profession. On the contrary, they usually expect that their impersonated roles will be opposed or rejected by their audience. Just as swindlers expect skepticism and opposition from their intended victims, so malingerers have traditionally expected skepticism and oppositions from physicians. However, as on the stage so also in real life, an audience's resistance to an actor's impersonated role is strongest when the play is first put on stage. After a run of initial performances, the actor is either accepted in his role— and the play goes on for a longer run; or he is rejected in it—and the play closes down. Moreover, the longer the actor plays his role, the less will his critics and audience scrutinize his performance: he is now "in." This is a familiar process in many phases of life. For example, if a student does well early in his courses and becomes defined as a good student, his teachers will scrutinize his subsequent performance much less closely than they will that of a bad student. In the same way, actors, athletes, financiers, and others of proven ability tend to be much more immune to criticism than those who are not yet so accepted.

The distinction between genuine and impersonated roles may be described in still another way, by making use of the concepts of instrumental and institutional groups and the criteria for membership in them.[16] Instrumental groups are based on shared skills. Membership in them, say in a Davis Cup team, implies that the person possesses a special skill. We consider this role genuine because such a person really knows how to play tennis. Institutional groups, on the other hand, are based on kinship, status, and other nonfunctional criteria. Membership in a family, say in a royal family, is an example. When the king dies, the crown prince becomes the new king. This transformation from nonking to king requires no new knowledge or skills; it requires only being the son of a dead king.

Impersonation may be summed up in one sentence; it is a strategy of behavior based on the model of hereditary monarchies. Implicit in this strategy is a deep-seated belief that instrumental skills are unimportant. All that is needed to succeed in the game of life is to "play a role" and gain social approval for it. Parents often hold up this model for their children to follow. When they do follow it, they soon end up with an empty life. When the child or young adult then tries to fill the void, his efforts to do so are often labeled as some form of "mental illness." However, being mentally ill or psychotic —or killing someone else or himself—may be the only games left for such a person to play.

A Summing Up

In playing a role, the actor's main task is to put on a good performance. If the role is genuine—by which I mean that it pertains to an *instrumentally* definable task, such as playing chess or driving a car—then successful role-playing simply means successful task mastery, and unsuccessful role-playing means unsuccessful task mastery.

If, however, the role is impersonated—by which I mean that it pertains to an *institutionally* definable task, such as convincing others that one possesses certain qualities whether one does or not—then the possibilities for failure are doubled. The person may fail, first, by putting on an inadequate performance and failing to persuade the audience to authenticate him in his impersonated role; and, second, by putting on a performance that is so convincing that the audience authenticates his impersonated role as his genuine role. I remarked on how this may happen to actors as well as to so-called mental patients. I might add here that this hazard is greatest for the competent and successful performer. In other words, those who play the games of hysteria or mental illness poorly or halfheartedly are likely to be repudiated in their roles by their families or physicians. It is precisely those who play these games most skillfully whose performances are likely to prove successful and whose identities will therefore be authenticated as sick—that is, as mentally sick. I submit that this is the situation in which most persons called mentally ill now find themselves. By and large, such persons impersonate* the roles of helplessness, hopelessness, weakness, and often of bodily illness—when, in fact, their actual roles pertain to frustrations, unhappinesses, and perplexities due to interpersonal, social, and ethical conflicts.

I have tried to point out the dangers which threaten such impersonators and those who accept their impersonations—the main danger being the creation of a culturally shared myth. I believe that "mental illness" is such a myth.

Contemporary psychiatry thus represents a late stage in the

---

* I do not wish to imply that this impersonation is always a consciously planned strategy, arrived at by deliberate choice among several alternatives—although often it is.

mental illness game. In its beginning stages—that is, before the end of the nineteenth century, when alienists aspired to be neurologists and neuropathologists—psychiatrists were violently opposed to those who impersonated the sick role. They wanted to see, study, and treat only "really" sick—that is, neurologically sick—patients. They believed, therefore, that all mental patients were fakers and frauds.

Modern psychiatrists have swung to the opposite extreme. They refuse to distinguish impersonated from genuine roles—cheating from playing honestly. In so conducting themselves, they act like the art expert, mentioned earlier,[17] who decides that a good imitation of a masterpiece is also a masterpiece.

Conceptualizing psychiatric illness on the model of medical illness, psychiatrists leave themselves no choice but to define psychiatric treatment as something that can be "given" only to persons who "have" a psychiatric illness! This leads not only to further unmanageable complications in conceptualizing the true nature of so-called psychiatric diseases and treatments, but also to an absurd dilemma with regard to persons who impersonate the role of the mentally sick patient.

Once a role is socially accepted, it must, in principle at least, be possible to imitate or impersonate it. The question then is: How shall the person who impersonates the role of mental patient be regarded—as malingering insanity or as insane? Psychiatrists wanted to claim such persons as patients so that they could "treat" them. They could do so only if those who pretended to be mentally sick were also conceptualized and defined as "sick"; hence, they were.

Thus, without perhaps anyone fully realizing just what was happening, the boundaries between the psychiatric game and the real-life game became increasingly blurred. The lonely, romantic movie fan, enchanted with his idolized actress on the screen, may gradually come to feel that she is actually becoming a close, lifelike, and intimate figure. What is needed for this is a convincing performance and a receptive audience.

And, indeed, just as men need a Marilyn Monroe, or women a Clark Gable, so physicians need sick people! I submit, therefore, that anyone who acts sick—impersonating this role—and does so vis-à-vis persons who are therapeutically inclined, runs the grave risk of being accepted in his impersonated role. And in being so accepted, he endangers himself in certain, often unexpected, ways. Although ostensibly he is requesting and receiving help, what is called "help" might be forthcoming only if he accepts the patient role and all that it may imply for his therapist.

The principal alternative to this dilemma lies, as I have suggested before, in abolishing the categories of ill and healthy behavior, and the prerequisite of mental sickness for so-called psychotherapy. This implies candid recognition that we "treat" people by psychoanalysis or psychotherapy not because they are sick but, first, because they desire this type of assistance; second, because they have problems in living for which they seek mastery through understanding of the kinds of games which they, and those around them, have been in the habit of playing; and third, because, as psychotherapists, we want and are able to participate in their "education," this being our professional role.

Finally, the concept of impersonation is useful for understanding the role not only of the psychiatric patient but also that of the psychiatric practitioner. The two are engaged in a reciprocal impersonation, each fitting into the role of the other like a key and a lock. The psychiatric patient impersonates, or is impressed into, the sick role: the so-called hysteric acts as if he were sick and invites medical treatment; the so-called paranoid is regarded as if he were sick and treatment is imposed on him against his will. In both cases, the person is defined, by himself or others, as a patient. Reciprocally, psychiatrists, psychoanalysts, and many clinical psychologists engage in a complementary act of impersonation: by accepting the problems of their clients as the manifestations of an illness, or by assigning such problems to the category of illness, they assume the roles of medical practitioners and therapists. This professional impersonation occurs also independently of the conduct of clients: it is actively fostered and supported by contemporary psychiatric, psychoanalytic, and psychological organizations and their members, and by other institutions and individuals, such as courts and schools, lawyers and educators.

The upshot is the professional credo of mental health professionals: that mental illness is like medical illness, and mental treatment like medical treatment. In fact, however, psychotherapists only look like doctors, just as hysterics only look like patients: the differences between the communicational interventions of psychotherapists and the physicochemical interventions of physicians constitute an instrumental gulf that no institutional dissembling can convincingly narrow.[18]

Until recently, this impersonation of the medical role by the psychiatrist and psychotherapist has served the apparent interests of both psychiatric patients and practitioners. Hence, not many concerned parties were left to protest this modern variation on the ancient theme of the emperor's clothes. I believe the time is now ripe to announce that the emperor is naked: in other words, that the medical aspects of psychiatry are just as substantial as was the fabric from which the emperor's legendary cloak was fashioned. As will be recalled, that material was so fine only the wisest could see it: to claim that the emperor was naked was, therefore, an affront against a powerful person as well as a self-confessed stupidity. It has been, and continues to be, much like this with psychiatry, whose similarities to medicine are so subtle that only the best-trained professional can see it: to claim that these similarities are insubstantial or nonexistent is thus an affront against the powerful social institutions of medicine and psychiatry, as well as a self-confessed stupidity. I hasten to plead guilty to both of these potential charges.

15 The Ethics of Psychiatry

The game-playing model of human behavior seems to me best suited for explicitly reintroducing ethical considerations into the study of psychiatry, psychology, and the so-called mental health professions. Games have payoffs or ends, such as winning a sum of money or besting an opponent, which constitute moral conceptions; and they must be played according to certain rules, with adherence to and deviance from the rules constituting further matters of moral concern. Whether a particular game is worth playing and whether particular rules are worth respecting and following are issues that often vex persons whose predicaments are now defined as psychiatric in character.

The game-playing model of behavior is also a useful bridge between ethics and psychoanalysis, and particularly between ethics and the theory of object relations, in which explanations are couched in terms of interactions between the self and others, the latter being called "objects."[1] In game theory, all the participants, whether self or others, are called "players," and their engagements, for which there is no special term in psychoanalysis, are called "games." Clearly, the perspectives of object relations and game-playing resemble each other at many points. In this concluding chapter I shall try to develop some of these similarities and point the way toward a synthesis of moral, psychoanalytic, semiotical, and social or game-playing approaches to an understanding of psychiatric problems in particular, and of personal conduct in general.

Object Relations and the Game Model

The similarities between object relations theory and game theory are most apparent in connection with the phenomena characteristically associated with the loss of objects and of games. Persons need stable and supporting objects: if they lose them, they tend to become depressed. Similarly, groups need stable and supporting games: if they lose them, they tend to develop anomie—a term popularized by Emile Durkheim,[2] who meant by it social apathy and disorganization as a result of a loss of previously valued aspirations, goals, or norms.[3]

A great deal of contemporary psychiatric and sociological writing rests on the premise that loss of objects and its vicissitudes characterize the frame of reference of personal conduct; and that loss of norms and its vicissitudes characterize the frame of reference of social conduct.[4] What I want to suggest now is that norms and normlessness also affect the individual; that, in other words, persons need not only other people but also rules worth following—or, more generally, games worth playing.

Men suffer grievously when they find no games worth playing, even though their object world might remain quite intact. To account for this, we must consider the relationship of the self to games. Otherwise, we are forced to reduce all sorts of personal misery and suffering to considerations of object relationships. At the same time, we might regard the loss of game as another, more comprehensive, aspect of what has heretofore been called loss of object. Furthermore, as the loss of a real or external object implies the loss of a player from the game—unless a perfect substitute for him can be found, which is unusual and unlikely—such loss inevitably results in certain changes in the game. It is evident, then, that "players" and "games" describe interdependent variables that together make up complex social systems—for example, families, organizations, societies, and so forth.

The connections between object and game outlined above may be illustrated by the following examples. A child that loses its mother loses not only an object—that is, a person invested with affection and other feelings—but is also precipitated into a human situation that constitutes a new game. The mother's absence means that other persons must care for some of the child's needs, and that he will henceforth have to relate to these persons.

Similar considerations hold for marriage. This game, traditionally conceived, lasts until death terminates it. So long as the players adhered to this rule, it provided them with great security against the trauma of game loss. It seems probable, indeed, that the institution of marriage has evolved—and has persisted as long as it has—not so much because it provides an ordered system of sexual relationships, nor because it is useful for child rearing, but rather because it provides men and women with an extremely stable human relationship, in the context of a relatively unchanging game. Marriage has achieved this goal better than probably any other institution except the organized religions, which tend also to be very stable. What many people find attractive about these games is that, having once learned how to play them, they can stop learning and changing.

Loss of a parent in childhood, or loss of a spouse in adulthood, are situations in which loss of object and loss of game go hand in hand. There are other situations, however, in which loss of object and loss of game occur separately—for example, the immigration of a whole family. In such a case, especially if the immigrants are accompanied by friends and servants, we have a situation in which people have lost certain important games without having lost significant personal objects. As a rule, such families either readily adapt themselves to new ways of living, a new language, and so forth—or go on living as if they had never left home.

The concept of learning, so clearly indispensable for any explanation of human behavior, is an integral part of game theory, but is not a part of object relations theory at all. One learns to play games, but one does not learn to have object relations. Certain key psychoanalytic concepts must thus be reinterpreted in terms of learning—a reinterpretation which is sometimes carried out by psychoanalysts quite casually and inexplicitly. For example, tranference might be viewed as a special case of "playing an old game." And so we find Greenacre, in a paper on this subject, remarking that "One thinks here of Fenichel's warning that not joining in the game is a principal task of handling the transference."[5]

Furthermore, although probably few analysts still believe that transference occurs only in the context of the psychoanalytic situation, many hold that this phenomenon pertains only to object relationships. I submit, however, that the characteristic features of transference can be observed in other situations as well, especially in the area of learned skills.[6] Thus, speaking a language with a foreign accent is one of the most striking everyday examples of transference. In the traditional concept of transference, one person (the analysand) behaves toward another (the analyst) as if the latter were someone else, previously familiar to him; and the subject is usually unaware of the actual manifestations of his own transferred behavior. In exactly the same way, persons who speak English (or any other language) with a foreign accent treat English as if it were their mother tongue; and they are usually unaware of the actual manifestations of their transferred behavior. Such persons think of themselves as speaking unaccented English: they cannot hear their own distortions of the language when they speak. Only when their accent is pointed out to them, or, better, only when they hear their recorded voices played back to them, do they recognize their linguistic transferences. These are striking parallels not only between the stereotyped behavioral acts due to previous habit, but also between the necessity for auxiliary channels of information outside the person's own self for recognizing the effects of these habits. This view of transference rests on empirical observations concerning the basic human tendency to generalize experiences.*

Further connections between the theory of object relations and game theory may be developed by re-examining affects and attitudes from the point of view of game-playing. From the standpoint of object relations, "being interested in" someone or something is an affect irreducible to other elements. Psychoanalysts call this "libidinal cathexis" or "investment" or "investment in objects." But from the standpoint of the experiencing person, objects do not even exist except insofar as they are invested with interest. Positive interest, such as love, is of course preferable to negative interest, such as hate, but either is preferable to no interest, such as apathy or indifference, which threatens the very existence of the personality or self.

To live meaningfully, man must be interested and invested in more than just objects. He must have games he finds worth playing. The principal affective manifestations of an eagerness to engage in life are curiosity, hope, and zest. As a loving attitude implies interest in persons—that is, in parents and children, wives and lovers—so a hopeful attitude implies interest in games—that is, in work and play, religion and social affairs.

Hope, then, is an expectation of successful participation in social interactions. This might imply winning, or playing well, or just enjoying the game. The point is that an unflagging

* A remarkably perceptive early formulation of this phenomenon was provided by Ernst Mach in 1885, who called it the "principle of continuity."[7]

interest in playing various games is an indispensable require-
ment for successful social living—that is, for what is often
referred to as "mental health." This is illustrated by the significance of work for psychological integrity, especially when
the occupation is self-selected and is socially valued. For
people who do not possess inherited wealth and who must
therefore work to earn a livelihood, doing a job they like and
doing it well is usually the most important game in their life.
Furthermore, by remaining interested in working, men can
avoid boredom and apathy on the one hand, and scrutiny of
the self and its objects and games on the other. In other words,
people who work might be said to be "playing" the work-
game, whereas the so-called idle rich "work" at playing. For
the latter, sports, travel, social gatherings, philanthropy, and
other activities provide outlets for their need for meaningful
games.

These remarks merely touch on the complicated subject of
the relationship between hope and religion, the essence of
which might be put as the question, "What should man be
hopeful about?" Without trying to answer this question here,
let me emphasize only that investing hope in religious faith is
perhaps one of the best psychological investments a person
can make. This is because by investing a small amount of hope
in religion—especially in the Christian religions, which promise lavish gratifications and rewards of all sorts—one gets back
a great deal. Few other enterprises, other than fanatical na-
tionalisms, promise as much. The rate of return on hope
invested in religion is thus much higher than on hope invested
in, say, rational work-a-day pursuits. Hence, those with small
capitals of hope may do best by investing their "savings" in
religion. And this indeed is what they often do.

Psychoanalysis and Ethics

In the foregoing pages, I have touched repeatedly on the
connections between ethics and psychiatry, psychoanalysis,

and the mental health professions, and have tried to make explicit the inexplicit moral values, judgments, and prescriptions inherent in psychiatric and psychoanalytic principles and practices. The ethical values embodied in, and enforced by, contemporary psychiatry—so-called general psychiatry—are too numerous and diverse to be encompassed in a brief discussion or to permit any kind of easy generalization. The situation is much simpler with respect to psychoanalysis, and I want to offer a few concluding remarks about the ethical values inherent in it and implemented through it.

First, what are the main sources of these values? I would briefly list them as follows: the tradition of medicine as a healing art; nineteenth-century science, and especially physics; philosophers, especially those of classical Greece and Rome and of the Enlightenment, and some moderns, such as Schopenhauer and Nietzsche; the great Western religions, especially Judaism and Roman Catholicism; and, of course, Freud's personal preferences and temperamental dispositions.[8]

And what is the nature or substance of these values? I would briefly identify them as rationalism, self-awareness, self-discipline, and the preservation of prevailing familial, social, and political arrangements. The idea that self-knowledge is a good is, of course, the ethics of rationalism and science applied to the self as a part of nature. An integral part of this scientific ethic is the principle that knowledge should be clearly stated and widely publicized and that it should never be kept a secret, especially from those who want to acquire it or might be affected by it. In particular, knowledge must not, according to this ethic, be kept secret by a small group and used as a source of power to mystify and control, stupefy and dominate, other individuals or groups. Although psychoanalysts espoused this scientific ethic in principle, they betrayed it in practice as soon as they had a chance to do so: when their numbers became sufficient to organize themselves into a group, they hastened to transform psychoanalytic thought from inquiry into dogma, and psychoanalytic practice from an instrument for liberating the individual into one for oppressing him.[9]

I wish to re-emphasize here that Freud never made explicit the moral values which animated his work and which he incorporated into the theory and practice of psychoanalysis. Indeed, what characterizes his voluminous writings—in contrast, as we shall see, to those of Adler for example—was his persistent effort to represent his work as purely "scientific" and "therapeutic." This is why it is so easy to answer the question, What is the psychoanalytic view of a *bad* human relationship or marriage? while it is quite impossible to answer its corollary, What is the psychoanalytic view of a *good* human relationship or marriage? In short, by couching his observations and interventions in the language of medicine and pseudo-medicine, Freud made it appear as if he were morally detached or neutral. But in the social sciences—or, generally, in human affairs—no such detachment or neutrality is possible. Moreover, nothing is easier than to show, point by point, which values Freud and other psychoanalysts supported, and which others they opposed. A few examples must suffice here: Freud not only "discovered" infantile sexuality, he also advocated the sexual enlightenment of children; he not only studied the effects of sexual seductions on children, he also opposed this practice; he not only speculated about the nature of homosexuality, but he also deplored it as a "perversion."

With respect to paired human relations, Freud believed that they always are, and should be, based on the domination of one partner and the submission of the other. His political beliefs were essentially Platonic, favoring an intellectual and moral elite dictatorially governing the masses. I have remarked earlier[10] on Freud's misogyny. His insistence that the psychoanalytic relationship between analyst and analysand be that of "a superior and a subordinate" is equally remark-able—and shocking.[11] He did not seem to regard genuine cooperation between equals as either possible or desirable.

As against Freud, Adler clearly articulated his concept of the morally desirable or "mentally healthy" human relation-ship.[12] It was characterized by a high degree of social interest and cooperativeness. He also stressed the values of truthful-ness and competence. At the same time, he placed less empha-sis than Freud on self-knowledge.

In short, whereas Freud disguised and obscured, Adler revealed and discussed, the moral values inherent in his obser-vations, theories, and therapies. I think this is one of the reasons for the different receptions that Freudian and Adlerian psychologies have received. Freud's work bore the stamp of the impartial, cool-headed natural scientist. It re-quired the work of many scholars to expose the values in-herent in Freudian psychology and psychotherapy. Not so for Adler's work, which from early on diverged from medicine and psychiatry, and even from psychotherapy, and became associated with child-rearing, education, and social reform.

I have suggested elsewhere that certain aspects of the psy-choanalytic procedure require a high degree of mutual co-operation between two relatively equal participants.[13] By this I mean that although analyst and patient are quite unequal with respect to certain skills and the knowledge of how to use them, they are, or should be, relatively equal with respect to power over each other.

If we judge by what psychoanalysts say, write, and do—and how else can we judge their work?—we would have to con-clude that there is not one psychoanalytic ethic but that there are two, each antithetical to the other. According to the one, the ethical ideal of psychoanalysis is paternalism: the relation-ship between analyst and analysand, and as many other rela-tionships as possible, should conform to the model of leader-follower, domination-submission. According to the other, its ideal is individualism: the relationship between analyst and analysand, and as many other relationships as possible, should conform to the model of cooperation and reciprocity between equals. Insofar as psychoanalytic practices are consistent with the latter ethic, I support them; and insofar as they are inconsistent with it, I oppose them.

In short, I believe that the aim of psychoanalytic therapy is, or should be, to maximize the patient's choices in the conduct of his life.[14] This value must be entertained explicitly and must be espoused not only for the patient but for everyone else as well. Thus our goal should not be to indiscriminately enlarge the patient's choices; this could often be achieved easily enough by reducing the choices of those with whom he interacts. Instead, our goal should be to enlarge his choices by enhancing his knowledge of himself, others, and the world about him, and his skills in dealing with persons and things. As psychiatrists and psychotherapists, whether of psychoanalytic or some other persuasion, we should thus try to enrich our world and try to help our patients to enrich theirs, not by diminishing the efforts and achievements of our fellow man, but by increasing our own.

Psychiatry as Social Action

The proposition that psychiatric operations are a species of social action—and hence, ultimately, a species of moral action —does not, I hope, require further proof. It is indeed difficult to see how this simple fact could have been so long and so successfully concealed from both popular and professional awareness. Psychiatrists do things with and to patients, and vice versa, and the things they do pertain to the moral convictions and conduct of each. Although the moral implications and practical impacts of psychiatric practices are more obvious in such interventions as involuntary mental hospitalization than in psychoanalysis, both of these practices, and all others, are, as I have tried to show throughout this book, instances of moral, political, and social action. To bring some order to an otherwise bewildering variety of psychiatric interventions, I propose to distinguish three classes of psychiatric actions, according to the psychiatrist's participation in the games of his patients, of their families, and of the society in which they all live.

1. The psychiatrist as theoretical scientist or ethicist. In this role, the psychiatrist acts as an expert on the game-playing behavior of psychiatric patients, families, groups, and the society in which they live: he shares his knowledge with those who hire him as an expert and who wish to learn from him as an authority.

2. The psychiatrist as applied scientist or ethicist. In this role, the psychiatrist acts as counselor, social repairman, or "therapist": he sorts out and classifies players according to their game-playing interests and skills and assigns them, with their consent, to games which they can, or ought to, play.

3. The psychiatrist as social engineer or controller of social deviance. In this role, the psychiatrist acts as priest and policeman, arbitrator and judge, parent and warden: he coerces and manipulates, punishes and rewards, and otherwise influences and compels people, often by relying on the police power of the state, to play, or to cease to play, certain games.

Another way of distinguishing among the various psychiatric interventions is by dividing them into two classes—voluntary and involuntary. The typical voluntary psychiatric interventions are psychoanalysis, the various types of individual and group psychotherapy, and a great variety of both office and hospital psychiatry employing psychological or physical methods of treatment with the informed consent of the patient. Typical involuntary psychiatric interventions are commitment or measures carried out under the threat of commitment, and psychiatric "diagnoses" and "treatments" imposed on persons by parents, schools, courts, military authorities, and other social or governmental agencies.

Although all of these interventions constitute interferences in the moral life of the so-called patient, they differ widely according to whether the intervention is sought by the client or is imposed on him against his will, and whether its aim and probable consequence is an enlargement or diminution of the client's freedom and self-determination.

I am opposed, on moral and political grounds, to all psychiatric interventions which are involuntary; and, on personal grounds, to all such interventions which curtail the client's autonomy. But, regardless of my moral, political, or personal preferences, I believe it is imperative that all of us—professionals and nonprofessionals alike—keep an open and critical mind toward all psychiatric interventions and, in particular, that we not accept or approve any psychiatric intervention solely on the ground that it is now officially regarded as a form of medical treatment.

Conclusions

It is customary to define psychiatry as a medical specialty concerned with the study, diagnosis, and treatment of mental illnesses. This is a worthless and misleading definition. Mental illness is a myth. Psychiatrists are not concerned with mental illnesses and their treatments. In actual practice they deal with personal, social, and ethical problems in living.

I have argued that, today, the notion of a person "having a mental illness" is scientifically crippling. It provides professional assent to a popular rationalization—namely, that problems in living experienced and expressed in terms of so-called psychiatric symptoms are basically similar to bodily diseases. Moreover, the concept of mental illness also undermines the principle of personal responsibility, the ground on which all free political institutions rest. For the individual, the notion of mental illness precludes an inquiring attitude toward his conflicts which his "symptoms" at once conceal and reveal. For a society, it precludes regarding individuals as responsible persons and invites, instead, treating them as irresponsible patients.

Although powerful institutional forces lend their massive weight to the tradition of keeping psychiatric problems within the conceptual framework of medicine, the moral and scientific challenge is clear: we must recast and redefine the problem of "mental illness" so that it may be encompassed in a morally explicit science of man. This, of course, would require a radical revision of our ideas about "psychopathology" and "psychotherapy"—the former having to be conceived in terms of sign-using, rule-following, and game-playing, the latter in terms of human relationships and social arrangements promoting certain types of learning and values.

Human behavior is fundamentally moral behavior. Attempts to describe and alter such behavior without, at the same time, coming to grips with the issue of ethical values are therefore doomed to failure. Hence, so long as the moral dimensions of psychiatric theories and therapies remain hidden and inexplicit, their scientific worth will be seriously limited. In the theory of personal conduct which I have proposed—and in the theory of psychotherapy implicit in it—I have tried to correct this defect by articulating the moral dimensions of human behaviors occurring in psychiatric contexts.

Epilogue

In Pirandello's play *The Rules of the Game* the following conversation takes place:

> LEONE: Ah, Venanzi, it's a sad thing, when one has learnt every move in the game.
> GUIDO: What game?
> LEONE: Why . . . this one. The whole game—of life.
> GUIDO: Have you learnt it?
> LEONE: Yes, a long time ago.[1]

Leone's despair and resignation come from believing that there is such a thing as the game of life. Indeed, if mastery of the game of life were the problem of human existence, having achieved this task, what would there be left to do? But there is no game of life, in the singular. The games are infinite.

Modern man seems to be faced with a choice between two basic alternatives. On the one hand, he may elect to despair over the lost usefulness or the rapid deterioration of games painfully learned. Skills acquired by diligent effort may prove to be inadequate for the task at hand almost as soon as one is ready to apply them. Many people cannot tolerate repeated disappointments of this kind. In desperation, they long for the security of stability—even if stability can be purchased only at the cost of personal enslavement. The other alternative is to rise to the challenge of the unceasing need to learn and relearn, and to try to meet this challenge successfully. Leone's problem is the dilemma of a man so far withdrawn from life that he fails to appreciate, and hence to participate in, the ever-changing game of life. The result is a shallow and constant life which may be encompassed and mastered with relative ease.

The common and pressing problem today is that, as social conditions undergo rapid change, men are called upon to alter their modes of living. Old games are constantly scrapped and new ones started. Most people are totally unprepared to shift from one type of game-playing to another. They learn one game or, at most, a few, and desire mainly the opportunity to live out life by playing the same game over and over again. But since human life is largely a social enterprise, social conditions may make it impossible to survive without greater flexibility in regard to patterns of personal conduct.

Perhaps the relationship between the modern psychotherapist and his client is a beacon that ever-increasing numbers of men will find themselves forced to follow, lest they become spiritually enslaved or physically destroyed. By this I do not mean anything so naïve as to suggest that "everyone needs to be psychoanalyzed." On the contrary, "being psychoanalyzed" —like any human experience—can itself constitute a form of enslavement and affords, especially in its contemporary institutionalized forms, no guarantee of enhanced self-knowledge and responsibility for either patient or therapist. By speaking of the modern psychotherapeutic relationship as a beacon, I refer to a simpler but more fundamental notion than that implied in "being psychoanalyzed." This is the notion of being a student of human living. Some require a personal instructor for this; others do not. Given the necessary wherewithal and ability to learn, success in this enterprise requires, above all else, the sincere desire to learn and to change. This incentive, in turn, is stimulated by hope of success. This is one of the main reasons why it is the scientist's and educator's solemn responsibility to clarify—never to obscure—problems and tasks.

I have tried to avoid the pitfalls of obscurantism which, by beclouding these problems, fosters discouragement and despair. We are all students in the metaphorical school of life. Here none of us can afford to become discouraged or despairing. And yet, in this school, religious cosmologies, nationalistic myths, and lately psychiatric theories have more often functioned as obscurantist teachers misleading the student than as genuine clarifiers helping him to help himself. Bad teachers are, of course, worse than no teachers at all. Against them, skepticism is our sole weapon.

Summary

The principal arguments advanced in this book and their implications may be summarized as follows.

1. Strictly speaking, disease or illness can affect only the body; hence, there can be no mental illness.

2. "Mental illness" is a metaphor. Minds can be "sick" only in the sense that jokes are "sick" or economies are "sick."

3. Psychiatric diagnoses are stigmatizing labels, phrased to resemble medical diagnoses and applied to persons whose behavior annoys or offends others.

4. Those who suffer from and complain of their own behavior are usually classified as "neurotic"; those whose behavior makes others suffer, and about whom others complain, are usually classified as "psychotic."

5. Mental illness is not something a person has, but is something he does or is.

6. If there is no mental illness there can be no hospitalization, treatment, or cure for it. Of course, people may change their behavior or personality, with or without psychiatric intervention. Such intervention is nowadays called "treatment," and the change, if it proceeds in a direction approved by society, "recovery" or "cure."

7. The introduction of psychiatric considerations into the

administration of the criminal law—for example, the insanity plea and verdict, diagnoses of mental incompetence to stand trial, and so forth—corrupt the law and victimize the subject on whose behalf they are ostensibly employed.

8. Personal conduct is always rule-following, strategic, and meaningful. Patterns of interpersonal and social relations may be regarded and analyzed as if they were games, the behavior of the players being governed by explicit or tacit game rules.

9. In most types of voluntary psychotherapy, the therapist tries to elucidate the inexplicit game rules by which the client conducts himself; and to help the client scrutinize the goals and values of the life games he plays.

10. There is no medical, moral, or legal justification for involuntary psychiatric interventions. They are crimes against humanity.

References

Preface to the Second Edition

1. See especially Thomas S. Szasz, *Law, Liberty, and Psychiatry; Psychiatric Justice; The Ethics of Psychoanalysis; Ideology and Insanity;* and *The Manufacture of Madness.*
2. See Thomas S. Szasz, Mental illness as a metaphor, *Nature,* 242: 305, 1973.
3. See Szasz, *The Ethics of Psychoanalysis.*

Epigraph

Karl R. Popper, Philosophy of Science: A Personal Report, in C. A. Mace, ed., *British Philosophy in the Mid-Century,* p. 177.

Introduction

1. Albert Einstein, *The World as I See It,* p. 30.
2. See, for example, Percy W. Bridgman, *The Nature of Physical Theory* and *The Way Things Are.*
3. See Charles W. Morris, *Signs, Language, and Behavior.*
4. See, for example, R. L. Gregory, On physical model explanations in psychology, *British Journal for the Philosophy of Science,* 4:192, 1953.
5. Karl R. Popper, *The Poverty of Historicism.*
6. Ibid., p. 160.
7. Ibid., p. 161.
8. Sigmund Freud, The Future of an Illusion (1927), in *The Standard Edition,* Vol. XXI, pp. 1–58.

269

9. See Karl R. Popper, *The Open Society and Its Enemies.*

1. Charcot and the Problem of Hysteria

1. See, for example, August B. Hollingshead and Fredrick C. Redlich, *Social Class and Mental Illness.*
2. Sigmund Freud, Charcot (1893), in *Collected Papers,* Vol. I, pp. 10–11.
3. Ibid., p. 11.
4. Ibid., pp. 12–13.
5. Georges Guillain, *J.-M. Charcot, 1825–1893.*
6. Axel Munthe, *The Story of San Michele.*
7. Freud, op. cit., pp. 18–19.
8. Ibid., p. 19.
9. Sigmund Freud, On the History of the Psycho-Analytic Movement (1914), in *The Standard Edition,* Vol. XIV, pp. 13–14.
10. Quoted in Guillain, op. cit., pp. 138–139.
11. Ibid., p. 174.
12. Ibid.
13. Ibid., p. 175.
14. Ibid., pp. 175–176.
15. Gregory Zilboorg, *A History of Medical Psychology,* pp. 362–363.

2. Illness and Counterfeit Illness

1. See Eilhard von Domarus, The Specific Laws of Logic in Schizophrenia, in Jacob S. Kasanin, ed., *Language and Thought in Schizophrenia,* pp. 104–114.
2. See Silvano Arieti, Schizophrenia, in Silvano Arieti, ed., *American Handbook of Psychiatry,* Vol. I, pp. 455–484.
3. See Chapter 7.
4. See Thomas S. Szasz, Malingering, *A.M.A. Archives of Neurology and Psychiatry,* 76:432, 1956.
5. Mortimer Adler, *What Man Has Made of Man,* p. 122.
6. See Thomas S. Szasz, The classification of "mental illness," *Psychiatric Quarterly,* 33:77, 1959.
7. James S. Chapman, Peregrinating problem patients: Münchausen's syndrome, *Journal of the American Medical Association,* 165:927, 1957.
8. Ibid., p. 933.
9. See Thomas S. Szasz, Commitment of the mentally ill, *Journal of Nervous and Mental Disease,* 125:293, 1957.
10. Sigmund Freud, Dostoevsky and parricide (1928), in *Collected Papers,* Vol. V, p. 224.

11. Eugen Bleuler, *A Textbook of Psychiatry* (1924), p. 191.
12. Kurt R. Eissler, Malingering, in G. B. Wilbur and W. Muenster-berger, eds., *Psychoanalysis and Culture,* pp. 252–253.
13. See also, Thomas S. Szasz, Moral conflict and psychiatry, *Yale Review,* 49:555, 1960.
14. For further discussion, see Chapter 13.

3. The Social Context of Medical Practice

1. August B. Hollingshead and Fredrick C. Redlich, *Social Class and Mental Illness.*
2. Mark G. Field, *Doctor and Patient in Soviet Russia,* pp. 146–148.
3. Ibid., p. 174.
4. See Thomas S. Szasz, On the theory of psycho-analytic treatment, *International Journal of Psycho-Analysis,* 38:166, 1957.
5. In this connection, see Field, op. cit., pp. 176–177.
6. Quoted in ibid., p. 159.
7. See Chapter 1.
8. See Thomas S. Szasz, Scientific method and social role in medicine and psychiatry, *A.M.A. Archives of Internal Medicine,* 101:228, 1958.
9. See, for example, Fyodor M. Dostoevsky, *Memoirs from the House of the Dead* (1861–62).
10. See Erik H. Erikson, *Childhood and Society.*
11. Field, op. cit., pp. 176–177.
12. See Walt W. Rostow, *The Dynamics of Soviet Society,* pp. 222–226.
13. See Field, op. cit., p. 174.

4. Breuer and Freud's *Studies on Hysteria*

1. See Ernest Jones, *The Life and Work of Sigmund Freud,* Vol. 1.
2. See, for example, F. J. Ziegler, J. B. Imboden, and E. Meyer, Contemporary conversion reactions, *American Journal of Psychiatry,* 116:901, 1960.
3. Joseph Breuer and Sigmund Freud, *Studies on Hysteria* (1893–1895), p. 5.
4. See Chapter 7.
5. In this connection, see Thomas S. Szasz, *Pain and Pleasure,* especially pp. 34–48.
6. Breuer and Freud, op. cit., pp. 143–144.
7. Sigmund Freud, Fragment of an Analysis of a Case of Hysteria (1905), in *The Standard Edition,* Vol. VII, pp. 16–17.
8. Breuer and Freud, op. cit., pp. 135–136.

9. Ibid., pp. 160–161.
10. Ibid., p. 166.
11. Kenneth M. Colby, *Energy and Structure in Psychoanalysis.*
12. Breuer and Freud, op. cit., p. 166.
13. See, for example, Felix Deutsch, ed., *On the Mysterious Leap from the Mind to the Body.*
14. See Bertrand Russell, *Human Knowledge*, pp. 44–53.
15. See, for example, Otto Fenichel, *The Psychoanalytic Theory of Neurosis.*

5. Hysteria and Psychosomatic Medicine

1. See John H. Woodger, *Physics, Psychology, and Medicine,* especially pp. 16–17.
2. See Thomas S. Szasz, *Pain and Pleasure,* pp. 51–81.
3. Moritz Schlick, On the Relation between Psychological and Physical Concepts (1935), in Herbert Feigl and Wilfrid Sellars, eds., *Readings in Philosophical Analysis,* p. 403.
4. Leon J. Saul, A Note on the Psychogenesis of Organic Symptoms, in Franz Alexander, Thomas M. French, et al., *Studies in Psychosomatic Medicine,* p. 85.
5. In this connection, see for example, Franz Alexander, *Psychosomatic Medicine,* and Felix Deutsch, ed., *On the Mysterious Leap from the Mind to the Body.*
6. Franz Alexander, Fundamental Concepts of Psychosomatic Research, in Franz Alexander, Thomas M. French, et al., op. cit., p. 3.
7. Ibid.
8. Ibid.
9. See, in this connection, Szasz, *Pain and Pleasure,* especially pp. 3–33.
10. See Gilbert Ryle, *The Concept of Mind.*
11. Alexander, op. cit., p. 9.
12. Szasz, op. cit., pp. 147–169.
13. Alexander, op. cit., p. 6.
14. Alexander, *Psychosomatic Medicine,* p. 42.
15. Ibid., p. 44.
16. See, for example, Sigmund Freud, *An Outline of Psychoanalysis* (1940), and Edward Glover, *Psychoanalysis.*
17. See, for example, Kenneth M. Colby, *Energy and Structure in Psychoanalysis,* and Eugene Pumpian-Mindlin, Propositions concerning energetic-economic aspects of libido theory, in Leopold Bellak, cons. ed., *Conceptual and Methodological Problems of Psychoanalysis, Annals of the New York Academy of Sciences,* 76:1038, 1959.

18. In this connection, see Jurgen Ruesch and Gregory Bateson, *Communication,* and Thomas S. Szasz, Language and Pain, in Silvano Arieti, ed., *American Handbook of Psychiatry,* Vol. I, pp. 982–999.
19. See Paul Bohannan, Translation, *The Listener,* 51:815, 1954.

6. Contemporary Views on Hysteria and Mental Illness

1. Otto Fenichel, *The Psychoanalytic Theory of Neurosis,* p. 194.
2. Ibid., p. 196.
3. Ibid., p. 216.
4. Ibid., p. 220.
5. John H. Woodger, *Physics, Psychology, and Medicine,* p. 57.
6. See Gilbert Ryle, *The Concept of Mind.*
7. Edward Glover, *Psychoanalysis,* p. 140.
8. Ibid., pp. 140–141.
9. Georg Groddeck, *The Book of the It* and *The World of Man.*
10. Harry S. Sullivan, *Conceptions of Modern Psychiatry,* p. 54.
11. Sigmund Freud, Five Lectures on Psychoanalysis (1910), in *The Standard Edition,* Vol. XI, p. 16.
12. See Chapter 13.
13. W. Ronald D. Fairbairn, Observations on the nature of hysterical states, *British Journal of Medical Psychology,* 27:105, 1954, p. 117.
14. See, for example, Linus Pauling, The molecular basis of genetics, *American Journal of Psychiatry,* 113:492, 1956.
15. See John R. Weinberg, *An Examination of Logical Positivism.*
16. See Richard von Mises, *Positivism.*
17. John J. Purtell, E. Robins, and M. E. Cohen, Observations on clinical aspects of hysteria, *Journal of the American Medical Association,* 146:902, 1951.

7. Language and Protolanguage

1. Hans Reichenbach, *Elements of Symbolic Logic,* p. 4.
2. See Thomas S. Szasz, *Pain and Pleasure,* especially pp. 82–104.
3. Alfred N. Whitehead and Bertrand Russell, *Principia Mathematica.*
4. Roman Jakobson, The Cardinal Dichotomy in Language, in Ruth Nanda Anshen, ed., *Language,* p. 163.
5. See, for example, Otto Fenichel, *The Psychoanalytic Theory of Neurosis,* pp. 14–15 and 46–51.
6. Sigmund Freud, The Unconscious (1915), in *The Standard Edition,* Vol. XIV, pp. 159–204.
7. See Eilhard von Domarus, The Specific Laws of Logic in Schizophrenia, in Jacob S. Kasanin, ed., *Language and Thought in Schizophrenia,* pp. 104–114; and Silvano Arieti, Schizophrenia, in

Silvano Arieti, ed., *American Handbook of Psychiatry*, Vol. I, pp. 455–484.

8. See Thomas S. Szasz, A contribution to the psychology of schizophrenia, *A.M.A. Archives of Neurology and Psychiatry*, 77:420, 1957.
9. For further discussion, see Chapters 10 and 12.
10. Reichenbach, op. cit., p. 19.
11. Joseph Breuer and Sigmund Freud, *Studies on Hysteria* (1893–1895), p. 178.
12. For further discussion, see Chapter 8.

8. Hysteria as Communication

1. Bertrand Russell, Introduction, in Ludwig Wittgenstein, *Tractatus Logico-Philosophicus*, p. 8.
2. Susanne K. Langer, *Philosophy in a New Key*, p. 70.
3. Ibid., pp. 76–77.
4. Margaret Schlauch, *The Gift of Language*.
5. See, for example, Robert L. Birdwhistell, Contribution of Linguistic-Kinesic Studies to the Understanding of Schizophrenia, in Albert Auerback, ed., *Schizophrenia*, pp. 99–124.
6. Langer, op. cit., p. 77.
7. Joseph Breuer and Sigmund Freud, *Studies on Hysteria* (1893–95), p. 136.
8. In this connection, see Thomas S. Szasz, *Pain and Pleasure*.
9. Anatol Rapoport, *Operational Philosophy*, p. 199.
10. Szasz, op. cit.
11. See Macdonald Critchley, *The Language of Gesture*, p. 121.
12. Sigmund Freud, Five Lectures on Psycho-Analysis (1910), in *The Standard Edition*, Vol. XI, p. 30.
13. Sigmund Freud, The Interpretation of Dreams (1900), in *The Standard Edition*, Vol. IV, p. 141.
14. Ibid., pp. 141–142.
15. See Sigmund Freud, Jokes and Their Relation to the Unconscious (1905), in *The Standard Edition*, Vol. VIII.
16. See Thomas S. Szasz, Recollections of a Psychoanalytic Psychotherapy, in Arthur Burton, ed., *Case Studies in Counseling and Psychotherapy*, pp. 75–110.
17. Sigmund Freud, The Interpretation of Dreams (1900), op. cit., and On dreams (1901), in *The Standard Edition*, Vol. V, pp. 631–686.
18. Sandor Ferenczi, To whom does one relate one's dreams? (1912), in Sandor Ferenczi, *Further Contributions to the Theory and Technique of Psycho-analysis*, p. 349.

19. See Thomas S. Szasz, The communication of distress between child and parent, *British Journal of Medical Psychology,* 32:161, 1959.
20. See Karl R. Popper, *The Open Society and Its Enemies.*

9. The Rule-Following Model of Human Behavior

1. R. S. Peters, *The Concept of Motivation,* p. 7.
2. See Thomas S. Szasz, A critical analysis of some aspects of the libido theory, in Leopold Bellak, cons. ed., *Conceptual and Methodological Problems in Psychoanalysis, Annals of the New York Academy of Sciences,* 76:975, 1959.
3. Sigmund Freud, Three Essays on the Theory of Sexuality (1905), in *The Standard Edition,* Vol. VII, pp. 123–245.
4. See Chapter 12.
5. Peters, op. cit., pp. 10–11.
6. Ibid., p. 14.
7. Ibid., p. 15.
8. James Strachey, The nature of the therapeutic action of psychoanalysis, *International Journal of Psycho-Analysis,* 15:127, 1934.
9. Ernest Jones, *The Life and Work of Sigmund Freud,* Vol. 3, p. 247.
10. See Philip Rieff, *Freud: The Mind of the Moralist.*
11. See Alfred Adler, *What Life Should Mean to You,* and Heinz L. Ansbacher and Rowena R. Ansbacher, eds., *The Individual Psychology of Alfred Adler.*
12. Sigmund Freud, The Antithetical Meaning of Primal Words (1910), in *The Standard Edition,* Vol. XI, pp. 153–162.
13. Thomas S. Szasz, *Pain and Pleasure,* pp. 162–163.
14. See Chapter 12.
15. See Chapter 15.

10. The Ethics of Helplessness and Helpfulness

1. See, for example, Sigmund Freud, The Future of an Illusion (1927), in *The Standard Edition,* Vol. XXI, pp. 1–58, and Civilization and Its Discontents (1930), ibid., pp. 59–148.
2. See especially, Alfred Adler, Selections from His Writings (1907–1937), in Heinz L. Ansbacher and Rowena R. Ansbacher, eds., *The Individual Psychology of Alfred Adler;* and Carl G. Jung, *Modern Man in Search of a Soul* (1933) and *Two Essays on Analytical Psychology* (1953).
3. Susanne Langer, *Philosophy in a New Key.*
4. Thomas S. Szasz, A contribution to the psychology of schizophrenia, *A.M.A. Archives of Neurology and Psychiatry,* 77:420, 1957.

5. Johann Christoph Friedrich von Schiller, Der Ring des Polykrates (1798), in *Werke*, Vol. I, pp. 176–179.
6. Luke 18:22–25.
7. Matthew 5:1–12.
8. Ibid., 6:34.
9. Matthew 19:23–30.
10. Luke 6:20–26.
11. Matthew 19:12.
12. See Heinrich Krämer and Jacob Sprenger, *Malleus Maleficarum* (1486).
13. See, for example, Sandor Ferenczi, The kite as a symbol of erection (1913), in *Further Contributions to the Theory and Technique of Psycho-Analysis*, pp. 359–360; Vermin as a symbol of pregnancy (1914), ibid., p. 361; Sigmund Freud, Three Essays on the Theory of Sexuality (1905), in *The Standard Edition*, Vol. VII, pp. 123–245; and Georg Groddeck, *The Book of the It* (1927).
14. Abraham Lincoln, From a letter (1858), in C. Morley and L. D. Everett, eds., *Familiar Quotations*, p. 455.
15. Matthew 19:30, 20:16; Mark 10:31; Luke 13:30.
16. See, for example, Bertrand Russell, A Psychoanalyst's Nightmare, in *Nightmares of Eminent Persons*, pp. 21–30.
17. See Thomas S. Szasz, The communication of distress between child and parent, *British Journal of Medical Psychology*, 32:161, 1959.
18. Sigmund Freud, Further recommendations on the technique of psycho-analysis (1913), *Collected Papers*, Vol. II, p. 346.
19. See Thomas S. Szasz, On the theory of psycho-analytic treatment, *International Journal of Psycho-Analysis*, 38:166, 1957.
20. Herbert Spencer, *The Man Versus the State* (1884), p. 78.
21. Ibid.
22. Ibid., p. 79.
23. Ibid.
24. Ibid., pp. 79–80.
25. Ibid., p. 80.
26. Geza Roheim, *The Origin and Function of Culture*.

11. Theology, Witchcraft, and Hysteria

1. See Gregory Zilboorg, *The Medical Man and the Witch During the Renaissance* and *A History of Medical Psychology*.
2. Heinrich Krämer and Jacob Sprenger, *Malleus Maleficarum* (1486).
3. Zilboorg, *The Medical Man and the Witch During the Renaissance*, p. 58.
4. Ibid., p. 153.
5. Zilboorg, *A History of Medical Psychology*, p. 155.

6. Ibid., p. 156.
7. See, for example, Geoffrey Parrinder, *Witchcraft.*
8. See Thomas S. Szasz, Commitment of the mentally ill, *Journal of Nervous and Mental Disease,* 125:293, 1957.
9. See Johan Huizinga, *The Waning of the Middle Ages.*
10. See, for example, Hans Vaihinger, *The Philosophy of "As If."*
11. See, for example, Richard Lewinsohn, *A History of Sexual Customs.*
12. See Siegfried F. Nadel, *Nupe Religion,* pp. 205–206.
13. See, for example, Parrinder, op. cit.
14. In this connection, see Talcott Parsons, Definitions of Health and Illness in the Light of American Values and Social Structure, in E. G. Jaco, ed., *Patients, Physicians, and Illness,* pp. 165–187.
15. Parrinder, op. cit., p. 54.
16. Ibid., p. 58.
17. Sigmund Freud, *New Introductory Lectures on Psycho-Analysis,* p. 183.
18. See, for example, Karen Horney, *New Ways in Psychoanalysis,* and Erich Fromm, *Sigmund Freud's Mission.*
19. Parrinder, op. cit., p. 79.
20. See Thomas S. Szasz, Moral conflict and psychiatry, *Yale Review,* 49:555, 1960.
21. A. Gallinek, Psychogenic disorders and the civilization of the Middle Ages, *American Journal of Psychiatry,* 99:42, 1942.
22. Ibid., p. 47.
23. Parrinder, op. cit., p. 68.
24. See Thomas S. Szasz, Psychiatry, ethics, and the criminal law, *Columbia Law Review,* 58:183, 1958.

12. The Game-Playing Model of Human Behavior

1. See George H. Mead, *Mind, Self, and Society* and *The Philosophy of the Act.*
2. See Jean Piaget, *Judgment and Reasoning in the Child, The Moral Judgment of the Child,* and *Play, Dreams, and Imitation in Childhood.*
3. Piaget, *The Moral Judgment of the Child,* p. 1.
4. Ibid., pp. 86–95.
5. Ibid., p. 16.
6. Ibid., p. 17.
7. Ibid., p. 18.
8. Ibid.
9. Matthew 5:5.
10. Ibid., 5:10.
11. See Thomas S. Szasz, Politics and mental health, *American Journal of Psychiatry,* 115:508, 1958, and Civil liberties and the mentally ill, *Cleveland-Marshall Law Review,* 9:399, 1960.

12. Piaget, *The Moral Judgment of the Child,* p. 250.
13. Ibid., p. 188.
14. See Thomas S. Szasz, Commitment of the mentally ill, *Journal of Nervous and Mental Disease,* 125:293, 1957, and Psycho-analytic training, *International Journal of Psycho-Analysis,* 39:598, 1958.

13. Hysteria as a Game

1. See Chapter 12.
2. Joseph Breuer and Sigmund Freud, *Studies on Hysteria* (1893–1895), pp. 22–23.
3. See Thomas S. Szasz, The myth of mental illness, *American Psychologist,* 15:113, 1960.
4. Harry Stack Sullivan, *Conceptions of Modern Psychiatry,* p. 203.
5. Ibid., pp. 204–206.
6. Ibid., pp. 207–208.
7. Ibid., pp. 209–210.
8. Ibid., p. 216.
9. Ibid., p. 228.
10. Sigmund Freud, On the History of the Psycho-Analytic Movement (1914), in *The Standard Edition,* Vol. XIV, pp. 14–15.
11. In this connection, see Joseph Fletcher, *Morals and Medicine,* especially p. 42.
12. See Thomas S. Szasz, Psycho-analytic training, *International Journal of Psycho-Analysis,* 39:598, 1958.
13. Sigmund Freud, General remarks on hysterical attacks (1909), *Collected Papers,* Vol. II, p. 100.

14. Impersonation and Illness

1. See George Herbert Mead, *Mind, Self, and Society,* and Erving Goffman, *The Presentation of Self in Everyday Life.*
2. Simone de Beauvoir, *The Second Sex,* p. 533.
3. In this connection, see Thomas S. Szasz, Psychiatry, psychotherapy, and psychology, *A.M.A. Archives of General Psychiatry,* 1:455, 1959.
4. Helene Deutsch, Some forms of emotional disturbance and their relationship to schizophrenia, *Psychoanalytic Quarterly,* 11:301, 1942; The impostor, ibid., 24:483, 1955.
5. Deutsch, The impostor, op. cit., p. 503.
6. Alfred Adler, Life-lie and responsibility in neurosis and psychosis (1914), in *The Practice and Theory of Individual Psychology* (1925), pp. 235–245.
7. Hans Vaihinger, *The Philosophy of "As If"* (1911).
8. Deutsch, The impostor, p. 504.

9. See especially Chapter 2, and Thomas S. Szasz, Malingering, *A.M.A. Archives of Neurology and Psychiatry*, 76:432, 1956.
10. See, for example, Thomas Mann, *Confessions of Felix Krull*, and D. W. Maurer, *The Big Con*.
11. In this connection, see Silvano Arieti and Johannes M. Meth, Rare, Unclassifiable, Collective, and Exotic Psychotic Syndromes, in Silvano Arieti, ed., *American Handbook of Psychiatry*, Vol. I, pp. 546–563, and H. Weiner and A. Braiman, The Ganser syndrome, *American Journal of Psychiatry*, 111:767, 1955.
12. S. Ganser, Über einen eigenartigen Hysterischen Dämmerzustand, *Archiv für Psychiatrie*, 30:633, 1898.
13. Arthur P. Noyes, *Modern Clinical Psychiatry*, Fourth Edition, pp. 505–506.
14. Fredric Wertham, *The Show of Violence*, p. 191.
15. In this connection, see especially Erik H. Erikson, The problem of ego identity, *Journal of the American Psychoanalytic Association*, 4:56, 1956; Ralph Greenson, Problems of identification, ibid., 2:197, 1954, and The struggle against identification, ibid., 2:200, 1954.
16. See Allen Wheelis, *The Quest for Identity*.
17. See Chapter 2.
18. See Thomas S. Szasz, Scientific method and social role in medicine and psychiatry, *A.M.A. Archives of Internal Medicine*, 101:228, 1958.

15. The Ethics of Psychiatry

1. See, for example, W. Ronald D. Fairbairn, *Psychoanalytic Studies of the Personality*.
2. Emile Durkheim, *The Elementary Forms of the Religious Life* (1912).
3. See Sebastian de Grazia, *The Political Community*.
4. See Robert K. Merton, *Social Theory and Social Structure*, Revised Edition, especially pp. 161–194.
5. Phyllis Greenacre, Certain technical problems in the transference relationship, *Journal of the American Psychoanalytic Association*, 7:484, 1959.
6. See Thomas S. Szasz, *Pain and Pleasure*, especially pp. 132–135.
7. Ernst Mach, *The Analysis of Sensations and the Relation of the Physical to the Psychical* (1885), p. 57; see also Thomas S. Szasz, Mach and psychoanalysis, *Journal of Nervous and Mental Disease*, 130:6, 1960.
8. In this connection, see David Bakan, *Sigmund Freud and the Jewish Mystical Tradition;* Richard La Pierre, *The Freudian Ethic;* and Philipp Rieff, *Freud: The Mind of the Moralist*.

9. See Bertrand Russell, A Psychoanalyst's Nightmare, in *Nightmares of Eminent Persons*, pp. 21–30; and Thomas S. Szasz, Psychoanalytic training, *International Journal of Psycho-Analysis*, 39: 598, 1958.

10. See Chapter 11.

11. Sigmund Freud, On the History of the Psycho-Analytic Movement (1914), in *The Standard Edition*, Vol. XIV, p. 49.

12. See generally Alfred Adler, *The Practice and Theory of Individual Psychology* (1925).

13. Thomas S. Szasz, On the theory of psycho-analytic treatment, *International Journal of Psycho-Analysis*, 38:166, 1957.

14. See Thomas S. Szasz, Recollections of a Psychoanalytic Psychotherapy, in Arthur Burton, ed., *Case Studies in Counseling and Psychotherapy*, pp. 75–110.

Epilogue

1. Luigi Pirandello, *Three Plays*, p. 25.

Bibliography

Adler, A. Selections from His Writings (1907–1937). In H. L. Ansbacher and R. R. Ansbacher (eds.), *The Individual Psychology of Alfred Adler*. New York: Basic Books, 1956.

———. Life-lie and Responsibility in Neurosis and Psychosis: A Contribution to Melancholia (1914). In A. Adler, *The Practice and Theory of Individual Psychology*. Translated by P. Radin, pp. 235–245. Paterson, N.J.: Littlefield, Adams, 1959.

———. *The Practice and Theory of Individual Psychology* (1925). Translated by P. Radin. Paterson, N.J.: Littlefield, Adams, 1959.

———. *What Life Should Mean to You* (1931). New York: Capricorn Books, 1958.

Adler, M. *What Man Has Made of Man: A Study of the Consequences of Platonism and Positivism in Psychology* (1937). New York: Frederick Ungar, 1957.

Alexander, F. Fundamental Concepts of Psychosomatic Research: Psychogenesis, Conversion, Specificity (1943). In F. Alexander, T. M. French, et al., *Studies in Psychosomatic Medicine*, pp. 3–13. New York: Ronald Press, 1948.

———. *Psychosomatic Medicine: Its Principles and Applications*. New York: W. W. Norton, 1950.

———, French, T. M. et al. *Studies in Psychosomatic Medicine: An Approach to the Cause and Treatment of Vegetative Disturbances*. New York: Ronald Press, 1948.

Ansbacher, H. L., and Ansbacher, R. R. (eds.). *The Individual Psychology of Alfred Adler: A Systematic Presentation in Selections from His Writings*. New York: Basic Books, 1956.

Arieti, S. *Interpretation of Schizophrenia*. New York: Robert Brunner, 1955.

―――. Schizophrenia. In S. Arieti (ed.), *American Handbook of Psychiatry*. Vol. I, Chapter 23, pp. 455–484. New York: Basic Books, 1959.

―――, and Meth, J. M. Rare, Unclassifiable, Collective, and Exotic Psychotic Syndromes. In S. Arieti (ed.), *American Handbook of Psychiatry*. Vol. I, Chapter 27, pp. 546–563. New York: Basic Books, 1959.

Bakan, D. *Sigmund Freud and the Jewish Mystical Tradition*. Princeton, N.J.: Van Nostrand, 1959.

Beauvoir, S. de. *The Second Sex* (1949). Translated and edited by H. M. Parshley. New York: Knopf, 1953.

Bellak, L. The Unconscious. In L. Bellak (cons. ed.), *Conceptual and Methodological Problems in Psychoanalysis. Ann. N. Y. Acad. Sc.,* 76:1066, 1959.

Birdwhistell, R. L. Contribution of Linguistic-Kinesic Studies to the Understanding of Schizophrenia. In A. Auerback (ed.), *Schizophrenia: An Integrated Approach*. Chapter 5, pp. 99–124. New York: Ronald Press, 1959.

Bleuler, E. *A Textbook of Psychiatry* (1924). Translated by A. A. Brill. New York: Macmillan, 1944.

Bohannan, P. Translation: A problem in anthropology. *The Listener,* 51:815, 1954.

Breuer, J., and Freud, S. Studies on Hysteria (1893–95). In *The Standard Edition of the Complete Psychological Works of Sigmund Freud*. Vol. II. London: Hogarth Press, 1955.

Bridgman, P. W. *The Nature of Physical Theory*. Princeton, N.J.: Princeton University Press, 1936.

―――. *The Way Things Are*. Cambridge, Mass.: Harvard University Press, 1959.

Burton, A. (ed.). *Case Studies in Counseling and Psychotherapy*. Englewood Cliffs, N.J.: Prentice-Hall, 1959.

Chapman, J. S. Peregrinating problem patients: Münchausen's syndrome. *J.A.M.A.,* 165:927, 1957.

Colby, K. M. *Energy and Structure in Psychoanalysis*. New York: Ronald Press, 1955.

Critchley, M. *The Language of Gesture*. London: Edward Arnold, 1939.

Deutsch, F. (ed.). *On the Mysterious Leap from the Mind to the Body: A Workshop Study on the Theory of Conversion*. New York: International Universities Press, 1959.

Deutsch, H. Some forms of emotional disturbance and their relationship to schizophrenia. *Psychoanalyt. Quart.,* 11:301, 1942.

―――. The impostor. Contribution to ego psychology of a type of psychopath. *Psychoanalyt. Quart.,* 24:483, 1955.

Domarus, E. von. The Specific Laws of Logic in Schizophrenia. In J. S.

Kasanin (ed.), *Language and Thought in Schizophrenia*, pp. 104–114. Berkeley and Los Angeles: University of California Press, 1944.

Dostoevsky, F. M. *Memoirs from the House of the Dead* (1861–62). Translated by Jessie Coulson. New York: Oxford University Press, 1956.

Durkheim, E. *The Elementary Forms of the Religious Life* (1912). Translated by J. W. Swain. New York: Macmillan, 1915.

Einstein, A. On the Methods of Theoretical Physics (1933). In A. Einstein, *The World as I See It*, pp. 30–40. New York: Covici, Friede, 1934.

Eissler, K. R. Malingering. In G. B. Wilbur and W. Muensterberger (eds.), *Psychoanalysis and Culture*, pp. 218–253. New York: International Universities Press, 1951.

Erikson, E. H. *Childhood and Society*. New York: W. W. Norton, 1950.

———. The problem of ego identity. *J. Am. Psychoanalyt. A.*, 4:56, 1956.

Fairbairn, W.R.D. *Psychoanalytic Studies of the Personality*. London: Tavistock Publications, 1952.

———. Observations on the nature of hysterical states. *Brit. J. M. Psychol.*, 27:105, 1954.

Fenichel, O. *The Psychoanalytic Theory of Neurosis*. New York: W. W. Norton, 1945.

Ferenczi, S. To Whom Does One Relate One's Dreams? (1912). In S. Ferenczi, *Further Contributions to the Theory and Technique of Psycho-Analysis*, p. 349. London: Hogarth Press, 1950.

———. The Kite as a Symbol of Erection (1931). In S. Ferenczi, *Further Contributions to the Theory and Technique of Psycho-Analysis*, pp. 359–360. London: Hogarth Press, 1950.

———. Vermin as a Symbol of Pregnancy (1914). In S. Ferenczi, *Further Contributions to the Theory and Technique of Psycho-Analysis*, p. 361. London: Hogarth Press, 1950.

Field, M. G. *Doctor and Patient in Soviet Russia*. Cambridge, Mass.: Harvard University Press, 1957.

Fletcher, J. *Morals and Medicine: The Moral Problems of: The Patient's Right to Know the Truth, Contraception, Artificial Insemination, Sterilization, Euthanasia*. Princeton, N.J.: Princeton University Press, 1954.

Freud, S. Charcot (1893). In *Collected Papers*. Vol. I, pp. 9–23. London: Hogarth Press, 1948.

———. Some Points in a Comparative Study of Organic and Hysterical Paralyses (1893). In *Collected Papers*. Vol. I, pp. 42–58. London: Hogarth Press, 1948.

———. The Interpretation of Dreams (I & II) (1900). In *The Stand-*

ard Edition of the Complete Psychological Works of Sigmund Freud.
Vols. IV and V, pp. 1–621. London: Hogarth Press, 1953.

————. Fragment of an Analysis of a Case of Hysteria (1905). In
The Standard Edition of the Complete Psychological Works of Sigmund Freud. Vol. VII, pp. 1–122. London: Hogarth Press, 1953.

————. Three Essays on the Theory of Sexuality (1905). In *The Standard Edition of the Complete Psychological Works of Sigmund Freud.* Vol. VII, pp. 123–245. London: Hogarth Press, 1953.

————. Jokes and Their Relation to the Unconscious (1905). In *The Standard Edition of the Complete Psychological Works of Sigmund Freud.* Vol. VIII, pp. 1–258. London: Hogarth Press, 1960.

————. General Remarks on Hysterical Attacks (1909). In *Collected Papers.* Vol. II, pp. 100–104. London: Hogarth Press, 1948.

————. Five Lectures on Psycho-Analysis (1910). In *The Standard Edition of the Complete Psychological Works of Sigmund Freud.* Vol. XI, pp. 1–55, London: Hogarth Press, 1957.

————. The Antithetical Meaning of Primal Words (1910). In *The Standard Edition of the Complete Psychological Works of Sigmund Freud.* Vol. XI, pp. 153–162, London: Hogarth Press, 1957.

————. Further Recommendations on the Technique of Psycho-Analysis (1913). In *Collected Papers.* Vol. II, pp. 342–365. London: Hogarth Press, 1948.

————. On the History of the Psycho-Analytic Movement (1914). In *The Standard Edition of the Complete Psychological Works of Sigmund Freud.* Vol. XIV, pp. 1–66. London: Hogarth Press, 1957.

————. The Unconscious (1915). In *The Standard Edition of the Complete Psychological Works of Sigmund Freud.* Vol. XIV, pp. 159–204. London: Hogarth Press, 1957.

————. The Future of an Illusion (1927). In *The Standard Edition of the Complete Psychological Works of Sigmund Freud.* Vol. XXI, pp. 1–58. London: Hogarth Press, 1961.

————. Dostoevsky and Parricide (1928). In *Collected Papers.* Vol. V, pp. 222–242. London: Hogarth Press, 1950.

————. Civilization and Its Discontents (1930). In *The Standard Edition of the Complete Psychological Works of Sigmund Freud.* Vol. XXI, pp. 59–148. London: Hogarth Press, 1961.

————. *New Introductory Lectures on Psycho-Analysis* (1932). New York: W. W. Norton, 1933.

————. *An Outline of Psychoanalysis* (1940). New York: W. W. Norton, 1949.

Fromm, E. *Sigmund Freud's Mission: An Analysis of His Personality and Influence.* New York: Harper & Row, 1959.

Gallinek, A. Psychogenic disorders and the civilization of the Middle Ages. *Am. J. Psychiat.,* 99:42, 1942.

Ganser, S. Über einen eigenartigen Hysterischen Dämmerzustand. *Arch. Psychiat.,* 30:633, 1898.

Glover, E. *Psychoanalysis.* London: Staples Press, 1949.

Goffman, E. *The Presentation of Self in Everyday Life.* Garden City, N.Y.: Doubleday Anchor, 1959.

Grazia, S. de. *The Political Community: A Study of Anomie.* Chicago: The University of Chicago Press, 1948.

Greenacre, P. Certain technical problems in the transference relationship. *J. Am. Psychoanalyt. A.,* 7:484, 1959.

Greenson, R. Problems of identification: Introduction. *J. Am. Psychoanalyt. A.,* 2:197, 1954.

————. The struggle against identification. *J. Am. Psychoanalyt. A.,* 2:200, 1954.

Gregory, R. L. On physical model explanations in psychology. *Brit. J. Phil. Sc.,* 4:192, 1953.

Groddeck, G. *The Book of the It: Psychoanalytic Letters to a Friend* (1927). London: C. W. Daniel, 1935.

————. *The World of Man: As Reflected in Art, in Words and in Disease.* London: C. W. Daniel, 1934.

Guillain, G. *J.-M. Charcot, 1825–1893: His Life—His Work.* Edited and translated by Pearce Bailey. New York: Paul B. Hoeber, 1959.

Hollingshead, A. B., and F. C. Redlich. *Social Class and Mental Illness: A Community Study.* New York: John Wiley, 1958.

Horney, K. *New Ways in Psychoanalysis.* New York: W. W. Norton, 1939.

Huizinga, J. *The Waning of the Middle Ages* (1927). New York: Doubleday Anchor, 1956.

Jakobson, R. The Cardinal Dichotomy in Language. In R. N. Anshen (ed.), *Language: An Enquiry into Its Meaning and Function.* Chap. IX, pp. 155–173. New York: Harper & Row, 1957.

Jones, E. *The Life and Work of Sigmund Freud.* Vols. 1, 2, 3. New York: Basic Books, 1953, 1955, 1957.

Jung, C. G. *Modern Man in Search of a Soul* (1933). Translated by W. S. Dell and C. F. Baynes. New York: Harvest, 1970.

————. *Two Essays on Analytical Psychology* (1953). Translated by R. F. C. Hull. New York: Meridian, 1956.

Kasanin, J. S. The Disturbance of Conceptual Thinking in Schizophrenia. In J. S. Kasanin (ed.), *Language and Thought in Schizophrenia, Collected Papers,* pp. 41–49. Berkeley and Los Angeles: University of California Press, 1944.

Krämer, H., and Sprenger, J. *Malleus Maleficarum* (1486). Translated, with an Introduction, Bibliography and Notes by the Rev. Montague Summers. London: Pushkin Press, 1948.

Langer, S. K. *Philosophy in a New Key* (1942). New York: Mentor Books, 1953.

LaPierre, R. *The Freudian Ethic*. New York: Duell, Sloan and Pearce, 1959.

Lewinsohn, R. *A History of Sexual Customs*. Translated by Alexander Mayce. New York: Harper, 1958.

Lincoln, A. From a letter (1858). In C. Morley and L. D. Everett (eds.), *Familiar Quotations*, Twelfth Edition, p. 455. Boston: Little, Brown, 1951.

Mach, E. *The Analysis of Sensations and the Relation of the Physical to the Psychical* (1885). Translated by C. M. Williams. Revised and supplemented from the Fifth German Edition by Sydney Waterlow, with a new Introduction by Thomas S. Szasz. New York: Dover Publications, 1959.

Mann, T. *Confessions of Felix Krull: Confidence Man* (1954). Translated by Denver Lindley. New York: Knopf, 1955.

Maurer, D. W. *The Big Con: The Story of the Confidence Man and the Confidence Game*. Indianapolis: Bobbs-Merrill, 1940.

Mead, G. H. *Mind, Self, and Society: From the Standpoint of a Social Behaviorist*. Edited, with an Introduction, by Charles W. Morris. Chicago: The University of Chicago Press, 1934.

———. *The Philosophy of the Act*. Chicago: The University of Chicago Press, 1938.

Merton, R. K. *Social Theory and Social Structure*. Revised and enlarged edition. Glencoe, Ill.: The Free Press, 1957.

Mises, R. von. *Positivism: A Study in Human Understanding* (1951). New York: George Braziller, 1956.

Morris, C. W. *Signs, Language and Behavior*. New York: Prentice-Hall, 1946.

Munthe, A. *The Story of San Michele* (1929). New York: Dutton, 1957.

Nadel, S. F. *Nupe Religion*. Glencoe, Ill.: The Free Press, 1954.

Noyes, A. P. *Modern Clinical Psychiatry*. Fourth Edition. Philadelphia: W. B. Saunders, 1956.

Parrinder, G. *Witchcraft*. Harmondsworth, Middlesex: Penguin Books, 1958.

Parsons, T. Definitions of Health and Illness in the Light of American Values and Social Structure. In E. G. Jaco (ed.), *Patients, Physicians and Illness*. Chapter 20, pp. 165–187. Glencoe, Ill.: The Free Press, 1958.

Pauling, L. The molecular basis of genetics. *Am. J. Psychiat.*, 113:492, 1956.

Peters, R. S. *The Concept of Motivation*. London: Routledge & Kegan Paul, 1958.

Piaget, J. *Judgment and Reasoning in the Child* (1928). Translated by Marjorie Warden. London: Routledge & Kegan Paul, 1952.

———. *The Moral Judgment of the Child*. Translated by Marjorie Gabain. Glencoe, Ill.: The Free Press, 1932.

————. *Play, Dreams and Imitation in Childhood.* Translated by C. Gattegno and F. M. Hodgson. London: William Heinemann, 1951.

Pirandello, L. The Rules of the Game (1919). Translated by Robert Rietty. In L. Pirandello, *Three Plays.* Introduced and edited by E. Martin Browne. Harmondsworth, Middlesex: Penguin Books, 1959.

Popper, K. R. *The Poverty of Historicism* (1944–45). Boston: Beacon Press, 1957.

————. *The Open Society and Its Enemies* (1945). Princeton, N.J.: Princeton University Press, 1950.

————. Philosophy of Science: A Personal Report. In C. A. Mace (ed.), *British Philosophy in the Mid-Century,* pp. 153–191. New York: Macmillan, 1957.

Pumpian-Mindlin, E. Propositions concerning energetic-economic aspects of libido theory: Conceptual models of psychic energy and structure in psychoanalysis. In L. Bellak (cons. ed.), *Conceptual and Methodological Problems of Psychoanalysis. Ann. N. Y. Acad. Sc.,* 76:1038, 1959.

Purtell, J. J.; Robins, E.; and Cohen, M. E. Observations on clinical aspects of hysteria. *J.A.M.A.,* 146:902, 1951.

Rapoport, A. *Operational Philosophy: Integrating Knowledge and Action.* New York: Harper & Row, 1954.

Reichenbach, H. *Elements of Symbolic Logic.* New York: Macmillan, 1947.

Rieff, P. *Freud: The Mind of the Moralist.* New York: Viking, 1959.

Roheim, G. *The Origin and Function of Culture.* New York: Nervous and Mental Disease Monographs, 1943.

Rostow, W. W. *The Dynamics of Soviet Society* (1952). New York: Mentor Books, 1954.

Ruesch, J., and Bateson, G. *Communication: The Social Matrix of Psychiatry.* New York: W. W. Norton, 1951.

Russell, B. Introduction to L. Wittgenstein's *Tractatus Logico-Philosophicus,* pp. 7–8. London: Routledge & Kegan Paul, 1922.

————. *Human Knowledge: Its Scope and Limits.* New York: Simon and Schuster, 1948.

————. A Psychoanalyst's Nightmare: Adjustment—A Fugue. In B. Russell, *Nightmares of Eminent Persons,* pp. 21–30. London: Bodley Head, 1954.

Ryle, G. *The Concept of Mind.* London: Hutchinson's University Library, 1949.

Saul, L. J. A Note on the Psychogenesis of Organic Symptoms (1935). In F. Alexander, T. M. French, et al., *Studies in Psychosomatic Medicine,* pp. 85–90. New York: Ronald Press, 1948.

Schiller, J. C. F. Der Ring des Polykrates (1798). In Schiller, *Werke.*

Vol. I, pp. 176–179. 12 Vols. Berlin-Leipzig: Th. Knaur Nacht, 1908.

Schlauch, M. *The Gift of Language* (1942). New York: Dover, 1955.

Schlick, M. On the Relation between Psychological and Physical Concepts (1935). In H. Feigl and W. Sellars (eds.), *Readings in Philosophical Analysis*, pp. 393–407. New York: Appleton-Century-Crofts, 1949.

Spencer, H. *The Man Versus the State* (1884). Boston: Beacon Press, 1950.

Strachey, J. The nature of the therapeutic action of psycho-analysis. *Internat. J. Psycho-Analysis*, 15:127, 1934.

Sullivan, H. S. *Conceptions of Modern Psychiatry*. The First William Alanson White Memorial Lecture. Washington, D.C.: The William Alanson White Psychiatric Foundation, 1947.

Szasz, T. S. Malingering: "Diagnosis" or social condemnation? Analysis of the meaning of "diagnosis" in the light of some interrelations of social structure, value judgment, and the physician's role. *A.M.A. Arch. Neurol. & Psychiat.*, 76:432, 1956.

――――. *Pain and Pleasure: A Study of Bodily Feelings*. New York: Basic Books, 1957.

――――. On the theory of psycho-analytic treatment. *Internat. J. Psycho-Analysis*, 38:166, 1957.

――――. A contribution to the psychology of schizophrenia. *A.M.A. Arch. Neurol. & Psychiat.*, 77:420, 1957.

――――. Commitment of the mentally ill: "Treatment" or social restraint? *J. Nerv. & Ment. Dis.*, 125:293, 1957.

――――. Psychiatry, ethics, and the criminal law. *Columbia Law Review*, 58:183, 1958.

――――. Scientific method and social role in medicine and psychiatry. *A.M.A. Arch. Int. Med.*, 101:228, 1958.

――――. Psycho-analytic training: A sociopsychological analysis of its history and present status. *Internat. J. Psycho-Analysis*, 39:598, 1958.

――――. Politics and mental health: Some remarks apropos of the case of Mr. Ezra Pound, *Am. J. Psychiat.*, 115:508, 1958.

――――. A critical analysis of some aspects of the libido theory: The concepts of libidinal zones, aims, and modes of gratification. In L. Bellak (cons. ed.), *Conceptual and Methodological Problems in Psychoanalysis. Ann. N. Y. Acad. Sc.*, 76:975, 1959.

――――. The classification of "mental illness": A situational analysis of psychiatric operations. *Psychiat. Quart.*, 33:77, 1959.

――――. Recollections of a Psychoanalytic Psychotherapy: The Case of the 'Prisoner K.' In A. Burton (ed.), *Case Studies in Counseling and Psychotherapy*. Chapter 4, pp. 75–110. Englewood Cliffs, N.J.: Prentice-Hall, 1959.

――――. Language and Pain. In S. Arieti (ed.), *American Handbook of*

Psychiatry. Vol. I, Chapter 49, pp. 982–999. New York: Basic Books, 1959.

————. The communication of distress between child and parent. *Brit. J. Med. Psychol.,* 32:161, 1959.

————. Psychiatry, psychotherapy, and psychology. *A.M.A. Arch. Gen. Psychiat.,* 1:455, 1959.

————. Mach and psychoanalysis. *J. Nerv. & Ment. Dis.,* 130:6, 1960.

————. The myth of mental illness. *American Psychologist,* 15:113, 1960.

————. Moral conflict and psychiatry. *Yale Rev.,* 49:555, 1960.

————. Civil liberties and the mentally ill. *Cleveland-Marshall Law Rev.,* 9:399, 1960.

————. *Law, Liberty, and Psychiatry: An Inquiry into the Social Uses of Mental Health Practices.* New York: Macmillan, 1963.

————. *Psychiatric Justice.* New York: Macmillan, 1965.

————. *The Ethics of Psychoanalysis: The Theory and Method of Autonomous Psychotherapy.* New York: Basic Books, 1965.

————. *Ideology and Insanity: Essays on the Psychiatric Dehumanization of Man.* Garden City, N.Y.: Doubleday Anchor, 1970.

————. *The Manufacture of Madness: A Comparative Study of the Inquisition and the Mental Health Movement.* New York: Harper & Row, 1970.

————. Mental illness as a metaphor. *Nature,* 242:305, 1973.

Vaihinger, H. *The Philosophy of "As If": A System of the Theoretical, Practical, and Religious Fictions of Mankind* (1911). Translated by C. K. Ogden. London: Routledge & Kegan Paul, 1952.

Weinberg, J. R. *An Examination of Logical Positivism.* London: Routledge & Kegan Paul, 1950.

Weiner, H., and Braiman, A. The Ganser syndrome: A review and addition of some unusual cases. *Am. J. Psychiat.,* 111:767, 1955.

Wertham, F. *The Show of Violence.* Garden City, N.Y.: Doubleday & Co., 1949.

Wheelis, A. *The Quest for Identity.* New York: W. W. Norton, 1958.

Whitehead, A. N., and Russell, B. *Principia Mathematica* (1910). Second edition, Vol. I. Cambridge, Mass.: Harvard University Press, 1950.

Woodger, J. H. *Physics, Psychology, and Medicine: A Methodological Essay.* Cambridge: Cambridge University Press, 1956.

Ziegler, F. J.; Imboden, J. B.; and Meyer, E. Contemporary conversion reactions: A clinical study. *Am. J. Psychiat.,* 116:901, 1960.

Zilboorg, G. *The Medical Man and the Witch During the Renaissance.* The Hideyo Nogushi Lectures. Baltimore: Johns Hopkins Press, 1935.

————. *A History of Medical Psychology.* In collaboration with G. W. Henry. New York: W. W. Norton, 1941.

Name Index

Subject Index

293

ABOUT THE AUTHOR

Thomas S. Szasz was born in Budapest in 1920 and came to the United States when he was eighteen. He took his B.A. and M.D. degrees at the University of Cincinnati, his psychiatric training at the University of Chicago, and his psychoanalytic training at the Chicago Institute for Psychoanalysis.

From 1950 to 1954, Dr. Szasz was a staff member at the Chicago Institute for Psychoanalysis and was in private practice in Chicago. In 1956, after two years of active duty in the Medical Corps of the Naval Reserve, he joined the faculty of the Upstate Medical Center of the State University of New York at Syracuse as Professor of Psychiatry. He has also been a Visiting Professor of Psychiatry at the University of Wisconsin and Marquette University and has lectured widely in colleges, law schools, and medical schools and to lay groups. He is a cofounder and Chairman of the Board of Directors of the American Association for the Abolition of Involuntary Mental Hospitalization.

Dr. Szasz is the author of nine books and over two hundred articles and reviews.